Reflexivity in French Rap

AF729178

Reflexivity in French Rap

More than a Mirror to the Republic

Emily Q. Shuman

OXFORD
UNIVERSITY PRESS

OXFORD
UNIVERSITY PRESS

Oxford University Press is a department of the University of Oxford. It furthers the University's objective of excellence in research, scholarship, and education by publishing worldwide. Oxford is a registered trade mark of Oxford University Press in the UK and in certain other countries.

Published in the United States of America by Oxford University Press
198 Madison Avenue, New York, NY 10016, United States of America.

© Oxford University Press 2026

All rights reserved. No part of this publication may be reproduced, stored in a retrieval system, transmitted, used for text and data mining, or used for training artificial intelligence, in any form or by any means, without the prior permission in writing of Oxford University Press, or as expressly permitted by law, by license or under terms agreed with the appropriate reprographics rights organization. Inquiries concerning reproduction outside the scope of the above should be sent to the Rights Department, Oxford University Press, at the address above.

You must not circulate this work in any other form
and you must impose this same condition on any acquirer.

Library of Congress Cataloging-in-Publication Data
Names: Shuman, Emily Q. author
Title: Reflexivity in French rap : more than a mirror to the republic / Emily Q. Shuman.
Description: [1]. | New York : Oxford University Press, 2026. |
Includes bibliographical references and index. |
Identifiers: LCCN 2025049433 (print) | LCCN 2025049434 (ebook) |
ISBN 9780197781579 paperback | ISBN 9780197781562 hardback | ISBN 9780197781609 |
ISBN 9780197781593 epub
Subjects: LCSH: Rap (Music)—France—History and criticism | Music and literature—France |
Rap (Music)—Social aspects—France
Classification: LCC ML3531 .S57 2026 (print) | LCC ML3531 (ebook) |
DDC 782.421649—dc23/eng/20260310
LC record available at https://lccn.loc.gov/2025049433
LC ebook record available at https://lccn.loc.gov/2025049434

DOI: 10.1093/9780197781609.001.0001

Paperback printed by Marquis Book Printing, Canada
Hardback printed by Lightning Source, Inc., United States of America

The manufacturer's authorized representative in the EU for product safety is Oxford University Press España S.A. of Parque Empresarial San Fernando de Henares, Avenida de Castilla, 2 – 28830 Madrid (www.oup.es/en or product.safety@oup.com). OUP España S.A. also acts as importer into Spain of products made by the manufacturer.

FSC
www.fsc.org
MIX
Paper | Supporting responsible forestry
FSC® C103567

Contents

Acknowledgments

It is hard to believe that this book project has finally come to fruition. I first need to thank Norm Hirschy, Rada Radojicic, and the team at Oxford University Press for their patience and support throughout this process. I am also indebted to the anonymous peer reviewers for immeasurably strengthening the final product with their feedback.

In many respects, this book is a reflection of the intellectual community I found at NYU's Institute of French Studies and Department of French Literature, Thought and Culture. The colleagues and friends I met there—of whom I must single out Danielle Beaujon, Tony Haouam, and Athena Fokaidis—have made and continue to make me a better scholar, educator, and person. I thank my committee, Cécile Bishop, Judith G. Miller, Frédéric Viguier, Hannah Freed-Thall, and Karim Hammou, for their encouragement and invaluable suggestions for improvement on the dissertation that became this book. I am especially grateful to Cécile Bishop for her intellectual rigor, mentorship, and belief in this project.

The dissertation research that became this book was supported by a Chateaubriand Humanities & Social Sciences fellowship, as well as a Henry M. MacCracken and a Dean's Dissertation Fellowship from the NYU Graduate School for Arts & Sciences. Portions of Chapter 1 make use of research conducted at the INA-Grand Est in Strasbourg in 2017 and at the Inathèque of the Bibliothèque nationale de France in 2018. I thank the staff of both centers for their help.

This book simply would not exist without the community of scholars, music journalists, artists, and devoted rap fans I found in Paris. One day in 2017, Karim Hammou generously replied to an e-mail from an American graduate student, sparking a collaboration for which I will always be thankful. There are not many reasons these days to be grateful for Twitter, but it did connect me with Emmanuelle Carinos Vasquez, who has been an immensely inspiring and supportive colleague, but above all, a brilliant friend. The experience co-organizing the seminar "Fight the Power? Musiques hip-hop et rapports sociaux de pouvoir" with Princia Andrianirina, Emmanuelle Carinos Vasquez, Keivan Djavadzadeh, and Karim Hammou indelibly shaped the paths of inquiry that led to this book. Work sessions with the seminar team and colleagues such as Marie Sonnette-Manouguian kept me going throughout the dissertation process, as did post-seminar *apéros* with many other colleagues whose work inspires these pages. I thank the CRESPPA for supporting the seminar over the years. This book was also nourished by two conferences in Paris (one physically, the other in spirit due to public health restrictions) to which I had the privilege of contributing. I am very appreciative of Paroma Ghose and my colleagues with the European HipHop Studies Network for their dedicated work putting together a successful annual meeting amid tough circumstances. I also thank all of those involved with the immensely inspiring Hip-Hop 360 exhibit and conference at the Philharmonie de Paris. I greatly appreciate Ouafae Mameche Belabbes and Raphaël Da Cruz for sitting down with me in a very early stage of this project to share their expertise as music journalists. I also thank Benoît Dufau and Emmanuelle Carinos Vasquez for discussing their experiences as co-organizers of the seminar "La Plume et le Bitume." Having concert buddies like Manue, Guéno, Selim, and many members of FC Contre-Attaque made this project much more than research.

Sections of this book's third chapter appeared in earlier versions in previous publications: "'Tout de noir vêtu': Skin and Surface in the Rap of Abd al Malik." *French Cultural Studies* 29, no. 3 (2018): 209–217; "Esthétique et performativité de la race dans 'Créature ratée' de Casey." *Itinéraires. Littérature, textes, cultures* 2020-3 (2021). I kindly thank the journal editors, special issue coordinators, and anonymous peer reviewers for their feedback and support. Many portions of the book have been workshopped over the years in seminars and at conferences across North America, France, the UK, and the Netherlands. The enriching conversations I was able to have with colleagues in these contexts no doubt left their mark on the final product.

Several colleagues graciously read and commented on chapter and manuscript drafts: Danielle Beaujon, Cécile Bishop, Emmanuelle Carinos Vasquez, and Karim Hammou. I am indebted to them for their keen eyes and encouragement in pushing me to clarify and fully commit to my ideas. Any inaccuracies remain fully my own.

I am very thankful to my colleagues at Radboud University for their kind support as I tried to balance navigating a new country, culture, and university system with writing this book. I deeply appreciate Rachel Gillett welcoming me to the Netherlands and sharing her insights. Work on this manuscript was made possible by an Early Career Research Development Grant from the Radboud Institute for Culture & History.

Throughout the dissertation and book writing process, the students I have had the pleasure of teaching at NYU, Université Paris-Est Créteil, and Radboud have been ever-constant reminders of why I do this. At a time when the foreign language departments, and the humanities more broadly, are under threat across the globe, their curiosity, enthusiasm, and ambition give this all a meaning that spreadsheets and audits can never fully capture. I am particularly grateful for the students of the "Politics of French Hip-Hop" course I taught at NYU, as well as guest speakers Éloïse Bouton and D' de Kabal. Their perspectives and passion made the classroom a fertile ground to explore the ideas that would become my dissertation and eventually this book.

Once a student of the French language and francophone cultures myself, I could never have predicted decades ago that my path would lead me here. Nevertheless, I had wonderful professors and teachers whose mentorship and examples laid the groundwork for this journey—Julie Baker, Olivier Delers, Sara Pappas, and Patricia Carlini.

I do not have the words to thank my parents for sticking by me through the stresses and rewards of an academic world I can never fully manage to explain. The same goes for Katie, with whom I am lucky to have shared many years of friendship, and my cousin Nicole, with whom I am proud to share some of the best traits of our grandmother. Many of my aunts and uncles, both those with insight into academia and those without, have been great sources of support. In humoring their long-distance aunt with weekly FaceTimes, my niece and nephew did more to keep me in this than they could ever know. Finally, while no longer with us, my grandparents are at the root of this book, not only because they gave me my first Muzzy tape to learn French, but also because they introduced me to literature, theater, and, unknowingly via their cable subscription, to the wonderful world of MTV.

Introduction

"A Little Soft for Rebel Music": Negotiating French Rap's Representational Space

In 1991, the French talk show *Ciel, mon mardi!* dedicated a full episode to rap. The show brought together rappers, music journalists, label representatives, and scholars to debate the genre's origins, creative processes, and themes, as well as the social identities of its performers. The opening voiceover presents rap as something that speaks about the street, comes from the working-class suburbs (*banlieues*), and is a token of recognition for the multiracial youth of those neighborhoods—the *blacks, blancs,* and *beurs.*[1] The voiceover further describes the music as "a mix of morality and violence, of evasion and rebellion, a means of getting out of a dead-end environment."[2] The introduction is emblematic of national television coverage of French rap in the early 1990s, which used the genre to discuss public order problems such as tagging and urban riots. In making rappers the visible face of those issues, television cemented an amalgamation between rap and a particular media figure: the racialized, working-class, suburban youth (*jeune de banlieue*).[3] As host Christophe Dechavanne repeatedly states, the episode's intent is to help the television audience discover these rappers they have heard so much about. In this regard, *Ciel, mon mardi*'s debate offers a crucial, early microcosm of the productive tension between conventions of reception, French rappers' meta-discourse on their craft, and the aesthetic techniques of rap performances that lies at the heart of this book.

The scope of the televised debate quickly tightens around rebellion and the bleak reality of the *banlieue.* From his seat amid the studio audience, Olivier Cachin, host of the television program *Rapline*, defines rap as poetry spoken over music. He traces its origins to the Black Power politics of Harlem's Last Poets. By his side, university professor Desdémone Bardin interjects that she

[1] This slogan—bringing together Black, white, and Arab identities—was a common way of evoking France's multiracial suburban youth throughout 1990s and eventually became synonymous with the victorious 1998 World Cup team.

[2] "*Un mélange de morale et de violence, d'évasion et de révolte, une façon de sortir d'un univers bouché.*" (All translations are my own unless otherwise stated.) Christian Vidalie, dir., *Ciel, mon mardi!*, TF1, February 5, 1991.

[3] Karim Hammou, *Une Histoire du rap en France* (La Découverte, 2014), 73–74.

Reflexivity in French Rap. Emily Q. Shuman, Oxford University Press. © Oxford University Press 2026.
DOI: 10.1093/9780197781609.003.0001

uses this style of vocal delivery in her English classes and that the virulent texts resonate with students. Both the journalist and the academic emphasize the value of radical activism and the historical struggle for racial justice in rap. Even though Cachin distinguishes between the music's aggressive themes and the mainstream media's image of rap as an instigator of destruction, Dechavanne routinely probes if rap is inherently violent by nature. To echo the host's desire to place the genre in definitive, intelligible boxes, a message on the screen prompts viewers at home to weigh in via Minitel on the question: "Is rap a culture?"[4]

The stakes of defining rap as the violent eruption of *banlieue* frustration quickly materialize for the participating rappers. Rock music journalist Jean-Pierre Sabouret turns in bemusement to MC Solaar, who had opened the episode with a performance of his hit single "Bouge de là," and asks in a dismissively sarcastic tone: "do you have the impression that you really expressed the revolt of suburban youth with what you just sang?"[5] Sabouret sharply distinguishes between the groove of Solaar's single, which he decidedly finds "a little soft for rebel music,"[6] and the "real" rap of groups like NTM that disrupt and disturb, even with their name, *Nique ta mère*.[7] Solaar, who would observe the rest of the show's debate almost exclusively in silence, retorts that there are many different ways of rapping. The elusive qualifications of "real rap" prove difficult to maintain, even for Sabouret's counterexample, as he later laments that NTM no longer have anything of substance to say.

Taking up this opposition, Dechavanne turns to Marseille natives IAM to adjudicate if rap exists to let off steam or to convey social messages. Akhenaton, going by the moniker "Chill," expresses distaste for the word "message," but nevertheless affirms that the purpose is to say something. IAM's remarks initially align with those of Sabouret and Bardin, for whom "commercial" music that breaks into the Top 50 serves as the foil for "real rap." The specter of Benny B, a hip-hop dancer and rapper from Brussels, and his breakout summer 1990 hit, "Vous êtes fous!" looms large here. Through music industry logics and collaborations, the song blended rap with dance music and relied heavily upon a chorus designed for commercial success.[8] Rather than ally himself with Sabouret, however, Akhenaton upholds Solaar's rebuttal that there is a

[4] *"Le rap, est-il une culture?"*

[5] *"T'as l'impression de vraiment exprimer la révolte des jeunes de banlieue avec ce que tu as chanté à tout à l'heure?"*

[6] *"Un peu molle pour une musique de révolte."*

[7] The name translates to "Fuck your mother."

[8] Karim Hammou, *Une histoire du rap*, 99.

range of light-hearted and serious lyrics, just as rap is musically comprised of a wealth of other genres, including jazz, funk, and soul. The rapper further rejects the creative constraints that accompany the emphasis on rap as rebel music: "we aren't going to limit ourselves to making songs about revolt on the pretext that it's rebel music."[9] As the late pioneer Lionel D interjects, within the element of revolt, there is a profound art from the *banlieue* that begs recognition. The invited rappers' insistence upon rap's aesthetic richness in the face of attempts to distill it into unequivocal, digestible terms remains constant throughout the episode.

Their arguments for aesthetic value meet the starkest challenge in the form of Dr. Gérard Zwang, whom the show credits as a musicologist. Using classical music references, Zwang presents rap as the heir to two forms: melodrama in its narration over percussion and *Ancien Régime* satirical songs in its political critique. Zwang's assertions that rap marks no innovation from these models and features rudimentary rhythms instantly transform him into the show's villain. Akhenaton responds that, while Zwang may just think of rap as *racaille* (riffraff) music, today he has "*racaille intelligente*" before him. His fellow group member, Shurik'n, challenges Zwang's historicization, rooting rap in practices of storytelling over drumbeats that long predate European composers. IAM channels these objections into their performance during one of the musical interludes. The group performs their ode to Pan-Africanism, "Red, Black and Green," which samples vocals from the Black American artists held up as models of politically valuable music throughout the episode, including Jungle Brothers and Gil Scott-Heron and Brian Jackson's "The Liberation Song (Red, Black and Green)." Within the metaphor of the three colors of Marcus Garvey's design for the Pan-African flag, IAM's lyrics bear witness to forms of systemic violence, whose red river of bloody oppression flows from the housing projects of Marseille back to the colonization of Africa. The allegories of violence resonate within the parameters of the show's debate, yet push against their limiting geographic and temporal scope.

IAM uses ad-libbed meta-commentary to hit back at Zwang's belittling remarks. Akhenaton inserts "100% intelligence" into the lyrics as a callback to his assertion that the musicologist finds himself faced with *racaille intelligente.* After the performance, Shurik'n cements the connection to the preceding debate with a direct remark to Zwang, with Sabouret also catching a stray bullet: "I think we've demonstrated that rap, it's something other than

[9] *"On ne va pas se cantonner à faire des chansons de révolte sous prétexte que c'est une musique de révolte."*

'I was on the street and got picked up by the cops.' Do we agree? And musically, it can also be violent."[10] While the performance of "Red, Black and Green" was a scheduled component of the show, IAM integrated the episode's talking points to assert their claims to aesthetic value. Zwang ultimately remained unconvinced, confidently predicting that, in ten years' time, no one would be talking about rap anymore.

Ciel, mon mardi! features the terms of debate that, over thirty years after Zwang's attempted clairvoyance, still shape critical conversations about rap in France. During the episode, rappers, journalists, and academics negotiated French rap's representational space and the limits of what it could embody in the social imaginary. The notion of "representational space" encompasses boundary maintenance—external from critics, industry professionals, political figures, and the media, as well as internal from rappers and their artistic collaborators—of the themes, repertoires, and sociopolitical import seen as inherent to rap.[11] Media representation and political instrumentalization filtered perception of the music through the *jeune de banlieue* figure, naturalizing a gaze that reads rap performances for indications of their informing context (the working-class suburbs and the racial and class alterity they signify). This amalgamation created specific expectations as to the types of experiences rap captures: delinquency, violence, and economic struggle. At the heart of the contention in the talk show was the relative weight of aesthetic and sociopolitical factors in defining what could, and should, be considered rap.

While much has changed since the 1990s, the frames of reception—or patterns of thinking about rap that shape its place in the French social imaginary—that I will explore in the following pages all feature in some form during *Ciel, mon mardi*'s debate. These frames include investments in French rap as poetic texts, belief in its innate capacity to enact violence, reliance on rappers as manifestations of the racial diversity that the colorblind French Republic officially disavows, lamentations that commodification crushes rap's true artistic nature, and reinforcements of the mainstream media as its principal antagonist. Rather than writing off these representations as distorted exterior gazes projected onto the musical genre, this book explores how French rappers channel these frames into their stylistic experimentations and claims to aesthetic value. At stake is the nuancing and expansion of French rap's representational space.

[10] *"Je crois qu'on a bien démontré que le rap, c'est autre chose que 'j'étais dans la rue et je me suis fait embarquer' on est bien d'accord? Et musicalement, ça peut être quelque chose de violent."*

[11] My understanding of representational space is indebted to Darby English's conceptualization of the term in the context of Black art, *How to See a Work of Art in Total Darkness* (The MIT Press, 2007), 34.

More than a Mirror: French Rap's Reflexivity

I argue that French rappers both redraw and re-entrench the boundaries of their representational space through reflexivity. I emphasize the duality of reflexivity—a look inward toward rap's stylistic conventions and rappers' creative labor, as well as a look outward toward anticipated reception and the social power dynamics that shape rap's value as a cultural product. Across the globe, rap is a popular culture object that many expect to hold up a mirror to the systemic injustices and paradoxes of its national context. France is no exception. French rap offers prisms through which alternative memories of the Hexagon's colonial past can emerge and which can expose the cracks of its postcolonial present.

Many French rappers proudly pursue this artistic vocation. Indeed, the second half of this book's title, *More than a Mirror to the Republic*, nods to Kery James' 2012 track "*Lettre à la République.*" The French-Haitian rapper's epistolary song functions as a "return to sender," tracing contemporary anti-immigrant sentiment, Islamophobia, and systemic racism back to French colonialism. Kery James raps: "*Loin des artistes transparents, j'écris ce texte comme un miroir/Que la France s'y regarde si elle veut s'y voir/Elle verra s'envoler l'illusion qu'elle se fait d'elle-même/J'suis pas en manque d'affection, comprends que je n'attends plus qu'elle m'aime.*"[12] The rapper powerfully likens his lyrics to a mirror that will reflect the French Republic's social realities, shattering its illusionary self-image as the nation of Enlightenment values and human rights. Yet, Kery James crucially insists that he and his fellow rappers are far from transparent, claiming an opacity and irreducibility for their artistry that is sometimes lost when critics frame rap uniquely as raw, no-holds-barred social commentary.

While honoring rap's specular qualities, this book makes the case for a pivot inward as well, to examine how rappers situate themselves within the French rap scene and how they articulate their artistic ambitions. I argue that the richest knowledge that rap produces about broader social forces such as racialization, commodification, and mediatization is entwined with reflexivity toward its aesthetic form and anticipated reception. It is the duality of reflexivity—a mirror held up to its social world *and* to itself—that captures rap in its complexities as a cultural product constantly drawing other art forms, media tropes, historical references, and political debates into its aesthetic

[12] "Far from transparent artists, I write this text as a mirror/that France looks in if she wants to see herself/She will see the illusion she makes of herself fly out the window/I'm not lacking affection, understand that I'm no longer waiting for her to love me."

practice. Rather than presume guaranteed strength and resistance in such *bricolage*, reflexivity acknowledges the self-conscious ways rappers negotiate the creative risks and rewards this strategy entails.

Rap is a musical genre particularly adept at reflexivity. This capacity emerges through lyrics in which rappers address listeners to comment upon themselves, what they are saying, or even the stylistic devices they are employing.[13] Such meta-commentary often extends to the music's aesthetic legitimacy and artistic nature.[14] Rap's overt intertextuality feeds into a self-referential community of practitioners, critics, and listeners likely to pick up on the genre's internal references, idiosyncrasies, and canonized traditions.[15] At the level of musical production, rap cites its own history, creates lineages of samples, and references peers to assert hip-hop authenticity.[16] This proclivity for self-historicizing within hip-hop culture[17] is matched only by its impassioned self-championing, capacity for self-critique, and restless internal creative force.[18]

In addition to these introspective turns, reflexivity stretches to the ways rappers riff on available modes of representation. This kind of representational play resonates in hip-hop culture's taste for sampling, remixing, and reappropriating existing cultural objects. Taking up Henry Louis Gates Jr.'s literary concept of "signifying," scholars retrace this taste for finding power in revising, commenting upon, or mimicking tropes through Black music history, African American literature, and West African storytelling figures such as tricksters and griots.[19] Imani Perry notably connects trickster consciousness to hip-hop's "subtextual discourse" that invokes shared knowledge to forge bonds with listeners, as well as uses elements of surprise to cleverly slip in social critique, particularly of white supremacy.[20] Reflexive techniques may also take into account reception by audiences that do not share rappers' lived experiences and social positions, as is the case with self-aware parody

[13] Anthony Pecqueux, *Voix du rap: essai de sociologie de l'action musicale* (L'Harmattan, 2007), 109.

[14] Richard Shusterman, *Pragmatist Aesthetics: Living Beauty, Rethinking Art*, 2nd ed. (Rowman & Littlefield Publishers, 2000), 232.

[15] Justin A. Williams, *Rhymin' and Stealin': Musical Borrowing in Hip-Hop* (University of Michigan Press, 2013), 12.

[16] Ibid., 20.

[17] "Hip-hop" refers to a broad cultural and artistic movement involving dance, graffiti, DJing, rap music, and even fashion. Within this range of practices, this book focuses exclusively on rap.

[18] S. Craig Watkins, *Hip Hop Matters. Politics, Pop Culture, and the Struggle for the Soul of a Movement* (Beacon Press, 2005), 5; Joseph G. Schloss, *Foundation. B-Boys, B-Girls, and Hip-Hop Culture in New York* (Oxford University Press, 2009), 3; Jeff Chang, *Total Chaos: The Art and Aesthetics of Hip-Hop* (Basic Books, 2006), x.

[19] Henry Louis Gates Jr., *The Signifying Monkey: A Theory of African-American Literary Criticism* (Oxford University Press, 1989); Russel A. Potter, *Spectacular Vernaculars: Hip-Hop and the Politics of Postmodernism* (State University of New York Press, 1995).

[20] Imani Perry, *Prophets of the Hood: Politics and Poetics in Hip Hop*. (Duke University Press, 2004), 30–31.

that anticipates white audiences fetishizing themes of racial discrimination and political struggle.[21]

Building upon rap's well-charted self-referentiality as a means of historicizing the genre and strengthening insider knowledge, I turn slightly outward to look at French rap's negotiations of its place in the social imaginary. With the frames of reception that orbit rap in the mix, reflexivity drifts from the security of in-group dynamics and shared knowledge within hip-hop scenes themselves, toward a means of grappling with dominant cultural scripts of artistry, risks of political and legal repression, racialization, market demands, and an increased media presence. As modes that span genres, there is an ambivalence to reflexivity, self-consciousness, and "meta" techniques. They can serve as motors of creativity, a means of asserting a place in an aesthetic tradition, signs of a genre's artistic maturity, strategies to maneuver around typecasting, imprints of industry logics, ways to pander to critics, or even the root of ironic, complacent detachment.[22] This book inscribes French rap's reflexivity within this tension, as a potential crux of aesthetic innovation and as a means of situated critique from within the larger cultural and media landscape. Reflexivity for French rappers is as much a means of building community with listeners and playing off shared knowledge as it is a means of reckoning with the stakes of the creative process, particularly one that actively draws other media and social power dynamics into its aesthetic form, rendering its reception susceptible to the symbolic weight of those forces.

Situating French Rap Within and Beyond the Hexagon

To better foreground French rappers' position in the cultural landscape and social imaginary, I will first situate rap's evolution in the Hexagon. Over the course of the 1980s, hip-hop culture's development in France began. In 1984, Sidney, the first Black host on French national television, animated *H.I.P. H.O.P.*, a short-format program dedicated to hip-hop culture, particularly dance. That same year, DJ Dee Nasty released the first French rap album, *Paname City Rappin'*, and later in 1989, co-hosted a radio show with Lionel D

[21] Katelyn E. Knox, *Race on Display in 20th- and 21st Century France* (Liverpool University Press, 2016), 142.

[22] For more on reflexivity and self-conscious aesthetics in other genres, see David Foster Wallace, "E Unibus Pluram: Television and U.S. Fiction," *Review of Contemporary Fiction* 13, no. 2 (1993): 151–194; Patricia Waugh, *Metafiction: The Theory and Practice of Self-Conscious Fiction (New Accents)* (Routledge, 2002); Werner Wolf, ed., *The Metareferential Turn in Contemporary Arts and Media. Forms, Functions, Attempts at Explanation* (Rodopi, 2011); David LaRocca, ed., *Metacinema: The Form and Content of Filmic Reference and Reflexivity* (Oxford University Press, 2021).

that would feature MC Solaar, NTM, and many other rappers from the Paris region.[23] After these initial forays, the early 1990s marked a crucial turning point in rap's national visibility. The working-class suburbs had returned to the spotlight after a series of riots in Lyon and Paris. Public policies invested in hip-hop culture as a means of both accessing marginalized experiences and combating social exclusion and delinquency in the *banlieues*. This political investment ambiguously portrayed hip-hop as both a product of social ills and its potential remedy. France's Minister of Culture during this period, Jack Lang, extolled a philosophy of cultural democracy that valorized hip-hop as a sociocultural practice of underprivileged groups that allows young people to positively construct their identities and socially integrate.[24] Throughout the 1990s, media, academic, and political figures typecast rappers as social messengers and ingrained the idea that true rap music channeled the gritty reality of *banlieue* life into a defiant, and often violent, expression of subjecthood in the face of marginalization.[25]

In the late 1990s, major record labels capitalized on artists' capacity to reliably represent the fantasized *banlieue* image. The 1994 Carignon law established quotas for French-language music on the radio, inciting some stations to orient themselves toward rap. Skyrock most notably adopted this strategy, and the station remains a major player—to the chagrin of many French rappers—in shaping commercial success, visibility, and aesthetic choices. In this period, the underground rap scene, bolstered by radio stations and major record labels, channeled the contestation, social exclusion, and violent revolt attributed to rap music into promotional efforts that Karim Hammou likens to a marketing of the margins.[26] These marketing strategies sought to convert rap's association with the *banlieue* and marginalized positions into commercial value.

While I begin with the critical moment of the 1990s, rap's place in the French cultural landscape has certainly not remained static since then. After a period of intense growth and investment from major record labels throughout the 1990s, the global music industry crisis of the 2000s, prompted in large

[23] Karim Hammou, "Forty Years of French Rap: Identities in Crescendo," trans. Katie B. Angus, in *Hip-hop en français. An Exploration of Hip-Hop Culture in the Francophone World*, ed. Alain-Philippe Durand (Rowman & Littlefield, 2020), 1–16.

[24] Loïc Lafargue de Grangeneuve, *Politique du hip-hop: Action publique et cultures urbaines* (Presses universitaires du Mirail, 2008), 12–14.

[25] See, e.g., Manuel Boucher, *Rap, Expression des Lascars. Significations et enjeux du rap dans la société française* (L'Harmattan, 1998).

[26] Karim Hammou, "Mainstreaming French Rap Music. Commodification and Artistic Legitimation of Othered Cultural Goods," *Poetics* 59 (December 2016), 77. Hammou borrows this theorization from Graham Huggan's work on postcolonial literature, *The Postcolonial Exotic: Marketing the Margins* (Taylor & Francis, 2001).

part by the proliferation of illegal online downloads, hit France, and rap in particular, hard. This period also saw orchestrated campaigns of legal and political denunciations of rap, particularly targeting lyrics critiquing postcolonial power dynamics[27] and systemic racism in France (Chapter 2). Since the mid-2010s, however, French rap's commercial prospects and place in the cultural landscape have greatly evolved. With the groundbreaking success of independent artists such as the duo PNL (Chapter 4) and Marseille phenomenon Jul, major record labels have largely abandoned offering rappers record contracts as the industry shifts to privileging distribution deals—a model that allows rappers to maneuver with a certain degree of artistic autonomy and allows key industry players to profit while mitigating risk.[28] This model rejoins a wave of growth in the French music industry, which has been significantly bolstered by urban music. This recently established meta-category—regrouping rap, R&B, soul, funk, and urban pop—represented close to 35% of the revenue from digital streaming and sales in 2017.[29] In an industry dominated by streaming platforms, urban music's physical sales grew significantly from 2015 onward. Between 2010 and 2015, the revenue generated by French rap multiplied by 2.5.[30]

Rap's place within the French public's cultural habits has expanded along with its commercial success. 2018 data from the Ministry of Culture attests to rap's mainstreaming, with the majority of the surveyed metropolitan France residents under fifty-five years of age, and 80% of the under 25 category listening to rap and/or contemporary R&B.[31] The taste for these genres, while remaining strongly anchored in the working class, has become a key fixture in the cultural practices of the middle class and is also present in the upper socioeconomic classes.[32] Furthermore, as taste has expanded and diversified across categories, *distaste* for rap has significantly declined, from 48% of the population in 2008 to 32% in 2018.[33]

[27] Keivan Djavadzadeh, "Colonialité du pouvoir, postcolonialité du rap: l'émergence et la répression d'un rap français structuré autour de la critique postcoloniale dans les années 2000," *The Postcolonialist* 3, no. 1 (2015): 1–9.

[28] Paco Garcia, "L'indépendance est morte, vive l'indépendance. Entre contraintes matérielles et enjeux symboliques: une analyse de l'évolution de 'l'indépendance' dans le rap en France," *Les Enjeux de l'information et de la communication* 22, no. 1 (2021): 19–34.

[29] Karim Hammou and Marie Sonnette-Manouguian, "Socio-économie de 'l'urbain' musical,'" in *40 ans de musiques hip-hop en France*, ed. Karim Hammou and Marie Sonnette-Manouguian (Presses de Sciences Po, 2022), 173–211.

[30] Ibid.

[31] Karim Hammou and Stéphanie Molinero, "Rap et RnB dans les pratiques culturelles en France," in *40 ans de musiques hip-hop*, 148.

[32] Ibid.

[33] Karim Hammou and Marie Sonnette-Manouguian, "40 ans de musiques hip-hop en France: (il)legitimation, institutionnalisation, et patrimonialisation," in *40 ans de musiques hip-hop*, 179.

However, despite commercial success, rap's cultural and aesthetic legitimacy is not secure. While rap has achieved economic durability in the French music industry, this value hinges upon the genre's exoticized image and the efforts of a circle of industry professionals from racial minorities.[34] Continued racial stereotyping of rappers and their music also fuels politicized controversies and legal action against rappers for their lyrics and music videos. Despite increased media recognition, the national press continues to reify artistic hierarchies between "good" and "bad" rap rooted in racialized and class-based notions of respectability.[35] Only a few artists, socially situated further from the racial and class stereotypes associated with rap, combine commercial success with institutional consecration. These ambivalences underscore persistent tensions between marginality and integration, between commercial value and aesthetic recognition, and between the delegitimizing effects of the music's perceived alterity and the legitimizing effects of proximity to the cultural mainstream.

Though it exclusively focuses on French rap, this book aims to negotiate the global and the local. Many hip-hop studies scholars have taken on what it means for rap and hip-hop culture to circulate from their Black American roots[36] and the streets of the Bronx and Harlem to practically every corner of the globe.[37] In attending to the scripts of artistry, aesthetic merit, and alterity in France that shape the performance and reception of the music, I join many studies that attest to the value of situating rap scenes in local histories of race-making and constructions of national belonging, and thus contest a straightforward process of Americanization.[38] This book's aim is not to identify what makes rap French,[39] nor is it to approach it primarily through the

[34] Ibid., 192.

[35] Marion Dalibert, "Du 'bon' et du 'mauvais' rap? Les processus médiatiques de hiérarchisation artistique," *Volume! La revue des musiques populaires* 17, no. 2 (2020): 83–97.

[36] Imani Perry, *Prophets of the Hood*, 10.

[37] Tony Mitchell, ed., *Global Noise: Rap and Hip Hop Outside the USA* (Wesleyan University Press, 2001); Murray Forman, *The 'Hood Comes First: Race, Space, and Place in Rap and Hip-Hop* (Wesleyan University Press, 2002); H. Samy Alim, Awad Ibrahim, and Alastair Pennycook, eds., *Global Linguistic Flows: Hip Hop Cultures, Youth Identities, and the Politics of Language* (Routledge, 2008).

[38] André J.M. Prévos, "The Evolution of French Rap Music and Hip Hop Culture in the 1980s and the 1990s," *The French Review* 69, no. 5 (1996): 713–725; Alain-Philippe Durand, ed., *Black, Blanc, Beur: Rap Music and Hip-hop Culture in the Francophone World* (Scarecrow Press, 2002); Alain-Philippe Durand, ed., *Hip-Hop en Français*; Felicia McCarren, *French Moves. The Cultural Politics of le Hip-Hop* (Oxford University Press, 2013). For global examples, Ian Condry, *Hip-Hop Japan: Rap and the Paths of Cultural Globalization* (Duke University Press, 2006); Alice Aterianus-Owanga, *"Le rap, ça vient d'ici!" Musiques, pouvoirs et identités dans le Gabon contemporain* (Éditions de la maison des sciences de l'homme, 2017); J. Griffith Rollefson, *Flip the Script: European Hip Hop and the Politics of Postcoloniality* (University of Chicago Press, 2017); Justin A. Williams, *Brithop. The Politics of UK Rap in the New Century* (Oxford University Press, 2021).

[39] For critical discussions of the Frenchness of an array of popular music genres, see Jonathyne Briggs, *Sounds French: Globalization, Cultural Communities & Pop Music, 1958–1980* (Oxford University Press, 2015); Gérôme Guibert and Catherine Rudent, eds., *Made in France: Studies in Popular Music* (Routledge, 2018).

lens of national identity. Rather, I critically examine debates surrounding rap in France and the ways rappers creatively work within them. As with the preceding retrospective on rap's development in France, each chapter is indebted to sociological and media studies approaches to French rap, as they provide a base from which I can plunge into individual performances. These case studies cover a diverse range of French rappers, from pioneering icons to influential players in the contemporary scene, but do not claim to exhaustively encompass the genre as a whole. While the first chapter engages distinctly French reference points for aesthetic value rooted in the nation's literary tradition, most of the conventions of reception explored in this book, such as campaigns to penalize the music (Chapter 2), expectations that rappers legibly perform racial difference (Chapter 3), critiques of rap's commodification (Chapter 4), and investments in its counternarratives to mainstream media (Chapter 5), readily connect to global debates.[40] I wish to strengthen dialogue between scholarship on French rap and global hip-hop studies, and to highlight the knowledge French rap contributes to critical conversations that extend beyond the borders of metropolitan France and the cultural industries centralized therein.[41]

Contesting French Rap's Marginality Through the Lens of Complicity

French rap's status as a widely consumed and increasingly routine cultural fixture complicates approaches that presume it suffers from incomprehension and sidelining. This echoes Paul Gilroy's oft-cited critique of academic criticism of hip-hop:

> Those who assert the marginality of Hip hop should be obliged to say where they imagine the center might now be. Hip hop's marginality is as official, as routinized, as its overblown defiance; yet it is still represented as an outlaw form. This is a mystery that aches to be solved.[42]

[40] Tricia Rose distills many of these debates in her book, *The Hip Hop Wars: What We Talk About When We Talk About Hip-Hop—And Why It Matters* (Basic Books, 2008).

[41] In the interest of reinforcing this dialogue, I have translated lyrics and primary source material from French to English. In respect for rappers' voices and the stylistic complexities of their lyrics that I cannot fully capture in translation, I keep their original French in the text, with English translations in the footnotes.

[42] Paul Gilroy, "'After the Love Has Gone': Bio-politics and Etho-poetics in the Black Public Sphere," *Public Culture* 7 (1994): 51.

Much scholarship on French rap emphasizes rappers' marginalized positions to highlight how the music challenges dominant models of citizenship and national identity. This line of inquiry reads rap against the colorblind ideology of Republican universalism, which refuses racial, ethnic, or religious identities as valid categories to organize social and political life in favor of the ideal of the abstract citizen.[43] In critique of these erasures, scholars value French rap for how it articulates hybrid identities inherited from postcolonial immigration and for how it disseminates alternative memories of French colonialism, as well as for its ability to give visibility to *banlieue* inhabitants.[44] Rooting rap's potential for critique in its marginality, however, is difficult to reconcile with the music's current place in the cultural landscape.

This book therefore takes into account rap's embeddedness in the economic forces, regimes of media representation, and broader artistic traditions of French society. I follow cultural theorist Stuart Hall's firm rejection of purist notions of popular culture's authenticity and autonomy from the larger field of social forces and the modern, capitalist cultural industries. Hall's historically rooted argument emphasizes the "double movement of containment and resistance" inherently inside popular culture, as it struggles against and operates within dominant culture's efforts to contain, reorganize, and recuperate it.[45] Therefore, while rap's cultural exclusion needs problematizing, so do its internal contradictions as a racialized form of popular culture.[46] The persistent roles that race and class play in its media coverage, place in the music industry, and legal battles require serious consideration of how forms of Othering shape the music's commercial and aesthetic value.

[43] Herrick Chapman and Laura L. Frader, eds., *Race in France: Interdisciplinary Perspectives on the Politics of Difference* (Berghahn Books, 2004); Alec G. Hargreaves, *Multi-Ethnic France. Immigration, Politics, Culture and Society*, 2nd ed. (Routledge, 2007); Tricia Danielle Keaton, Tracey Denean Sharpley-Whiting, and Tyler Stovall, eds., *Black France/France Noire. The History and Politics of Blackness* (Duke University Press, 2012).

[44] See Veronique Helenon, "Africa on Their Mind: Rap, Blackness, and Citizenship in France," in *The Vinyl Ain't Final: Hip Hop and the Globalization of Black Popular Culture*, ed. Dipannita Basu and Sidney J. Lemelle (Pluto Press, 2006); Charles Tshimanga, "Let the Music Play: The African Diaspora, Popular Culture, and National Identity in Contemporary France," in *Frenchness and the African Diaspora: Identity and Uprising in Contemporary France*, ed. Charles Tshimanga, Ch. Didier Gondola, and Peter J. Bloom (Indiana University Press, 2009); Nathalie Etoke, "Black Blanc Beur: Ma France à moi," *Nouvelles Études Francophones* 24, no. 1 (2009): 157–171; Lara Dotson-Renta, "'On n'est pas condamné à l'échec': Hip-hop and the *Banlieue* Narrative," *French Cultural Studies* 26, no. 3 (2015): 354–367; Pierre-Alain Clement, "La signification du politique dans le rap. L'exemple du 'rap de fils d'immigrés' (1997–2012)," *Cultures et conflits* 97 (2015): 123–141; Chong J. Bretillon, "'Double Discours': Critiques of Racism and Islamophobia in French Rap," in *Post-Migratory Cultures in Postcolonial France*, ed. Kathryn Kleppinger and Laura Reeck (Liverpool University Press, 2018).

[45] Stuart Hall, "Notes on Deconstructing the Popular," in *Essential Essays, Volume 1*, ed. Stuart Hall and David Morley (Duke University Press, 2018), 348, 357.

[46] Stuart Hall, "What Is This 'Black' in Black Popular Culture?" *Social Justice* 20, no. 1/2 (1993): 108.

In this regard, I join efforts in hip-hop studies scholarship to critically probe the ambivalences of rap's position in the cultural field. Tricia Rose's foundational work *Black Noise* lays out the tension between US rap's social critique, dominant media constructions of blackness, and music industry imperatives.[47] Through a postcolonial lens, studies of national and transnational rap scenes explore how rappers contest marginalization, systemic injustice, and lingering effects of colonial histories, yet also stress the need to move away from fetishizing rap's resistance in light of its increasingly valued place in the global cultural industries.[48] As both J. Griffith Rollefson and George Lipsitz argue, rap and hip-hop culture fuel their creative force from the paradoxes of their postcolonial societies *and* from their ability to work within alienating global economic and political systems.[49]

I propose to examine rap's entangled relationship with the media landscape, cultural industries, and social forces that shape its representational space as one of complicity.[50] I emphasize less complicity's moral and legal implications than I do its rarer, yet more neutral signification of "bound together." Its English etymology derives from the Latin *complicāre,* meaning "to fold," by way of modern French, where the word *complicité* holds dual meanings of participation in illicit activity and rapport, affinity, or harmony.[51] The notion of French rap's complicity in the designation of its representational space intentionally chips away at investments in the musical genre's marginalization and autonomy. I am interested in how complicity's sense of "bound together" sheds light on the reflexive ways French rappers and their artistic collaborators work within the cultural scripts, political debates, industry imperatives, and media logics that frame the music's commercial and aesthetic value.

Reflexivity, complicity, and representational space thus maintain a dynamic relationship throughout the chapters that follow. Through reflexivity, French rappers grapple with their complicit co-construction of their representational space. Rappers acknowledge the risks and rewards of aesthetically integrating various expectations of them into their performances,

[47] Tricia Rose, *Black Noise. Rap Music and Black Culture in Contemporary America* (Wesleyan University Press, 1994), 104.

[48] See, e.g., Cristina Moreno Almeida, *Rap Beyond Resistance: Staging Power in Contemporary Morocco* (Palgrave Macmillan, 2017).

[49] J. Griffith Rollefson, *Flip the Script,* 5; George Lipsitz, *Dangerous Crossroads: Popular Music, Postmodernism, and the Poetics of Place* (Verso, 1994), 34.

[50] I have developed the notion of French rap's complicity in its uses of sexual fantasy and humor vis-à-vis the police and the far right: Emily Q. Shuman, "Fantasies of Power: Sex, Humour and Complicities in French Rap," *Modern & Contemporary* France 33, no.4 (2025): 523–540. DOI: https://doi.org/10.1080/09639489.2025.2519085.

[51] *Oxford English Dictionary*, s.v. "complicity (n.), Etymology," July 2023, https://doi.org/10.1093/OED/1013833844.

and further use reflexivity to implicate their audience in those stakes. Rap's proclivity for self-referentiality and in-group dynamics aligns with understandings of complicity as a tool in other cultural fields, such as literature. Building upon Pierre Bourdieu's notion of complicity between authors, critics, and audiences in upholding the literary field's commonsense beliefs,[52] Helen Craske stretches the term to comprise reflexive, self-referential play between authors in a socio-literary network, as well as authorial strategies of self-promotion and self-defense.[53] The idea of complicity encompassing self-positioning and meta-level aesthetic techniques will be essential to its relationship in this book to French rap's reflexivity toward its dominant frames of reception. The web of artistic collaborations, citational play, common cultural reference points, and shared antagonists that emerge through the following chapters attests to the entangled dynamics between internal and external actors reworking and reinforcing French rap's doxa.

Rather than conveying moral judgment or disqualifying its artistry, complicity figures as a potential motor driving French rap's introspection and evolutions. Nor does complicity negate French rap's capacity for critique of the systems in which it is embedded. I take inspiration here from work in art history and media studies that sees recognizing complicity as a fruitful starting point for critique in neoliberal, late-stage capitalist, and media-saturated contexts in which autonomy and clearly delineated moral and political positions prove elusive. Artists may very well offer alternative forms of expression, but they operate from within these systems, whether that participation be voluntary, critical, or contradictory.[54] Art that "plays in the system" holds ambivalent effects, but nevertheless poses essential questions about the potential for resistance from entangled positions.[55] While the art world differs substantially from rap in terms of institutional support, aesthetic recognition, and cultural legitimacy, investments in both rap and fine art's oppositionality rely on eliding their situatedness within the cultural industries. Complicity therefore moves past an idealized notion of rap's autonomy that is ultimately incompatible with its evolving place within the broader fields of media and cultural production.

[52] Pierre Bourdieu, *The Rules of Art: Genesis and Structure of the Literary Field*, trans. Susan Emanuel (Stanford University Press, 1996), 227–228.

[53] Helen Craske, *Complicity in Fin-de-siècle Literature* (Oxford University Press, 2024), 9, 138.

[54] Johanna Drucker, *Sweet Dreams: Contemporary Art and Complicity* (Chicago University Press, 2005), 17.

[55] Anna Watkins Fisher, *The Play in the System: The Art of Parasitical Resistance* (Duke University Press, 2020), 5.

Close Reading French Rap: Between Aesthetics and Politics

The attention to lyrics, sound, and visual culture in my close readings reflects the arsenal that rappers and their artistic collaborators—beatmakers, music video directors, photographers—have at their disposal to reflexively engage with not only the nature of the performance but also the mechanisms that value or devalue it. This multimodal approach[56] challenges a tendency in scholarship on French rap to situate rappers' engagement with cultural, political, and media discourses at the level of the lyrics. Each chapter pulls from music and mainstream journalism, academic criticism, and political rhetoric to establish patterns of thinking about French rap. I then delve into individual rap performances to close read how they reflect critical awareness of the frames of reception to which they are exposed. This move demonstrates that the performances are far from mere responses or reactive counterattacks, but artistically ambitious and stylistically complex objects in their own right. The lens of reflexivity therefore signals creative choices behind French rap performances, while foregrounding the aesthetic experiences and understandings of social power dynamics they afford.[57]

As its title indicates, this book seeks balance between attention to rap's interventions in political and social issues on the one hand, and its self-positioning and aesthetic techniques on the other hand. I follow the lead of the rappers in my corpus, who intertwine commentary on their stylistic innovations with reflections on how social forces shape perceptions of their music. Through this balancing act, I wish to move away from the instrumentalization of aesthetics in cultural studies as a means to a political end, such as advancing social messages or raising collective awareness of systemic injustices.[58] My emphasis on rap aesthetics does not, however, advocate for a return to the Kantian notion of an autonomous aesthetic and a disinterested appreciation of form, but rather for an aesthetic embedded in the social world.[59] My interdisciplinary close readings tease out the ways

[56] Carol Vernallis calls for this blend to bridge music video aesthetics with their political and media contexts, *Experiencing Music Video: Aesthetics and Cultural Context* (Columbia University Press, 2004); *The Media Swirl, Politics, Audiovisuality, and Aesthetics* (Duke University Press, 2023).

[57] My emphasis on affordances, or aesthetic elements' inherent constraints and possibilities that act and are acted upon as they encounter social and political structures, pulls from Tia DeNora's sociology of music approach and Caroline Levine's literary new formalism; Tia DeNora, "Music into Action: Performing Gender on the Viennese Concert Stage, 1790–1810," *Poetics* 30 (2002): 19–33; Caroline Levine, *Forms: Whole, Rhythm, Hierarchy, Network* (Princeton University Press, 2015).

[58] Jonathan Sterne, "The Burden of Culture," in *The Aesthetics of Cultural Studies*, ed. Michael Berubé (Blackwell Publishing, 2005), 90.

[59] Musicologist Adam Krims argues that if close reading explores how music's sensorial pleasure circulates and functions in the world as part of the greater web of cultural, social, and economic life, it can avoid reifying the ideology of aesthetic autonomy, *Music/Ideology: Resisting the Aesthetic* (Gordon and

rap performances draw in other forms such as literature and audiovisual media, and make mechanisms of legal penalization, commodification, and racialization perceptible as aesthetic components of its whole. While this approach does not ultimately escape the imbrication of aesthetics and politics, it does hold aesthetic techniques in the position to produce knowledge about social forces, and not solely the other way around.

Stuart Hall famously defined his own interest in popular culture through a political lens, emphasizing it as both the site and the stake to be won or lost in the "struggle for and against a culture of the powerful."[60] Within this strategic battle for position, Hall argues that "the meaning of a cultural form and its place or position in the cultural field is not inscribed inside its form. Nor is its position fixed once and forever."[61] In emphasizing the affordances of French rap performances, I do not argue that their meaning lies purely at the level of form. Aesthetic techniques cannot dictate the politics of reception. I posit reflexivity as a tool for French rappers to navigate their music's unmoored position in the cultural field and its susceptibility to interpretations they can seek to shape, but that ultimately lie beyond their control.

Throughout the book, I refer most often to rap "performances." On a practical level, this term reflects the diverse objects in my corpus, including recorded songs, music videos, album covers, and live performances. While I strive to recognize rappers' collaborations with other artists such as beatmakers and music video directors, the term "performance" acknowledges that this book's focus is not on production logics but rather on the cultural object that is put out into the world for interpretation. Far from being a mere catch-all, the term purposefully draws from performance studies[62] to capture the potential for play and innovation with established scripts, repertoires, and aesthetic traditions on the one hand, and, on the other hand, the constraining effects of generic conventions, industry logics, and social power dynamics such as race and gender.

Each performance represents a particular stylistic exercise best understood in the context of the artist's idiosyncratic signature, not as an interchangeable stand-in for French rap as a whole. However, rather than focus

Breach, 1998), 6–7. See also Adam Krims, *Rap Music and the Poetics of Identity* (Cambridge University Press, 2000).

[60] Stuart Hall, "Notes on Deconstructing the Popular," 360.

[61] Ibid., 356.

[62] Elin Diamond's classic formulation defines performance as "always a doing and a thing done," *Performance and Cultural Politics* (Routledge, 1996), 1. Different chapters will engage with different theories of performativity, notably regarding the material effects of discourse (Chapter 2), and the social, perceptual processes of racialization (Chapter 3).

on personae,[63] or constructed star personalities, I borrow the term "posture" from literary studies, where it designates the positioning of an author within the literary field. An individual writer's posture emerges through their work, self-representation in the media, critical reception, and relation to existing cultural myths surrounding "the author" as a figure in the social imaginary.[64] Shifting from literature to rap—which will be problematized in Chapter 1—"posture" reflects the crucial role of self-positioning within the rap scene in the complicit interaction between frames of reception and reflexive aesthetic techniques.

With all its mirror imagery, this book is also intended as a reflexive critical exercise toward my work as a scholar and toward approaches to rap in my field of French cultural studies. If I am drawn here to the reflexive, it may very well be because, as Richard Dyer observes, meta-discursive moments in art align with my "meta" activity as a critic.[65] Yet, it also reflects my relationship to the music as a listener who has often found confidence in rap—and who has come to navigate the role my whiteness, gender, and middle-class upbringing in the US play in that sensation. My interest in reflexivity also stems from how rap has shaped my own self-questioning as new artists and voices have accompanied the discovery of new facets of myself. The close readings that follow inevitably reflect my own critical ears and eyes, but, in turning toward what the performances offer up for aesthetic appreciation, entertainment, community building, and knowledge production, I hope they will also convey the enjoyment and stimulation I have found therein. Instead of writing from the position that French rap is doomed to be misunderstood and marginalized, and therefore desperately needs defending, I seek to leave space for the creative ways it plays off and challenges expectations, including my own.

Chapter Outline

The interplay between reflexivity, complicity, and representational space spelled out over the course of the next five chapters captures French rap's aesthetic maturity, commercial success, and instable artistic legitimacy. The first two chapters are structured as mirror-like reflections, encompassing both legitimizing and delegitimizing investments in rap lyrics as text. These chapters investigate frames of reception that seek to determine rap's

[63] Richard Dyer, *Stars* (Bloomsbury, 1979); Philip Auslander, "Performance Analysis and Popular Music: A Manifesto," *Contemporary Theatre Review* 14, no. 1 (2004): 1–13.
[64] Jérôme Meizoz, *Postures littéraires. Mises en scène modernes de l'auteur* (Éditions Slatkine, 2007), 45.
[65] Richard Dyer, *The Culture of Queers* (Routledge, 2002), 201.

assimilability within established cultural scripts of artistry. Chapter 1 focuses on a potent legitimizing gesture in France—likening rap to the nation's literary patrimony. Conferring authorial status to rappers comes with the creative privileges of poetic license, aesthetic sophistication, and perceived distance from politically charged referents. I explore press coverage and academic criticism to demonstrate that, underneath the ostensible focus on poetic dexterity with the French language, literary parallels invoke notions of virtuosity shaped by race, class, and norms of respectable masculinity. I then delve into the postures and performances of MC Solaar, Médine, and Booba. While their strategies differ, each rapper proves cognizant of the racialized parameters of inclusion in France's pantheon. Through this awareness, they contend with the weight of literary parallels in demarcating French rap's representational space and negotiate the ways in which engaging with the literary can both bolster and undermine their own positioning in the rap scene.

Chapter 2 takes up the flip side of focus on French rap as text. It examines legal and political campaigns to penalize lyrics as performative discourse capable of inciting violence toward the French Republic and its institutions, notably the national police. Through bills and debates in the National Assembly, as well as trials against French rappers, this second chapter explores the contested issues of referentiality, truth claims, and artistic responsibility that underlie efforts to typecast rappers as ideal culprits in times of social tension. I close read performances from Tandem, La Rumeur, Sniper, and Youssoupha that stage these mechanisms of penalization, in many instances as reflections upon their own legal battles. Their aesthetic techniques underscore the ambivalent effects of drawing the legal sphere's discursive codes, evidentiary requirements, and subject positions into the creative process. On the one hand, aestheticizing these parameters carves out space to expand the scope of testimony, accusations of injustice, and community-building gestures in rap. On the other hand, blurring boundaries between rap performances and courtroom arguments risks entrenching rap's representational space around a reactive, defensive position vis-à-vis state power.

Chapter 3 grapples with the expectation that rap perform the politicized work of reflecting the racial diversity that the colorblind French Republic disavows. The chapter moves from early French media and academic reception that turned to rappers as the visible faces of racialized *banlieue* youth, to French cultural studies scholarship that, in critique of colorblind universalism's blind spots, similarly invests in rap's representability of France's multiracial society. I argue that approaches that posit French rappers' racial difference as a self-evident starting point risk flattening the intricate ways rappers engage with racialization as a performative, perceptual process that their music and visual culture can shape. Chapter 3 thus turns this frame of reception back onto itself by centering performances from Médine, Abd al Malik, and Casey that draw in the racializing gaze and aesthetically trouble the intelligibility of race. Through stylistic devices, they expose the interpretive work the racializing gaze requires and hinge the rapper–audience relationship on negotiating the ethical stakes of that work. Inviting the alienating power of the gaze into the performance ultimately provides the grounds for these rappers' aesthetic experimentations, anti-racist positions, and connections to their audiences.

From this point, the book sinks further into French rap's embeddedness in the logics of the cultural industries and media landscape. Building upon Chapter 3's demonstration of how rap music and visual culture articulate perceptual processes of racialization, Chapter 4 explores performances that intertwine staging alterity with commentary on rap's commodified nature. The chapter begins by exploring critiques of rap's adherence to capitalist values. This lens often dismisses rap's artistic merit, or, for Leftist commentators, constructs a hierarchy between rap that seeks out commercial success and rap that remains true to its supposed vocation of social commentary. Chapter 4 complicates this opposition by tracing how rap's perceived marginality informs its commercial value. In performances by PNL, Alpha Wann, and Shay, the central metaphor of the illicit drug trade ties together formal elements that make marginality perceptible with those that comment upon commodification. The illicit allows these rappers to assert their captivating hold on the audience and right to profit from that influence, as well as reflect on the vulnerable process of submitting their persons, emotions, and creative labor to market logics.

The fifth and final chapter takes up rap's immersion in the media landscape. This chapter problematizes the portrayal of rap as a counternarrative to mainstream media discourse. I instead posit the relationship between rap and media as one of complicity, in which rap may offer opposition to mainstream media frames, but does so by integrating the norms and logics of those same media. Keny Arkana, NTM, Médine, and Vald take rap's embeddedness in the larger media landscape as a starting point for the creative process and find their conceptual strength and coherence in the norms that govern that landscape. In so doing, they adopt various strategies and stances toward media logics' relative weight in shaping their music's representational space.

These five chapters progress toward a deeper understanding of rap's place in the media and cultural landscapes in France. They build toward a greater sense of the genre's aesthetic complexity and agency, moving beyond a restricted relationship of response to social exclusion. From each chapter's move from a frame of reception to instances of artistic reflexivity, a complicit relationship emerges in which rappers harness expectations of the genre into complex postures and stylistic exercises. This book ultimately seeks a path between the fetishization of rap's marginality and ability to hold up a much-needed mirror to its society on the one hand, and the complacent view of rap as merely a product and reflection of its environment on the other.

Chapter 1
Literary Litmus Tests
Rap Artistry and the Figure of the Author

In the spring of 2016, students at France's prestigious École normale supérieure (ENS) invited the rapper Casey to their seminar on the stylistics of French rap—"La Plume et le bitume."[1] One of the seminar's main objectives was to offer an aesthetic approach to rap in the presence of the artists themselves, providing rappers with a platform to construct their own discourse on their craft. The co-organizers, Emmanuelle Carinos Vasquez and Benoît Dufau, selected rappers for whom language and writing played a central part in the creative process and who were more likely to "play along" with the seminar's premise and offer detailed, introspective reflection on their artistic choices.[2] When the organizers asked how she felt upon receiving the invitation, Casey replied with her signature frankness,

> *Ça me soûle toujours un peu parce que je sais que les caméras qui étaient là-bas que j'ai virées ou des gens viennent juste parce qu'on est à l'ENS. En dehors de ça ils n'en ont rien à foutre du rap. Tout d'un coup, on est adoubé par le fait de venir parler du rap ici. On acquiert quelques titres de noblesse en parlant à l'ENS. Ça me gonfle un peu. Ça, je ne peux rien y faire, c'est très français. La France aime la littérature et la France a l'impression que tout ce qui est de l'ordre de l'intellect et de la culture se passe dans les grandes écoles et non pas dans les bistrots et pas dans les halls d'immeubles. Mais ça c'est un truc français à la con, tu vois.*[3]
>
> It always gets on my nerves a bit because I know that the cameras that were over there that I kicked out, or people come just because it's at the ENS. Outside of that they don't give a damn about rap. All of a sudden, we're knighted by coming to talk

[1] The name is an homage to Booba's "Le Bitume avec une plume." The seminar, which ran from 2014 to 2017, was organized in two parts: a preparatory session close reading a given artist's lyrics, followed by a session in that rapper's presence.
[2] Interviews by the author with Emmanuelle Carinos Vasquez and Benoît Dufau, January 25, 2020; February 12, 2020.
[3] École normale supérieure—PSL, "Rencontre avec la rappeuse Casey," YouTube video, 26:34, May 2, 2016, https://www.youtube.com/watch?v=jJsqvpG6Gfk.

Reflexivity in French Rap. Emily Q. Shuman, Oxford University Press. © Oxford University Press 2026.
DOI: 10.1093/9780197781609.003.0002

> about rap here. We acquire some kind of nobility in talking at the ENS. That annoys me somewhat. But I can't do anything about that, it's very French. France loves literature and France has the impression that everything that is intellectual or cultural comes through prestigious schools and not from bistros and not from the entrance halls of apartment buildings. But that's just a stupid French thing, you see.

Exasperated, Casey attributes the media and public enthusiasm around the seminar in large part to its institutional setting. The intense focus on the *grande école*,[4] as she intimates, reproduces the notion that elite academic establishments reserve the privilege to recognize virtuosity. This privilege, Casey argues, posits working-class spaces such as bistros and social housing projects as antithetical to knowledge production. The ENS's symbolic weight made the seminar more than an exchange between rappers and academic analyses of their work; it was a head-on collision with deeply ingrained cultural beliefs about artistic and intellectual value in France.

For Casey, there is something decidedly French about the legitimizing power of academia and literature. Indeed, in France, literature enjoys the distinct ability to embody the nation's history and self-image. The bond between the literary canon and national identity goes hand in hand with the elevation of the writer as a public figure imbued with moral authority.[5] Over the course of the late 18th and 19th centuries, beliefs in the French language's superiority and natural ability to express rational thought strengthened the link between individual literary genius and the collective genius of the French nation.[6] For authors from France's former colonies who choose to write in French, postcolonial power dynamics complicate the pursuit of the nation's literary ideal. The literary institution's mechanisms of distinction and the authors' own quests for recognition hinge upon extra-literary criteria that transform their texts into pretexts to address sociopolitical issues. These processes reaffirm France's desired status as the nation uniquely able to inspire, nourish, and reward literary genius both within and beyond its borders.[7] A given author's perceived difference therefore conditions not only their inclusion within France's literary self-image but also their own self-positioning vis-à-vis that tradition. As a musical genre conflated with the racialized *jeune de banlieue* figure, rap encounters a similar tension between aesthetic and extra-aesthetic criteria in the recognition of its creative talent.

[4] In the French higher education system, *grandes écoles* are highly selective establishments with competitive entrance exams. They offer three- to five-year degrees equivalent to a master's.

[5] See Priscilla Parkhurst Clark, *Literary France: The Making of a Culture* (University of California Press, 1987).

[6] Ann Jefferson, *Genius in France: An Idea and its Uses.* (Princeton University Press, 2014), 52.

[7] Kaoutar Harchi, *Je n'ai qu'une langue, ce n'est pas la mienne. Des écrivains à l'épreuve* (Pauvert, 2016), 289.

Before the ENS amphitheater, Casey derisively laid out how the literary fashions the script by which rappers must perform artistry:

> *Surtout en France, il est de bon ton de dire qu'on a été influencé par les livres. Parce que ça fait genre on a lu. Du coup, on est intelligent. Ça, il faut le dire en France. Si vous voulez escroquer la France, faut qu'un rappeur dise qu'il a lu des livres. Comme certains qui disent qu'ils adorent Roland Barthes, qu'ils lisent ça toute la journée, qu'ils adorent Brel, avec des vestes en velours.*[8]

> Especially in France, it's good form to say you've been influenced by books. Because that gives the impression you've read. So you're intelligent. You have to say that in France. If you want to scam France, a rapper has to say that he's read books. Like some that say they love Roland Barthes, that they read that all day long, that they love Brel, with velour suits.

The rapper mocked her peers who all too willingly play into the required literary and musical references necessary for acceptance into the realm of highbrow culture. The recipients of these performed homages stretch from the literary critic and semiotician Roland Barthes to a monument of the *chanson française* musical tradition, Jacques Brel. Casey's choice of the verb "to scam" acknowledges that rappers have some leeway to take the codes of the cultivated artist and create their own representational strategies for media visibility and critical acclaim. The velour suit-clad caricature she depicts underscores the importance of self-presentation in the performance of the rapper-intellectual figure. Ridiculing this figure enables Casey to fine-tune her own posture in contrast. Compared to the calculating rappers that "scam" France, she subtly positions herself as more authentic, not only in her cultural references—during the seminar, she cites the Martinican writers and political figures Frantz Fanon and Aimé Césaire—but also in her ability to see through this charade of cultural capital. Nevertheless, despite differences in strategy, Casey's reflections suggest common ground in the French rap scene: a collective consciousness of the cultural parameters of artistic recognition that individual rappers can choose to take, leave, or indeed, scam.

This chapter examines the ways France's literary tradition informs journalistic and scholarly criticism of rap. It focuses on the mechanisms of reception and cultural reference points through which critics negotiate rap's Frenchness and attempt to bring the genre into the fold of the nation's cultural patrimony. This negotiation takes place through strategic parallels to France's great authors

[8] "Rencontre avec la rappeuse Casey," 38:16.

and renowned singer-songwriters. Inclusion within that pantheon rests upon a series of litmus tests measuring the right doses of masterful sublimation of the French language, critical distance from lyrical content, and artistic self-awareness. While the parameters of such tests may seem creative in nature, they prove to be shaped by race, gender, and class. Parallels to the literary canon thus reveal a great deal about how and under which conditions rappers' perceived marginality can be made assimilable into existing cultural idioms of coolly detached, observant, misunderstood, tortured, or even obscene poetic genius.

To borrow Casey's language, I analyze how the literary's "knighting" function and privileged status work their way into French rappers' aesthetic claims and strategies of self-representation. Such strategies reveal nuanced and diverse relationships between rap and France's literary heritage that encompass homage, provocation, identification, blunt dismissal, and profit-minded exploitation. My objective is not to determine to what extent rap shares formal qualities with literature or poetry, but rather to examine how critics recognize and how rappers perform artistry against the blueprint of virtuosity provided by France's revered authors. Analyzing how these literary relationships infuse songs, visual culture, and postures challenges critical focus on French rap as text. Instead, these analyses reveal productive interaction between the cultural power of the literary on the one hand and rap's specific aesthetic codes, constraints, and musical roots on the other. In shifting the conversation away from potential formal or thematic parallels between rap and literature, this chapter homes in on the enduring role perceived marginality plays in determining a given rapper's authorial status.

Literature, Language, and the Frenchness of Popular Music

A distinct writing style and mastery of the language's supposedly innate poetic qualities have a longer history of securing the Frenchness of popular music, particularly in contrast with mass popular culture imported from the United States. This has been the case for the *chanson française*, a genre that has eluded clear definition in musical terms.[9] Over the course of the late 1950s and the 1960s, critics converged on the genre's lyrical qualities and lineage with French literary traditions as its distinguishing characteristics.[10]

[9] See Peter Hawkins, *Chanson: The French Singer-Songwriter from Aristide Bruant to the Present Day* (Ashgate, 2000).
[10] Jonathyne Briggs, *Sounds French,* 47.

The exceptionality of *chanson's* textual sophistication found weight in opposition to globalized, Anglo-American popular music and its French imitations, such as the rock and roll–inspired genre known as *yé-yé*.[11] Looking back even further, the primacy of lyrics, self-consciousness, and masterfully channeled emotion in *chanson* marks a strategic distinction from the emphasis on dance and the body in racialized music hall styles such as jazz and the Revue nègre, which included Josephine Baker's performances.[12] Unlike these latter musical styles and their foreign models, *chanson's* artistic merit resided in its perceived proximity to a longer French history of oral poetry and storytelling.

Awareness of the power of literature and poetry factored into the self-representation of the three canonical artists who came to embody the *chanson française*, Jacques Brel, Georges Brassens, and Léo Ferré, as they put renowned poets to music or published their own lyrics in poetry collections. For David Looseley, this strategic self-fashioning culminated in the enduring singer-songwriter trope combining social observations, literary skills, the "outsider" status of 15th-century wandering poets like François Villon, and, at times, the emotional force of Edith Piaf.[13] *Chanson*'s patrimonialization therefore draws upon existing archetypes of the artist, which singer-songwriters themselves sought out through the specific poets and aesthetic traditions with which they experimented—bohemian, anti-establishment figures of the Modernist canon and anarchic Surrealists for Ferré, or an eclectic blend of traditional and obscure poets for Brassens.[14] These references were integral to their aesthetic projects and evolving sociopolitical stances.

Perhaps unsurprisingly, then, *chanson* often joins literature as a common point of comparison for French rap, and an equally contested one at that. For some, the emphasis on lyrics indicates rap's solubility within the *chanson française* tradition.[15] However, rap's rhythmic complexity, Black American roots, and portrayals of social exclusion have fueled scholarly debate over the directness of its link to *chanson*.[16] For example, whereas the earliest instances of rap in French in the 1980s mirrored *chanson's* nonchalant vocal style, preference for melodic intonation, and use of homophonic syllables at the end of

[11] The name "yé-yé" stems from the repetitive "yeah yeah" chorus of American rock and roll.

[12] David Looseley, "Authenticity and Appropriation: A Discursive History of French Popular Music," in *Imagining the Popular in Contemporary French Culture*, ed. Diana Holmes and David Looseley (Manchester University Press, 2013), 56.

[13] David Looseley, *Popular Music in Contemporary France: Authenticity, Politics, Debate* (Berg, 2003), 58–62.

[14] Peter Hawkins, "The Re-Invention of the French Singer-Songwriter in the Liberation Years: Léo Ferré and the French Poetic Heritage in Popular Song," in *The Singer-Songwriter in Europe: Paradigms, Politics, and Place*, ed. Isabelle Marc and Stuart Green (Routledge, 2016), 153–163.

[15] David Looseley, "Authenticity and Appropriation," 75.

[16] Christophe Rubin, "Le rap est-il soluble dans la chanson française?" *Volume! La revue des musiques populaires* 3, no. 2 (2004): 29–42.

each measure, pioneers such as NTM, IAM, and MC Solaar quickly worked to make their flows polyrhythmic.[17] Rather than resolving this issue of inheritance, I look at how these reference points come together in the reception and performance of French rap. This angle sheds light on the push and pull between marginalization and recognition that conditions rap's inclusion within national parameters of artistry.

Since the early days of the genre's implantation in France, commitment to the French language and literary traditions has been a crucial factor in negotiating its adaptability to the Hexagon and distinction from its American predecessor. In a 1990 interview ahead of the release of the compilation *Rapattitude*, the television program *Rapido* asked the groups NTM and Assassin whether they had originally tried to rap in English to mimic their American forerunners. For the rappers, the use of French was obvious. Their audience was French, after all, and lyrical dexterity came naturally in their native language.[18] The specter of the United States persisted through the late 1990s in the mainstream press, which depicted French rap as an unsubtle copycat imprisoned by its admiration for the American pioneers.[19] Journalists regretted that the themes of bellicosity, materialism, and communitarian identity politics—plagues that originated in American rap—subsequently infected the French scene.[20] At the same time, praise of certain rappers' creativity with the French language and extensive reservoirs of literary references emerged as a means to distinguish artists from the Americanized pack. Indeed, scholars cite French rap's engagements with literature and the Republican public school philosophy among its most distinguishing factors from its US counterpart.[21]

Both academic scholarship and national press coverage have traditionally privileged the textual form of French rap lyrics. A few notable exceptions emphasize the interaction between the music, the rapper's flow, rhyme schemes, and lyrical stylistic devices.[22] The emphasis on text

[17] Idir Mahiou, "Du flow binaire au flow polyrythmique, 'de la rime scolaire à la rime rappeuse': une histoire des performances formelles dans le rap en France de Chagrin d'amour à Ärsenik," *Itinéraires. Littérature, textes, cultures* 2020-3 (2021), DOI: 10.4000/itineraires.9222.

[18] *Rapido*, "Interviews de membres de 93 NTM," Footage filmed in 1990. Consulted at the Inathèque, Bibliothèque nationale de France in December 2018.

[19] "*Prisonnier de son admiration pour les pionniers américains*," Stéphane Davet, "MC Solaar, héritier rappeur du dandysme à la française," *Le Monde*, June 11, 1997.

[20] "*Les poses guerrières, l'obsession matérialiste, la paranoïa communautaire avaient fini par recouvrir le hip-hop d'une chape de plomb*," Stéphane Davet, "Les Transmusicales accueillent un hip-hop nouveau, progressiste et poétique," *Le Monde*, December 2, 1999.

[21] Bettina Ghio, *Sans Fautes de frappe: rap et littérature* (Le Mot et Le Reste, 2016), 19; Christian Béthune, *Le rap, une esthétique hors la loi* (Éditions Autrement, 2003), 214.

[22] Jean-Marie Jacono, "Pour une analyse des chansons de rap," *Musurgia* 5, no. 2 (1998): 65–76; Christophe Rubin, "Le texte de rap: une écriture de la voix," *Actes du 22ème colloque d'Albi* (CALS-CPST, 2002), 267–276; Christian Béthune, *Pour une esthétique du rap* (Klincksieck, 2004); Julien Barret, *Le rap ou l'artisanat de la rime* (L'Harmattan, 2008); Emmanuelle Carinos Vasquez and Karim Hammou, eds., *Perspectives esthétiques sur les musiques hip-hop* (Presses universitaires de Provence, 2020).

translates to efforts to determine rap's filiation within France's literary and poetic traditions. The structure of rap's verses, its creative use of slang, syntactic innovations, and intense emotions motivate parallels to revered poets such as Victor Hugo, Charles Baudelaire, and Arthur Rimbaud.[23] Not unlike *chanson* singer-songwriters, rappers have adapted literary and poetic texts to music, or taken inspiration from literary figures to engage with those forms of writing themselves.[24] Literary patrimony also appears within rap songs through parody, intermedial sampling, paraphrasing, and allusion. Within these performances, literary figures serve as reference points through which rappers can claim artistic legitimacy or reject the very pertinence of canonical literature.[25] Literature thus makes its way into rap's broader game of reflexivity to distinguish rappers' own writing processes.[26]

Comparisons to both literature and *chanson* rooted in deftly crafted writing and aestheticized language enable a distinctly French understanding of what rap should be. In these encounters with cultural patrimony, historic tropes of creative genius collide with notions of authenticity and virtuosity specific to rap and its place in the French social imaginary. While *chanson* artists drew from archetypes of the poet as a tortured soul, errant bohemian, or observant outsider, the link between marginality and artistry plays out differently in the case of a racialized genre such as rap. To explore that link, this chapter moves through the cases of MC Solaar, Médine, and Booba. Across these three case studies, the rappers' postures and meta-commentary seek out, interrogate, provoke, or flout the parameters of artistic recognition at the intersection of France's literary canon and rap's aesthetic criteria. In so doing, they negotiate the susceptibility of their critical reception to the gravitational pull of the literary and its norms of creative genius. MC Solaar, Médine, and Booba adopt markedly different strategies that nevertheless play off their complicit relationship to the literary, where complicity signifies a state of entanglement and room to work within literary comparisons as a convention of reception.

[23] Thomas Deslogis, "Comment le rap français a réécrit (et dépassé) l'Histoire de la poésie," *Les Inrocks*, June 12, 2016, https://www.lesinrocks.com/musique/rap-francais-a-reecrit-depasse-lhistoire-de-poesie-65047-12-06-2016/.

[24] E.g., Abd al Malik, *Camus, l'art de la révolte* (Fayard, 2016); Vîrus x Jehan-Rictus, *Les Soliloques du Pauvre* (Livre-CD) (Au Diable Vauvert, 2017). For more on rapper-authors, see Stève Puig, "Redefining Frenchness Through Urban Music and Literature: The Case of Rapper-Writers Abd al Malik and Disiz," in *Post-Migratory Cultures in Postcolonial France*, ed. Kathryn Kleppinger and Laura Reeck (Liverpool University Press, 2018).

[25] Nina Rolland, "'Dans la rue et le bitume ne poussent que les fleurs du mal': jouer et déjouer Charles Baudelaire et sa poésie dans le rap français," *Itinéraires. Littérature, textes, cultures* 2020-3 (2021), https://doi.org/10.4000/itineraires.9377.

[26] Florian Alix, "'Stendhal me connaît pas': reconnaissances littéraires et pratiques transmédiales dans le rap français," *XXI/XX- Reconnaissances littéraires* 1, no. 1 (2020): 187–207.

Putting their reflexivity in conversation with their reception brings to light the role perceived alterity plays in the bestowal or denial of authorial status. Reflexivity further highlights the creative ways rappers blend claims of aesthetic innovation with critical awareness of what they represent in French society to probe the contours of their representational space.

MC Solaar: French Rap's Literary Litmus Test

With the release of his first single, "Bouge de là" in 1991, Claude M'Barali, alias MC Solaar, became one of French rap's first and biggest mainstream successes. As evidenced by this book's opening vignette, from his earliest national television appearances, MC Solaar found himself set apart from his peers in the emerging public debate over French rap's aesthetic complexity, cultural distinctiveness, and political radicality. Within this debate, NTM served as the hardcore foil for the danceable swing of Solaar's music. NTM would fuel this opposition themselves by explicitly dismissing the rap credentials of Solaar's hit single due to its pop-like structure destined for mainstream radio play, as well as its lack of substantive message, which rendered the song borderline infantile in their eyes.[27] NTM's dismissal points to how the interplay between form and content secures the addictive, harmless air of Solaar's single.

"Bouge de là" imagines mundane interactions in which Solaar provides surprisingly impolite answers that prompt his interlocutor to tell him to go away. For example, the double-entendre of *descendre* (to take downstairs or to kill) risks fatal consequences for his neighbor's pet dog: "*Ma voisine de palier, elle s'appelle Cassandre/Elle a un petit chien qu'elle appelle Alexandre/Elle me dit, 'Claude MC est-ce que tu peux l'descendre?'/J'ai pris mon Magnum, j'ai dû mal comprendre.*"[28] The bassline's groove, coupled with Solaar's relaxed flow elongating the final syllable of each line, packages this dialogue as cheeky wordplay and jesting misunderstandings. Solaar's emphasis on semantic surprise diverged from the notion that rap needed something to say, and that something needed to be equally shocking in form and content. While for some, the song's lack of subversive intent ruled it out as rap, its beat offered significant hip-hop credentials. In what would become a lasting collaboration, DJ Jimmy Jay crafted the beat for "Bouge de là" around a sample of "The Message" by

[27] "*'Bouge de là', c'est pas du rap—c'est construit comme un morceau de variétés: y'a plus de refrains que de couplets. Ensuite, OK c'est un aut' genre, mais bon . . . ça dit rien quand même. C'est pour les enfants à la limite.*" Cited in Karim Hammou, *Une Histoire du rap*, 160.

[28] "My neighbor, her name's Cassandra/She's got a little dog she calls Alexander/She tells me, 'MC Claude can you take him out?'/I grabbed my Magnum, I must have misunderstood."

British funk group Cymade. In addition to securing the ludic nonchalance of Solaar's lyrics, the sample placed the rapper in a musical lineage with major figures in US hip-hop who had previously sampled the song's breakbeats, including DJ Kool Herc, Grandmaster Flash, and De La Soul. The song inscribed Solaar within a style of rap heavily influenced by funk, soul, and jazz,[29] setting the tone for the distinct blend of sound and meticulously crafted lyrics that would cement his status as both the embodiment of cool and the poet of French rap.

Through the interaction between lyrical inventiveness, sonic citations from across what Paul Gilroy calls "the Black Atlantic,"[30] commercial success, and national media attention, "Bouge de là" laid the foundation for lasting investment in MC Solaar's exceptionality. MC Solaar's awareness of that exceptionality, particularly in the form of boastful ego trips in his lyrics, has fueled vastly different critical interpretations. Scholars have read these reflexive moments of braggadocio as lingering influences of US rap that undercut the rapper's poeticized slang and detached attitude that otherwise favor his inclusion within *chanson*;[31] instances of rap's existential and pedagogical poetic functions, but which prove too egocentric to qualify as social contestation;[32] or indeed "malicious linguistic play" that serves as covert anticolonial rebellion.[33] On the one hand, canonizing Solaar at all costs within French literary and musical heritage flattens the crucial role that US rap, jazz, soul, and funk play in his critical reception, creative process, and posture. Rather than vestiges of his American counterparts, Solaar's strategies of self-promotion suggest a keen awareness of the points of overlap between poetic consecration and the racialized appeal of his cool approach to social observation. On the other hand, politicized readings of the rapper's form elide the role reverence to the canon plays in his posture, as well as his efforts to distance himself from the potentially divisive critiques of his peers. Solaar's frequent recourse to ego trips, the musical traditions his songs sample, and the visual references for his album covers demonstrate a dual desire to assert the literary qualities of his lyrics *and* the authenticity of his contemplative style within Black music history. As I will argue, these two aesthetic projects work together to frame Solaar's consecration in French literary culture as an exceptional feat,

[29] In the US context, borrowing from jazz carved out a seemingly more sophisticated "jazz rap" subgenre in the early 1990s. Justin A. Williams, *Rhymin' and Stealin,'* 48.

[30] Paul Gilroy, *The Black Atlantic: Modernity and Double-Consciousness* (Harvard University Press, 1993).

[31] Peter Hawkins, *Chanson*, 209.

[32] Isabelle Marc Martínez, *Le rap français. Esthétique et poétique des textes* (1990–1995) (Peter Lang, 2008), 183, 214.

[33] Geoffrey Baker, "Preachers, Gangsters, Pranksters: MC Solaar and Hip-Hop as Overt and Covert Revolt," *The Journal of Popular Culture* 44, no. 2 (2011): 243.

demonstrating the openness and cultural eclecticism of both the rapper and laudatory critics from the national press.

For Solaar, media prominence at a critical juncture in the negotiation of French rap's representational space created opportunities to craft meta-discourse around his eclectic and erudite sources of inspiration. A 1992 television interview at the Château de Versailles suggests Solaar's awareness that praise for his lyrics' aesthetic complexity comes through performing reverence toward France's patrimony and language. The interview opens with the instrumental music of his first album's eponymous track, "Qui sème le vent récolte le tempo," and a tracking shot of the rapper swaggering through the palace gardens. He appears dressed in a baggy, khaki ensemble, a large, wooden, ornamental necklace, and a hat inspired by West African wax prints, the visor flipped up in 1990s hip-hop style. With the palace squarely in the background, Solaar connects his stage name to Louis XIV's use of the sun to visualize his power. He blends the two monikers to assert that "King Solaar" is here.[34] After a freestyle of "Bouge de là," Solaar affirms his desire to create a purely French rap that resists the urge to copy its US counterpart. In the same breath, he notes the ragamuffin influences that help him make the language "swing," as well as his commitment to writing in coherent, correct French, much like the poets who once performed at Versailles. The rapper touches on the mythic status of the Sun King's court and its role in projecting French cultural prestige to the world. The historical setting becomes a visual metaphor for Solaar's Frenchness, while the soundtrack and the rapper's styling maintain enough distance to frame him as the fresher, yet unlikely heir to the nation's poetic tradition.

Throughout the 1990s, the national press solidified Solaar's singularity as the poet of French rap for his intelligent texts and passion for words and ideas. Prestigious institutions, such as the *Académie française*, the official council for all matters pertaining to the French language, reinforced this distinction by awarding him the 1998 *Grande médaille de la chanson française* for "*l'ensemble de ses chants poétiques*" (the whole of his poetic songs). The rapper's own narrative of his creative process plays into this consecration. References to bookshops, public libraries, dictionaries, and novels pepper his interviews. Testimonies from Solaar's collaborators corroborate his scholarly approach, describing him as a character that speaks like a dictionary and communicates in quotes.[35] For *Le Monde*, the rapper's deep love for words renders his music

[34] Gérard Bar-David, dir., "MC Solaar à Versailles," *Ramdam*, France 3, January 13, 1992.

[35] Jean-Baptiste Vieille, "Prose Combat, histoire d'un classique," *Abcdrduson*, April 24, 2021, https://www.abcdrduson.com/special/mc-solaar-prose-combat/.

"a new virtuoso variation on language and literature" that distances the "author-rapper" from "rapper-motormouths" caught up with sociopolitical issues and animosity toward authority figures, such as NTM and IAM.[36] In bestowing authorial status on Solaar, the critic recognizes the rapper's stated literary influences, including novelist Georges Perec, revered for his wordplay, and poet Francis Ponge, celebrated for his meticulous descriptions of quotidian objects. Solaar's verbal agility allows him to "seduce those who only expected monotone aggression from hip-hop," and therefore go beyond the usual audience of *banlieue* youth.[37] References to key literary figures, while rooted in specific formal qualities, also illustrate Solaar's unique ability to put critical distance between himself and the supposed straightforward emotionality and social myopia of his musical genre.

Le Monde frames the rapper's widespread appeal and inventive wordplay as exceptional by highlighting all the ways in which, at first glance, he ticks the prerequisite boxes for rappers: a young Black man born in Dakar, equipped with an Americanized stage name, and leader of a *banlieue* posse.[38] Solaar is therefore also distinct in his ability to rise above the stereotypes of his racial identity and neighborhood—qualities that easily could have made him yet another caricatured rapper. The newspaper thus wonders if he isn't rather the rightful heir to the "good old French tradition" of dandy singers such as Serge Gainsbourg and Jacques Dutronc.[39] The grounds for these parallels lie in their shared talent for double-edged language, sentimentality, and an ironic detachment that thinly veils their intelligence and social consciousness. The emphasis on Solaar's dandyism further intertwines a sense of refined, stylish self-presentation with this mastery of French's literary qualities. The mention of the rapper's racial identity, birthplace, and *banlieue* upbringing underscores the meaningfulness of his integration into this French brand of nonchalance, while maintaining a sense of racialized coolness.

The interplay between literary patrimony and aesthetic contemplation in MC Solaar's critical reception is best exemplified by a 1998 televised interview filmed in the Bibliothèque de l'Arsenal, the site of Charles Nodier's

[36] "*Nouvelle variation virtuose sur le langage et la littérature . . . Claude MC paraît vouloir s'inscrire plus résolument dans la lignée des chanteurs dandys de la bonne tradition française Gainsbourg, Dutronc plutôt que celle des rappeurs-tchatcheurs en prise avec le contexte politique et social contemporain, comme NTM ou IAM.*" Stéphane Davet, "MC Solaar."

[37] "*Son agilité verbale a séduit ceux qui n'attendaient du hip-hop qu'une agression monocorde.*"

[38] "*A première vue, Solaar a satisfait aux critères d'usage: jeune black né à Dakar en 1969 de parents tchadiens, au pseudonyme américanisé (de son vrai nom Claude M'Barali), leader d'une bande (le 500 One Posse) de banlieue (Villeneuve-Saint-Georges) . . .* "

[39] The comparison to Gainsbourg finds echoes in Solaar's 1994 single "Nouveau western," which samples Gainsbourg and Brigitte Bardot's "Bonnie and Clyde." Solaar's 2017 album also features an ode to the singer and his provocative persona, "Super Gainsbarre."

literary salon, which once hosted the likes of Victor Hugo, Alfred de Vigny, and Alphonse de Lamartine.[40] The journalist's invocation of these literary giants and the ornate first editions in the background add to the chorus of comparisons between Solaar and France's great authors. However, the journalist explicitly presents the location as Solaar's choice, which frames the parallel as the result of the rapper's authentic literary passion. As the interview focuses on Solaar's artisanal grasp on the French language, the association with renowned authors solidifies the rapper's place among those with the rare capacity to elevate everyday language to its true poetic potential. Solaar's description of his writing process accentuates the musicality of language that he seeks, as well as the intended academic content, such as references to Nietzsche, that could help listeners like his young cousin study for their *baccalauréat* (the national exams secondary school students take at the end of their studies). Solaar passed the *bac* himself and went on to study applied foreign languages at the Sorbonne's Jussieu campus. The rapper explains in the interview that he seeks to make thought-out songs, with the classic format of French school essays: thesis, antithesis, and synthesis. To emphasize his music's argumentative substance, Solaar evokes the lasting impact of one of France's central institutions—the Republic's free, secular, public school.

This pedagogical mission joins the rapper's stated desire to privilege language that brings people together, rather than use politically charged words such as *banlieue, voyou, jeune maghrébin,* and *bande de jeunes*, which he feels would exclude or alienate listeners.[41] On the one hand, in renouncing these divisive terms, Solaar dismisses the value of political and media rhetoric that uses and misuses them until they become fantasized projections detached from reality. On the other hand, the rapper subtly differentiates himself from his peers who employ these discursive devices to comment on their social world, and profit from their charged connotations for shock value. Solaar affirms his singularity within the French rap scene, thanks to his desire to poeticize language and render his listeners—in his words—more "aesthete." MC Solaar's self-positioning and national media coverage map out the terms of his inclusion in the literary tradition: performed reverence for the canon, an expository style inherited from French schools, and the right dose of observant detachment that allows him to sublimate social situations that would otherwise make him a rap cliché.

Solaar's awareness of these conditions does not only play out in the media. Ego trips about his dexterity with the French language and boastful

[40] Pierre Dugowson, dir., *Les grands entretiens du cercle*, France 2, May 5, 1998.
[41] "Suburb, thug, young North African, gang of young people."

recognition of the critical acclaim this talent affords him are omnipresent in his music from his first album. *Qui sème le vent récolte le tempo*, which would sell over 300,000 copies and earn Solaar his first of five *Victoires de la musique*—France's national music awards—features multiple tracks that both revel in his poetic consecration and duel with the delegitimizing effects of this commitment to form in the eyes of some of his peers. In "À temps partiel," Solaar accentuates his academic success by mixing the acronyms of various diplomas with skills specific to rap. These achievements attest to his discipline, which, capitalizing on the phonetic similarity between the military call to attention and the expression for police custody, he opposes to the unruliness of *banlieue* violence: "*Garde-à-vous, fixe, discipline de l'armée/Garde-à-vue, rixes, indiscipline dans les cités.*"[42] While Solaar insists that he isn't seeking to be sanctimonious, just strictly stating facts—"*pas moralisateur, stricte réalité*"—he makes it clear that his intellectual rigor sets him apart from both "*les rebelles à temps partiel*" (part-time rebels) and "*les penseurs par intérim*" (interim thinkers). The rapper brings together his love for music, artisanal approach to writing, and astute observational skills to distinguish himself: "*Musicologue et mélomane/Pose, compose, recompose, décompose/En linguiste structuraliste de la nouvelle prose.*"[43] In the final verse, Solaar roots this "poetic, rhythmic, angelic" approach to music within a specific sonic lineage by citing jazz as the spark behind rap's success: "*Si le rap excelle, le jazz en est l'étincelle.*" Through the ego trip of "À temps partiel," Solaar spells out a clear vision of his unique contribution to French rap, rooted in a studied approach to language, clear-sighted commentary on *banlieue* strife, and devotion to musical genres such as jazz.

While this style of braggadocio negotiates Solaar's claims to both poetic prowess and rap authenticity, negative judgments as to the supposedly commercial nature of his music and his nice guy, teacher's pet (or kid-friendly, to recall NTM's perspective) persisted, and added fuel to the rapper's second album, *Prose Combat*. The track "Temps mort" proposes a time-out to address such negativity. The sampled jazz saxophone of Lou Donaldson and the meditative loop of piano notes reinforce the tone of measured reflection. Solaar frames his verses as a *comptine*, or nursery rhyme, in which he encounters hostility ranging from hateful far-right rhetoric to an imagined scene with a model who critiques his song about the fashion industry, "Victime de la mode." Solaar's signature mix of serious and ludic registers

42 "Attention, set, army discipline/Police custody, brawls, lack of discipline in the projects."
43 "Musicologist and music lover/Place, compose, recompose, decompose/As a structuralist linguist of the new prose."

feeds these scenarios into the overarching moral of the story. The rapper takes the higher ground and proposes that the haters he's hidden in the lyrics take the song as a philosophical tale, an invitation to step back, reflect, and work on their critical thinking skills: "*Si je t'ai plaqué dans ce texte/C'est pour que tu voies ton attitude une fois sortie du contexte/Alors prends ça comme un conte philosophique/Prends du recul pour qu'avance ton sens critique.*" He explicitly opposes himself to hardcore rap in this regard: "*L'autodidacte n'est pas didactique ça c'est le hardcore.*"[44] In this sense, *Prose Combat*, whose title marries the literary with a spirit of contestation, further refines Solaar's emphasis on subtlety and reflection as a way to distance himself from the genre's perceived norms.[45]

The album's twelfth track marks the most salient inscription of this approach within a racialized notion of cool. "À dix de mes disciples" frames Solaar as the savior of politically engaged music—somewhere between Buddha and his ten disciples or Jesus, whose twelve followers would match the song's position in the track list. The producer, Boom Bass, opens the beat with sampled vocals from Jungle Brothers' "Done by the Forces of Nature": "Black man, black heart, black soul." The beat samples a squealing saxophone from James Brown's longtime band, the J.B.'s. The sampled song, "The Grunt," again places Solaar in esteemed company from across the Atlantic, including Public Enemy, Erik B. & Rakim, 2 Live Crew, and Wu-Tang Clan, who had previously sampled the song's saxophone and breakbeat. Over the clamor of the drums, Solaar laments that France has abandoned the revolutionary spirit of the May 1968 protests and that socially conscious music had given way to pop music: "*L'esprit de 68 aujourd'hui se dissipe/On jette l'éponge, tandis qu'ils lançaient des pavés/La chanson engagée laisse place la variet'.*"[46] Solaar seemingly seeks to shore up his own place in that tradition of socially conscious artists and to hit back at those for whom his broad appeal would exclude him from such a lineage.

The rapper broadens the scope of this tradition beyond France, as he shouts out one of Senegal's first hip-hop groups, Positive Black Soul, before coining the neologism "radiocool" for his style. The sonic signature of "À dix de mes disciples" canonizes Solaar's radical coolness in Black music history, stretching from the United States to Senegal and back to France. In the second

[44] "The autodidact isn't didactic, that's the hardcore." For more on the opposition between Solaar's "inoffensive" approach and hardcore rap's "violent" critiques, see Laurent Béru, "Le rap français, un produit musical postcolonial?" *Volume!* 6, nos. 1–2 (2008): 61–79.

[45] Solaar's original title, *L'art subtil du prose combat*, was an homage to a Perec essay introducing the "subtle art" of the Chinese boardgame Go. Jean-Baptiste Vieille, "Prose Combat."

[46] "Today the spirit of '68 is dissipating/We're throwing in the towel, whereas they threw pavestones/ Committed music is making way for pop."

verse, Solaar returns to his professed reverence toward jazz, which he hails as the evolving, humanist, and revolutionary music that lifts rap out of its fossilization: "*Il sort de la sclérose grâce au J.A.Z.Z.*" While laudatory, the rapper's nostalgic nods to jazz reactivate a longer history of Black French communities devising self-representation strategies vis-à-vis the exoticizing enthusiasm surrounding the musical genre and Black American performers' arrivals in France.[47] In a new era, Solaar's musical influences factor into his performance of a soft, cerebral, and "respectable"[48] Black masculinity as a means of maneuvering around racist stereotypes and the perceived clichés of violence and machismo in American rap music.[49]

Prose Combat's cover artwork encapsulates the interaction between aesthetic refinement, critical distance, and racialized coolness that secures Solaar's posture. On the back cover (see Fig. 1.1), Solaar poses on the littered steps of a public transportation station. The graffitied sign behind him reads, "Trains to Victoria," transporting the album holder to London. The photographer, Philippe Bordas, chose the South London suburb of Brixton, particularly for its history of riots pitting the predominantly Afro-Caribbean residents against the police in the 1980s. The specific overground station further places Solaar in the musical heritage of the Black Atlantic, as it was also the location where Guyanese-British artist Eddy Grant wrote the hit song, "Electric Avenue."[50] These details would have remained obscure for many who purchased the album, which blunts the potential provocation of its setting. The image's foreign, urban setting nevertheless leaves enough visual clues to reinforce the particularities of race, cultural heritage, and class that render MC Solaar's cool demeanor and poetic mastery remarkable for critics.

MC Solaar's consecration as the poet of French rap hinges on his meticulous writing process, as well as on the ironic detachment and double-edged wordplay that earned him comparisons to *chanson* and literary figures. These qualities find value in the national press against the backdrop of rap's stereotypical image, as well as Solaar's racial identity, immigrant background, and *banlieue* upbringing. For critics, the rapper's exceptionality lies in his ability to reflect

[47] See Rachel Anne Gillett, *At Home in Our Sounds. Music, Race, and Cultural Politics in Interwar Paris* (Oxford University Press, 2021).

[48] Respectability describes social, behavior-disciplining efforts to combat negative, racist stereotypes with alternative public images and self-identities rooted in moral worth and self-restraint. See Mitchell Duneier, *Slim's Table. Race, Respectability, and Masculinity* (University of Chicago Press, 1992).

[49] Clara Heysch de la Borde, "Les codes d'une masculinité 'cool': discours et performance de genre dans les clips du rappeur MC Solaar," *Genre en séries: cinéma, télévision, médias* 15 (2023), https://doi.org/10.4000/ges.3904.

[50] Jean-Baptiste Vieille, "Prose Combat."

Fig. 1.1 Artwork for the 1994 album *Prose Combat*

on his social context and sublimate language, where his peers lose themselves in the urgent emotionality of their social message. Solaar's lyrical references, ego trips, and meta-commentary on his creative process lay claim to poetic virtuosity and honor France's intellectual traditions. These techniques reveal a keen awareness of his privileged position in negotiating rap's place in France's cultural patrimony.

Solaar's performances oscillate between riding the wave of that recognition and repelling digs from peers who question the legitimacy of his approach. The rapper's lyrical shoutouts, samples, and visuals claim both authenticity and distinctiveness in the rap scene by situating his work within transatlantic Black music history. His vision of reasoned, instructive messages, anchored in jazz, funk, and soul, accentuates the mechanisms of racialization that were always present, albeit more implicitly, in critical celebrations of his measured nature. Only looking at Solaar's literary homages thus occults his efforts to inscribe his rap within Black musical traditions, as well as the role such efforts play in his consecration. The blend of these two claims—literary virtuosity and meditative reflection—cements Solaar's place at the pinnacle of French rap's poetic potential and as the standard for calm, cool, and collected social commentary.

Médine: Self-Granted Patrimony and Denounced Double Standards

MC Solaar's status as the benchmark for literary consecration has left such a lasting mark on French rap's place in the cultural landscape that fellow rappers draw him into their own reflexive gestures. In his 2015 song "MC Soraal," Médine reimagines Solaar's hit "Bouge de là" to explore how norms of tone, respectability, and reasoned debate condition rap's inclusion in the French literary tradition. Born Médine Zaouiche in the port city of Le Havre, Médine is known for his politically engaged music that addresses a range of injustices, including racism, Islamophobia, and colonial violence, both within and beyond his paternal grandparents' native Algeria.[51] Médine's political stances and past affiliations have been fodder for intense media controversy. In the mid-2010s, those scrutinized affiliations included Kémi Séba, a Pan-Africanist essayist and former leader of a Black supremacist and antisemitic group, Dieudonné, the controversial comedian accused of antisemitism and Holocaust denial, and Alain Soral, a far-right essayist close to Dieudonné. "MC Soraal" blends Soral's name with MC Solaar's moniker to assert that media reception places rappers on either side of a rigid binary: benevolent lyricist or hostile polemist. Médine's reflections on the parameters of palatability in turn set up a fine line between homage and provocation in his own strategic references to the nation's great authors.

Proof, Médine's trusted beatmaker, creates a sense of urgency with high-pitched string instruments before cutting out to a brief, yet salient sample of the baseline from "Bouge de là." This isolated musical quotation casts Solaar's shadow over the performance and makes his role as a foil explicit. Médine's hoarse vocal delivery repeats, "*On m'a dit 'Bouge de là,'*"[52] to reinforce a dimension of hostile exclusion that evacuates the playfulness of Solaar's hit. The single's cover artwork further cites that of Solaar's *Prose Combat*, with key divergences that reflect the tone of Médine's performance. Médine poses in a similar transport station, with now graffiti-free signs behind him (see Fig. 1.2).

[51] Chapters 3 and 5 feature detailed discussion of these subjects in Médine's music. For more on his approach to postcolonial memory, see Katelyn E. Knox, "Rapping Postmemory, Sampling the Archive: Reimagining 17 October 1961," *Modern & Contemporary France* 22, no. 3 (2014): 381–397.

[52] "They told me 'get out of here.'"

Fig. 1.2 Still from Lyric Video for Médine's "MC Soraal"

Unlike Solaar's relaxed pose, Médine sits upright and stares down the camera with a furrowed brow. Whereas Solaar's image evokes nonchalance, Médine is alert and ready to confront those who would order him to move.

The song's lyrical structure accentuates the comparison. Each line begins with "*entre*" (between) and offers diametric oppositions to suggest that Médine situates himself somewhere on a continuum between extremes. Through these binaries, the rapper reflects on the relationship between perceived artistic value and meaningful contribution to social debates: "*Entre l'orateur, la grande gueule, le bon album et la bonne œuvre*" and later, "*Entre artiste prodige et pur produit hard-discount/Trouve-moi entre la rime riche et l'art de pauvre!*"[53] Médine evokes contrasting notions of rhetorical style, cacophony, good albums, and good works that link artistic judgments with social impact and persuasive potential. He exploits the figurative language of wealth in aesthetic critique to situate himself somewhere between the rich rhyme schemes characteristic of classical French poetry and the poor man's sense of art.

Within this oppositional logic, MC Solaar assumes his exemplary function as the standard for elevated language and reasoned discourse that bridges social divides instead of deepening them. Through a reference to Robert Louis Stevenson's 1886 novella, Médine positions Solaar as the Doctor Jekyll to Alain Soral's Mr. Hyde: "*Entre Doctor Solaar et Mister Soral!*" Rather than follow in Solaar's consensus-seeking footsteps, Médine channels his fellow rapper's acclaim to sharply refuse rigid binaries and advocate for a plurality of approaches within rap's representational space. In the outro, Médine lays claim

[53] "Between orator, big mouth, the good album and good works"; "Between prodigious artist and pure discount product, find me between rich rhymes and poor art."

to a literary lineage typical of Solaar's critical reception, as he denigrates the quality of other rappers' lyrics and compares his own to Marcel Proust: "*Hé, fini les prout'lines/Retour aux lignes de Proust.*"[54] Within a song that doubles down on his biting, less unifying tone, the self-attributed literary comparison pushes back against the perceived distance between Médine and consecrated artists like MC Solaar.

The title of Médine's 2017 album, *Prose Élite*, pursues provocative play on the literary's legitimizing power, and nods yet again toward MC Solaar's *Prose Combat*. At first glance, *Prose Élite* claims poetic virtuosity, yet the title is also a clever play on words with *prosélyte*, or proselytizer. Médine's wordplay hints at literature's venerated status in France, while riffing on right-wing fears of proselytism and communitarianism in the nation's Muslim population. These fears have taken up significant space in public debate on *laïcité,* a legal principle of secular neutrality and freedom of conscience emerging from the 1905 separation of Church and State. Many of Médine's songs address Islamophobia and the constantly moving goalposts of integration when it comes to *laïcité*. These performances have often been met with controversy, as was the case with 2015's "Don't Laïk," which will feature in Chapter 5 for its aesthetic entanglement with mainstream media forms. Two years later, *Prose Élite*'s semantic polyphony blended claims to poetic genius with an artistic commitment to provoking debate. Such an ethos sharply diverges from the model of contemplative social commentary of Solaar's *Prose Combat.*

The album's eponymous song channels literary and religious references to explore tensions between form, content, tone, and the rapper's hold over his audience. Médine asserts his linguistic dexterity while distinguishing his craft from that of an author: "*Je cause comme un bouquin, je suis pas écrivain/Mais j'décris la vie urbaine en alexandrins/Cruciverbiste, j'craque le vernis/Tellement de choses à dire que j'déborde de la ligne.*"[55] The rapper frames his ability to describe urban life through terminology for poetic meter, yet the vivid images he uses defy scholastic adherence to structure. His passion for words—likened to that of a crossword puzzle enthusiast—cracks the veneer of his descriptions. The sheer quantity of things he must get off his chest leads him to lose control and spill over the edge, either the physical lines of the page or the metaphorical line governing acceptable speech.

The chorus plays on religious signifiers to probe the effects of his overflowing pen on his audience: "*Musique argotière, prêtre des paliers, pasteur des prévenus/*

[54] "Lame punchlines are over, return to the lines of Proust."

[55] "I talk like a book, I'm not a writer/But I describe urban life in alexandrines/Cruciverbalist, I crack the varnish/So much to say that I spill over the lines."

Ce soir j'suis seul en scène/j'rappe où j'ai pas pied, j'prêche mes convaincus."[56] Further playing off political anxieties over proselytism, Médine dons various Christian clergy titles, but mixes them with references to the legal system and to housing project landings—associated in the media imaginary with loitering or drug dealing. Pursuing this faith-based imagery, Médine affirms he's both taking risks as he raps and preaching to the choir, using the *convaincus* nickname for his fan base. The nickname ironically repackages charges of heavy-handed messaging and communitarianism. "Prose Élite" suggests that while Médine's wordplay often takes him out of his depth, his loyal audience follows—a claim sure to press the buttons of those who fear his ambitions to convert. The religious framing of his relationship to his audience renders his claims to elite prose all the more troubling for a model of rap's literary virtuosity rooted in measured observations à la Solaar. Médine flouts that model's ideal of artistic detachment, foregrounding the intense conviction with which he "preaches" his message.

The title's polysemy finds visual expression in the album cover, which features a photograph of the rapper in the form of a street advertising poster pasted on an austere concrete wall (see Fig. 1.3).[57] Extended exposure to the elements has torn the poster, revealing a black-and-white photograph of Victor Hugo layered underneath. The juxtaposed portraits join the two men by their facial hair in a move that parallels Médine's 2008 song "Code Barbe," in which he toys with the idea of the beard as a shifting signifier depending on whose face it covers (see Chapter 3). He raps in "Code Barbe" about how the beard, as a marker of Muslim religiosity, becomes an overdetermined symbol of omnipresent threat through Islamophobic logics. On the cover of *Prose Élite,* Victor Hugo's beard serves as a foil for Médine's. On the face of a revered author, the beard signifies perspicacity and timeless virtuosity. By merging their two faces, Médine suggests that the violent connotations sutured to his own image make it so that his artistic contributions will not be met with the same veneration.

Yet, the juxtaposed portraits also visualize a parallel between Médine's claims to elite prose and Hugo's frequent writings on poetic genius as a strategy to claim that designation for himself. Declared a traitor to France and exiled under Napoleon III, Hugo tied poetic genius to the ability to disconcert, to transgress boundaries, and to be attackable.[58] Additionally

[56] "Slang music, priest of the corridor, preacher of defendants/Tonight I'm alone on stage, I'm rapping out of my depth, I'm preaching to the choir."

[57] The album cover for *Prose Élite* and music video for the title track feature artwork by visual artist Hugues Anhès' project AFFICHEZ-VOUS.

[58] Ann Jefferson, *Genius in France*, 81–82.

Fig. 1.3 Cover art for the 2017 album *Prose Élite*

considered an enemy of the Catholic Church for his impassioned defense of secular education, Hugo's massively attended state burial in the Pantheon marked the Parisian sepulcher's transmutation from a religious site to a secular monument to the nation's great men. Hugo's presence on the album cover thus suggests an artistic kinsmanship that, given the author's consecration as a Republican icon, would provoke the detractors for whom the very qualities that render Médine "attackable" put him at odds with France's secular values.

However, the cover's staging and street poster aesthetic make it a more ambiguous visual than an homage to one of France's most prolific pens. Médine envelops his patrimonial references within rap's spatial imaginary of the street. Rather than inserting himself into spaces of elite culture to claim the merit of his prose, Médine absorbs a literary giant into the codes of popular culture. The rapper's likeness is layered over Hugo's, just as new advertisements replace outdated ones, or as political campaigners supplant their rivals' posters. Médine thus treads a fine line between reverence and arrogance, between citing Hugo as an influence and claiming to take his place as a symbol of virtuosity.

The album's title track reinforces Médine's appropriative ambitions, as he raps that he and his fellow artists have their own references, but grant themselves "yours," presumably addressing the gatekeepers of cultural patrimony: "*On a nos propres références/Les tiennes, on se les octroie*." The punchline is bookended with lines linking French rappers to revered figures. The rapper likens the *chanson* singer-songwriters Brassens, Brel, and Ferré to "La Ligue," using the nickname for the trio he forms with Kery James and Youssoupha.[59] Médine goes on to play off Mac Tyer's real name, "Socrate," to assert that his fellow rapper is his kind of national philosopher.[60] The punchline is thus emblematic of Médine's posture vis-à-vis the literary. Refusing a strategy of reverence akin to MC Solaar's, the rapper tactically alludes to the canon as a means of denouncing the rigid strings attached to parallels between rap and literature. Granting himself such parallels further goads detractors, for whom his tone, lyrical content, and what he represents in the social imaginary make him fundamentally incompatible with the nation's elite prose tradition.

Anchoring his taste for provocation within the literary tradition equips Médine to confront those detractors. The rapper's invitation to the "La Plume et le Bitume" seminar in 2017 provoked complaints from current and former ENS students, as well as online vitriol from the far right. The following year, Médine had to cancel his concerts at the Bataclan, one of the sites of the November 2015 terrorist attacks, after vocal protests from far-right and right-wing politicians, as well as from some associations of victims' families. Proponents of canceling the concerts cited the lyrics to "Don't Laïk" as supposed incitements to murder, and narrowed in on Médine's 2005 album *Jihad*, without the context of its subtitle: "*le plus grand combat est contre soi-même*" (the biggest combat is against oneself). Médine notably announced a change of concert venue through the song "Brassens," an ode to the artist celebrated as both the epitome of *chanson*'s literary nature and as the heir to the protest song genre.

In 2021's "Voltaire," Médine again reflected on the Bataclan controversy by joining claims to literary patrimony with "MC Soraal's" suggestion that inclusion in the canon rests on normative expectations of tone and content. Médine returns to Victor Hugo—"*C'est maître Victor Hugo qui disait qu'être contesté, c'est être constaté*"[61]—to find company in employing provocation as

[59] After initially collaborating on Kery James' 2013 track, "Contre nous," the informal trio have long teased an elusive collective album.

[60] "Your philosopher of France/Me, my Socrates lives in the 9.3 (Seine-Saint-Denis region)." Both Youssoupha and Mac Tyer will feature in Chapter 2.

[61] "It's the master Hugo who said that to be contested is to be noticed."

a strategy to gain public attention. The chorus further references a song that Gavroche sings in Hugo's *Les Misérables*. In the novel, Gavroche's tune rings out during the failed 1832 uprisings against the restored monarchy, at a time when the elite feared Voltaire and Rousseau's nefarious influence on the rebellious poor. Gavroche chastises paranoid censorship that exaggerates the writers' hold over the population. Médine, performing from a time in which Voltaire and Rousseau's patrimonial places are secure, inverses their role in the chorus: "*C'est ni d'la faute à Voltaire, ni d'la faute à Rousseau/Mais c'est jamais pour nos frères qu'on sépare l'œuvre de l'homme.*"[62] Voltaire and Rousseau now stand in as ironic benchmarks, measuring how far France has come in recognizing creative liberties, yet still selectively withholds these privileges. Médine claims that separating the artwork from the man never applies to "our brothers,"[63] a term of affection that indicates solidarity either in terms of shared profession (fellow rappers) or shared social backgrounds.

"Voltaire" further reflects on how aesthetic form and emotional resonances condition the conferral of poetic license. The track, co-produced by Proof, incorporates piano played by Sofiane Pamart, an increasingly sought-after collaborator for French rappers. The first verse and the chorus turn to Auto-Tune to allow for a sung delivery over the piano melodies. Médine's use of pitch-correcting technology relies on its perceived ability to evoke emotional subjectivity, particularly for masculine artists.[64] The sentimentality in his voice accompanies introspective lyrics that put forth his own view of his music and the surrounding polemics. In the second verse, as the beat's hi-hats become more salient, Médine abandons Auto-Tune for a flow highlighting the hoarseness of his voice. The shift accompanies a change in lyrical tone, from rhetorical musings to targeted accusations of double standards in the media's treatment of his music.

This move resonates with the outro's sample of an interview with Casey, in which she unequivocally summarizes the colonial mindset behind critiques of raw, emotional responses to systemic discrimination:

> *C'est à dire que si tu es en colère, c'est que tu n'es pas capable de raisonner logiquement. Puisque, en tout cas en Occident, la colère, c'est l'ennemi de la réflexion. Ça, c'est un truc paternaliste, tu vois. C'est une façon de dire qu'en gros tu es primitif,*

[62] "It's neither Voltaire's fault nor Rousseau's/But it's never for our brothers that we separate the man from the artist."

[63] Debates over the significations of "*nos frères*" will be at the heart of Chapter 2's discussion of the trial against the group La Rumeur.

[64] Catherine Provenzano, "Making Voices: The Gendering of Pitch Correction and the Auto-Tune Effect in Contemporary Pop Music," *Journal of Popular Music Studies* 31, no. 2 (2019): 65.

> *tu ne sais pas organiser ta pensée. C'est une façon de te disqualifier, de disqualifier le discours. Et c'est une façon aussi de s'assurer un certain confort. C'est à dire "je veux bien t'entendre mais dis-le-moi gentiment que ça n'soit pas trop inconfortable." Non, des fois c'est juste un crachat dans ta gueule, tu vois, que j'ai envie de t'envoyer pour que tu comprennes.*
>
> That's to say that if you're angry, it's because you're not capable of reasoning logically. Since, in any case in the West, anger is the enemy of reflection. That's a paternalistic thing, you see. A way of saying more or less that you're primitive, that you don't know how to organize your thoughts. It's a way of disqualifying you, of disqualifying your discourse. And it's also a way of ensuring a certain comfort. That's to say, "I want to hear you, but say it to me nicely so that it's not too uncomfortable." No, sometimes it's just a glob of spit in your face that I want to send you, so that you get it.

The sampled interview, as well as the mix of vocal and musical styles, explores norms dictating the audibility of social critique. Within the context of the song's patrimonial references, Médine argues that the creative privileges of authorship rest on perceived inoffensiveness. His reception indicates that the literary's power to recognize rap artistry is mediated by tone and image. To ponder these double standards, Médine takes it upon himself to craft his own parallels between literature and rap that refuse a hierarchical reverence, instead enveloping each genre within the other's codes. Blurring these boundaries fuels the rapper's pursuit of provocation and self-conscious testing of the tenuous relationship between political radicality and artistry. It further drives his introspective performances when he comes up against the limits of that relationship.

Booba: Obscene Poetics, Outsourced Consecration

As the litmus test for French rap's literary value, MC Solaar came to define the genre's poetic potential through not only dexterous wordplay but also artistic detachment from hot-button social issues. Médine instrumentalizes literary and *chanson* traditions to confront the expectation of measured reflection. He lays out how tone, form, and what one embodies in the social imaginary can deny the capacity for aestheticized language. For his part, the rapper Booba provides a more paradoxical case of critical appeal, posture, and racialized poetic genius. Born Élie Yaffa in the Hauts-de-Seine region west of Paris to a white French mother and a Senegalese father, Booba first made his mark on French rap as half of the duo Lunatic, which he formed with the rapper

Ali. After the success of Lunatic's first album, *Mauvais Œil*, Booba launched a critically and commercially successful solo career. He also set off on entrepreneurial adventures that include the record labels Tallac and 92i (subsidiaries of Universal Music Group France) and a whiskey brand, as well as the now-defunct streetwear label Ünkut and OKLM media group.

Since the mid-2000s, Booba has resided in Miami and has long embraced the aesthetics and postures of US rap. As a member of the short-lived, yet influential collective Time Bomb (1996–1998), Booba's avowed New York influences inspired evolutions in flow for French rap, including a greater turn to assonance, paronomasia, tonic intonations, and accelerations that gave the effect of chopping up the language.[65] His music's themes of bellicosity and machismo, inspired by US rap, echo in the beefs he has maintained with fellow rappers, including La Fouine, Rohff, and Kaaris.[66] Alongside the rapper's Americanized, materialistic, and combative public image, critics laud the poetics of his lyrics. This recognition does not come *despite* his lyrics' perceived violence and vulgarity, but rather harnesses these qualities to posit Booba as the misunderstood, obscene bad boy of France's literary tradition. These attributes feed dual, complicit strategies of self-distinction. In the first, critics frame their recognition of Booba's virtuosity as a provocative act of criticism. In the second, the rapper plays hot and cold with the literary establishment.

Booba's 2004 album *Panthéon* asserts his place in French cultural patrimony, all while showcasing his adherence to Americanized values. The monument that gives the album its name lurks in the background of the album's bronze-tinted cover. Under the official inscription of its façade—*Aux grands hommes, la patrie reconnaissante* (To great men, the nation is grateful)—the Pantheon serves as the final resting place for the Republic's exemplary statesmen, writers, and artists, including, as previously mentioned, Victor Hugo. Despite its connotations of glory, Booba's album cover shrouds the monument in the shadow of a hazy, setting sun, suggesting its chapter of cultural history is ending (see Fig.1.4). A barren forest and two ominous crows separate the national temple from the rapper, who stands prominently in the foreground. Booba's face is similarly obscured in shadow, this one cast by a flat-brimmed hat. He stands shirtless at an angle

[65] See Julien Barret, *Le rap ou l'artisanat de la rime*, 144; Rémi Wallon, "'Va te faire niquer toi et tes livres': Time Bomb, le triomphe d'un rap français bête et méchant," *Revue critique de fixxion française contemporaine*, 5 (2012): 119; and Genono, "Time Bomb Explose!" *Vice*, July 7, 2014, https://www.vice.com/fr/article/6va8mr/time-bomb-explose-revolution-rap-francais.

[66] This last clash came to a head in 2018 with a brawl in the Orly airport that resulted in not only legal consequences for each, but protracted, theatrical challenges to an MMA-style combat that played out for years on social media.

Fig. 1.4 Cover art for the 2004 album *Panthéon*

to the camera, catching his tattooed arms and pectoral muscles in the glow of the light. The cover immortalizes Booba's physical strength and dedication to his body, and thus plays with the supposed incongruity between these attributes and the intellectual contributions of those immortalized in the Pantheon.

From within his enclosed fist, Booba's chain emits a blinding beam of light that cuts up toward the Pantheon. The image links him to the Republic's most revered figures through the "bling-bling" aesthetic associated with US rap and, more broadly, through the profit-driven, American mindset often held up as the antithesis to France's conception of culture. The emphasis on the rapper's muscular form recalls how *chanson* secured its cerebral, literary Frenchness against the focus on dance in contemporaneous musical trends from across the Atlantic. Such a conflict of values harmonizes with the Pantheon's historical role as the stage for ideological divisions, with different regimes entombing, expelling, and moving bodies according to their respective repertoires of national heroes. Whether *Panthéon* asserts Booba's place among the nation's literary greats or seeks to usurp them, it does so by showcasing his stalwart attachment to materialism and physical strength, qualities that flout established scripts of creative genius.

The self-styled Duke of Boulogne flaunts his "uncultured" posture and the vulgarity of his lyrics that trouble elitist notions of refinement. The 2006 song "Le Duc de Boulogne" plays up this crass irreverence. The beat, produced by Nazbrok, uses a harpsichord to sonically evoke the Baroque tradition and plunge listeners into the ornate *châteaux* where nobles would have enjoyed the talents of prodigious composers. Booba quickly clashes with this *Ancien Régime* ambiance through incisive, bodily imagery at France's expense: "*Mon rap prend de la protéine, soulève v'là les haltères/Je fais des dons d'urine pour que la France entière se désaltère/L'Afrique, c'est la terre, à leur santé je déblatère.*"[67] Booba's ego trip uses muscular imagery to link his rap's power to his own physical force, before boasting, with a mix of largesse and pretentiousness that mocks noble attitudes, that he generously donates his urine to meet France's thirst. "*Urine*" both creates internal rhyme with "*protéine*" in the preceding line and, in eschewing a cruder term, parodies the elite's more formal register. Implicitly invoking the histories of slavery and colonial violence that generated the nobility's wealth, the rapper dedicates the submissive position in which he places France to the African continent. Despite France's humiliated position, the idea of quenching thirst implies the nation's near-physiological need for his blend of brute force, disrespect, and obscenity.

Booba continues to blend registers of language to exacerbate the shock value of his self-bestowed aristocratic title. In the second verse, the rapper acknowledges his penchant for breaking with decorum and the impact that disregard has on the upper classes: "*Baby, fais-moi la bise puis suce-moi la bite!/OK, je suis vulgaire les bourges en chopent des ulcères/Quand ils écoutent ce qui sort de ma bouche, c'est le son dangereux du ter-ter.*"[68] Booba once again shifts his tone, this time toward an imagined woman whom he smooth talks into giving him a kiss on the cheek, before abruptly telling her to perform oral sex on him. Without missing a beat, the rapper owns his heterosexist vulgarity and revels in the distress it causes the bourgeoisie.[69]

In the third verse, Booba extends this distress to the political class. He boasts of all the work he will create for then-Minister of the Interior Nicolas Sarkozy, as well as his unparalleled sophistication on the mic: "*Toute l'équipe à Sarko,*

[67] "My rap takes protein/lifts hella weights/I give donations of urine so all of France can quench its thirst/ Africa's the land, to their health I'm spouting off."

[68] "Baby, give me a kiss on the cheek then suck my dick!/OK, I'm vulgar, the bourgeoisie get ulcers over it/ When they listen to what comes out of my mouth, it's the dangerous sound of the hood."

[69] Benoît Dufau, "Humour et violence dans le rap français," in *Le sens de l'humour. Style, genres, contextes*, ed. Florence Leca-Mercier and Anne-Marie Paillet (Academia-l'Harmattan, 2018), 305.

j'la ferais bien tapiner/Au micro, j'suis un des négros les plus raffinés."[70] As the next chapter will explore, Sarkozy was a major figure in campaigns to penalize rap for perceived insults toward the Republic. The choice of the verb "*tapiner*" implies arduous labor, or, more specifically, sex work, and thus suggests a sexualized sense of domination over the politician that rejoins the song's explicit imagery. Booba harnesses these connotations to reassert his performance's refined nature and to root that sophistication in his blackness. His awareness that, for this section of society, his music is nothing more than the threatening sound of racialized *banlieue* youth factors into the song's provocative claim to nobility through explicit disregard for respectability and upper-class norms of polite speech.

Despite such revelry in his lyrics' ability to disgust, Booba's proclivity for obscene, trenchant lyrical imagery attracted scholarly praise relatively early in his career. In 2003, Thomas A. Ravier published an article entitled "Booba ou le démon des images" in the prestigious academic journal, *La Nouvelle Revue Française*. Ravier coined a new stylistic device to describe Booba's poignant poetics: *métagore*. A particular brand of metaphor, *métagores* are "comparisons that have no business existing, and, immediately, an appearance, venomous, retinal, abrupt, brutal, that are impossible to get out of your head."[71] Ravier's analysis breaks from past acclaim for rappers' literary merits by rooting the value of Booba's style in the brutal, noxious nature of his language and the psychosomatic effects it can produce.

The piece's structure implies that Ravier is all too aware of how provocative this gesture is in the pages of a renowned journal of literary criticism. He stages a dialogue in which "traditional" critics probe him about "his" Booba, express bemusement at the rapper's moniker, allude to the *banlieue*, and inquire as to whether writing over a beat is indeed literary. In this dialogue, Ravier plays up the foreignness Booba represents for academia, as well as the preconceived notions of the *banlieue* that potentially impede close analysis of his lyrics. The possessive adjective ascribing Booba to Ravier positions the critic within an in-group of fans, but in opposition to his peers due to his defense of the rapper. However, Ravier is far from excluded from the literary circles he addresses, and it is precisely this inclusion that heightens his article's provocation. The critic punctuates his abrupt writing style with passing mentions to writers

[70] "All of Sarko's team, I'd make them work/On the mic I'm one of the most sophisticated n*ggas." (A note on translation: while the French word "*négro*" translates directly to the dated English term "negro," Black French rappers use it in a manner that resembles Black anglophone rappers' use of the n-word.)

[71] "*Des rapprochements qui n'ont pas lieu d'être et, immédiatement, une apparition, vénéneuse, rétinienne, brusque, brutale, impossible à se retirer de la tête,*" Thomas A. Ravier, "Booba ou le démon des images," *La Nouvelle Revue Française*, no. 567 (October 2003): 40.

whose visions of literature, in his view, correspond to Booba's lyrics: immediate, fast-paced, riddled with poignant images, and enriched with musicality. The writers, including Proust, Mallarmé, Céline, and Artaud, speak to those with a certain literary culture who can situate these names within the field. Yet the chosen references—Ravier stresses that even Proust had his moment as a pariah—situate Booba among misunderstood revolutionaries and controversial figures, reinforcing the idea that his music's aesthetic value is indissociable from his marginality.

In the wake of Ravier's article, many critics have applauded Booba's poetic genius. Such accolades describe the multitude and depth of the rapper's stylistic devices and pursue comparisons to Céline and Baudelaire through their potent, sensual, and shocking images, as well as through the misunderstandings and backlash that accompany such atypical artistry. These analyses reproduce Ravier's self-distinction by underscoring the authors' academic and literary credentials that enable them to break down the formal or philosophical complexity of Booba's lyrics. They simultaneously highlight the seemingly taboo nature of their appreciation for the rapper in their professional and social circles.[72] Despite the growing corpus of publications arguing for the poetry of Booba's music, critics continue to preface their analyses with acknowledgments of the materialism, obscenity, and physicality that make the rapper such an unconventional candidate for the Pantheon.

These qualities do indeed hold delegitimizing effects, as was the case in a less-than-laudatory album review that described Booba as "a mix of exacerbated animality and materialism" with "a voice of lava and a pen full of vitriol."[73] However, these same qualities are integral to celebrations of the rapper, as in a "textual analysis from a well-read fan" in the pages of *Libération*, which accentuates Booba's exacerbated virility and describes his album as bubbling with testosterone.[74] The focus on Booba's imposing body invokes persistent stereotypes of Black masculinity as dangerous in its potentially aggressive strength and as closer to a more natural, "primitive" state.[75] The racialized repertoire of physicality and violence sharply contrasts the more cerebral, emotionally vulnerable figure of the tortured artist.

While defending Booba's literary merit occupies scholars and journalists, the rapper does little to encourage these academic enterprises. When asked

[72] Alexandre Chirat, *Booba. Poésie, musique et philosophie* (L'Harmattan, 2015); Arnaud Sagnard, "L'autre affaire Booba, le tabou littéraire," *L'Obs*, September 4, 2018, https://bibliobs.nouvelobs.com/actualites/20180904.OBS1773/l-autre-affaire-booba-le-tabou-litteraire.html.

[73] "*Booba est un mélange d'animalité et de matérialisme exacerbés. Voix de lave et plume au vitriol . . .*" Julien Bordier, "Futur, un Booba sombre et musclé," *L'Express*, December 10, 2012.

[74] Clément Bénech, "Booba, Faim de reparties," *Libération*, April 20, 2015.

[75] Pap Ndiaye, *La Condition noire: essai sur une minorité française* (Calmann-Lévy, 2008), 215.

in a 2016 television interview how it felt to have his writing compared to that of Céline or studied in university lecture halls, the rapper replied that he had never read the author's work, but would perhaps get around to it on the airplane, or when time allowed. He instead likened this recognition to a sort of "miracle," claiming, "even I don't know how I do it. I don't really read books, I don't have a diploma, but I have a brain, we'll say. And I use it."[76] Booba's stance toward literary praise has fluctuated throughout his career, ranging from professed flattery that Ravier, someone so far removed from rap, was able to understand his music so well, to resistance to textual analyses of his lyrics.[77] The rapper has likened such painstaking exercises to slow-motion replays in football matches—something is lost from the immediacy of the live action.[78] Booba's own descriptions of his influences have mirrored this equivocation. Although he most often plays up his disregard for books and negative experiences in the classroom, the rapper has fleetingly evoked the impression poetry left on him as a pupil. In a 2008 interview with *Vice*, Booba recalled his interest in poetry's images and quatrain rhymes, namedropping Rimbaud's "Le Dormeur du val," and linking this early fascination to his own attention to syntax. He was, however, quick to add that he loves just talking shit and saying impulsive things.[79]

Booba's desecration of the literary rejoins his New York rap influences and metaphorical depictions of criminality to secure his singularity within the French rap scene, and specifically his distance from MC Solaar.[80] Rather than discouraging close reading, the rapper's ambivalence toward literature plays an integral role in his critical acclaim. Several punchlines have become near-canonical references to accentuate the academic non-conformity of poetic analyses of Booba's lyrics. These traditional citations include Lunatic's 2000 song "Hommes de l'Ombre," in which Booba recounts negative experience with the French Republican school and emphatically dismisses its attempts to instill in him literary appreciation and Enlightenment values: "*Et à l'école ils m'disaient d'lire, voulaient m'enseigner qu'j'étais libre/Va t'faire niquer toi et tes livres.*"[81] Another oft-cited lyric from Lunatic's 1996 song "Le crime paie" offers

[76] "*Même moi je ne sais pas comment je fais. Je ne lis pas vraiment de bouquins, je n'ai pas de diplôme. Mais, voilà, j'ai un cerveau, on va dire. Et je m'en sers.*" "Booba, De la Prison à Harvard," *Sept à huit*, TF1, May 22, 2016.

[77] Rémi Wallon, "Booba," *Vice*, November 20, 2008, https://www.vice.com/fr/article/vdwmy9/booba-187-v2n11.

[78] Thomas Stélandre, "Booba, le cru et l'écrit," *Libération*, November 24, 2013, https://next.liberation.fr/musique/2013/11/24/booba-le-cru-et-l-ecrit_961653.

[79] "*En même temps j'adore dire de la merde, des trucs impulsifs.*" Rémi Wallon, "Booba."

[80] Rémi Wallon, "'Va te faire niquer toi et tes livres,'" 118.

[81] "And at school they told me to read, wanted to teach me that I was free/Go fuck yourself, you and your books."

a more ambiguous relationship to poetry: "*Mon rap, un poème sans poésie.*"[82] Booba acknowledges that his music takes the form of poetry, perhaps in the use of verses or rhyme schemes. Yet, he evacuates any claim to poetic qualities in terms of his lyrical content, which bears no resemblance to poetry's romanticized ideal. As a routine fixture in Booba's critical reception, this line facilitates investments in his rap as radical, vulgar poetry. Perhaps most paradoxically, critics praising the aesthetic complexity of Booba's lyrics cite his most overt rejection of that recognition in 2015's "Temps mort 2.0": "*Fuck être un lyriciste négro, j'suis là qu'pour ramener les chèques.*"[83] In clear dismissal of attempts to anoint his texts, Booba obstinately plays up his singular drive for economic gain. Rather than discourage poetic analyses of his music, these lyrics play an essential role therein, feeding a sort of *je t'aime . . . moi non plus* relationship between the rapper and his well-read admirers.

For Booba, this performed disregard maintains the coherence of his posture, as openly seeking out literary acclaim and showing reverence to the canon would complicate his particular performance of virility and pursuit of Americanized ideals. However, in 2018, after years of playing coy with the "poet" label and outsourcing his consecration, Booba embraced the literary appeal of his lyrics in a way befitting of his entrepreneurial spirit. The Duke of Boulogne gave his blessing for a limited-edition collection of over six hundred of his punchlines. The volume, entitled *Le bitume avec une plume. Un puzzle de mots et de pensées*, retailed for three hundred euros and exclusively at the Parisian concept store *NOUS*. The graphic designers at the project's origin, Romain d'Abrigeon and Pierre Delort, visualized Booba's lyrics with illustrations including an ornate crypt for French hip-hop, shackled bodies of enslaved people, and the public transport line of the rapper's youth—the RER C—graffitied with one of his preferred nicknames, "Kopp." In a full circle moment, the duo solicited a preface from Ravier, who doubles down therein on his accolades of Booba despite persistent condescension toward rap among the literary and political elite. These paratextual elements reinforce the literary value and potency of the rapper's lyrical imagery. Booba's role in the rarified collection was far from limited to the exalted punchlines that filled its pages. Éditions Tallac, a branch of the rapper's imprint under Universal Music Group, published the volume. The imposed scarcity and astronomical price tag of the literary product thus align with Booba's businessman ethos.[84]

[82] "My rap, a poem without poetry."
[83] "Fuck being a lyricist, n*gga, I'm here to bring home checks."
[84] Four years after this limited release, Booba published a slimmed-down version of the tome as an accessibly priced paperback.

A short publicity video for the collection encapsulates the volume's blend of aesthetic and entrepreneurial ambitions.[85] The black-and-white video plunges viewers into the production process, zooming in on the smooth texture of the ink, the grace with which the pages fall into place, the bobbing gears of the printing press, and the hands that meticulously seal the binding. The video packages the collection as a sleek, artisanal, luxury good. Close-ups of excerpted punchlines, including the eponymous "*J'suis le bitume avec une plume*" that adorns the spine, envelop Booba's lyrics in this carefully crafted product. The minimalistic background music uses a reverberating gong to punctuate shots of the printed text and illustrations, adding a solemn, epic, and perhaps ominous, tone. The video ends with a close-up of a hand shutting the cover to reveal the title. The hand lingers there as one would place their hand on a religious text to swear an oath, adding a sacred air to the volume. Far from being an about-face toward his emphatic dismissal of France's literary tradition, Booba's embrace of his poetic status harmonizes with the materialism and dogmatic drive for profit that made his pantheonization so alluring and polarizing in the first place.

* * *

Through the case studies of MC Solaar, Médine, and Booba, this chapter traced the role race, class, religion, and norms of respectable, heterosexual masculinity play in granting rappers the creative privileges of authorial status. Each rapper adopts a different strategy of self-presentation toward the validating power of the literary—reverence for MC Solaar, self-granted parallels for Médine, and outsourced consecration masked as disregard for Booba. Their self-conscious performances tease out the stakes of literary parallels for their own position in the French rap scene. While Solaar enjoys poetic consecration, on a second front, he grapples with the challenges his style of wordplay poses for his authenticity in the eyes of some of his peers. For Médine, drawing his own literary and *chanson* comparisons reinforces his provocative style, clashes with double standards in French rap's reception, and reflects upon the limits of his approach within those clashes. Booba ostensibly flouts the literary to shore up an avowedly Americanized, capitalist posture. While the literary is legitimizing for many critics and rappers, it nevertheless poses unique opportunities and obstacles when it meets the codes of rap artistry. The three rappers analyzed in this chapter reflexively work with these

[85] Le bitume avec une plume, "Le Bitume avec une plume/Teaser," YouTube video, 1:04, November 24, 2018, https://www.youtube.com/watch?v=_K4JJVM40fM&t=60s.

opportunities and obstacles, maintaining complicity between their postures and literary frames of reception as they navigate their representational space. The cases of MC Solaar, Médine, and Booba delineate the ways public image and tone condition critical investments in French rap as text. The following chapter will take up the flipside of this selective mechanism of legitimization and examine how rappers operate within the negative, even punitive reception of their lyrics as surface-level texts incapable of sublimated language, and thus capable of real-world harm.

Chapter 2
Poetic Injustice
Staging the Penalization of French Rap

The selective consecration of French rappers as authors worthy of the nation's great literary tradition invokes a particular form of ownership over a text. Such ownership allows for critical distance from the text's content and for figurative language that sublimates quotidian social realities. As the previous chapter showed, this sense of masterful control, artistic detachment, and measured social commentary operates along sliding scales of marginality and literariness. The delicate alchemy of those two qualities renders a rapper commensurable with long-held French notions of creative genius. Yet, in the shadow of the aesthete rapper lurks a boogeyman figure: the rapper whose music collapses critical distance and spills into unbridled emotion and symbolic violence always at risk of becoming real. As a critical trope, such a rapper not only lacks textual ownership and vision but veers sharply into artistic irresponsibility. This chapter deals with that shadowy figure and the underside of investments in French rap as text.

I return first to Casey's appearance at the seminar, "La Plume et le Bitume," to expose the double-edged sword that anoints certain rappers for their literary approaches, while confining the genre as a whole to transparent transcriptions of lived experience. Discussing her verse in the song "Ce soir je brûlerai . . . " by Asocial Club, Casey seizes the opportunity to make a forceful statement about her performance's allegorical nature:

> *C'est toujours jouissif de brûler quelque chose, de façon symbolique, bien sûr. On accuse toujours les rappeurs de violence mais ça va, c'est des mots. On n'a rien brûlé en vrai. . . Les rappeurs, on n'est pas des auteurs, nous. Tout ce qu'on dit c'est du premier degré. On ne projette rien. Si je dis "je vais les égorger," c'est sûr que je vais les égorger.*[1]
>
> It's always enjoyable to burn something, symbolically of course. One always accuses rappers of violence but it's fine, they're words. We didn't really burn anything.

[1] "Rencontre avec la rappeuse Casey," 18:07.

Reflexivity in French Rap. Emily Q. Shuman, Oxford University Press. © Oxford University Press 2026.
DOI: 10.1093/9780197781609.003.0003

Rappers, we're not authors. Everything we say is literal. We don't project anything. If I say, "I'm going to slit their throats," surely I'm going to slit their throats.

The rapper evokes the pleasure in *symbolically* burning something, echoing the emotional release of the song's verses in which she and her fellow group members—AL, Vîrus, and Prodige—recount frustration with the labor market, class-based discriminations in the cultural sector, public school teachers with white savior complexes, and disenchantment with organized politics. Each rapper ends their verse by declaring intent to set fire to the institution symbolizing their respective grievance. After briefly reveling in catharsis, Casey assuages those who would take her comments literally with a playfully patronizing reminder of rap's verbal nature.

To dismiss observers who would grant a great deal of power to rap as speech acts that portend violent actions in the real world, Casey offers a more innocuous conception of words and their power: "*it's fine*, they're *words*." The sarcasm with which she parrots face-value interpretations of her lyrics, coupled with the fact that she sits in an amphitheater with the invitation to expertly dissect those same lyrics, makes such literal readings ring absurdly false. Underneath this layer of ridicule, however, lies a paradoxical view of words as both motive of indictment and proof of innocence. Whether it's the belief in rap lyrics' violent, material effects or the defense of their symbolic nature, Casey's remarks suggest that these conflicting viewpoints nevertheless converge to ensure the debate plays out in the realm of speech and text.

Casey roots the stubborn pigeonholing of rap to life writing and literal declarations of criminal intent in the conflation of rappers and racialized authors of destructive acts:

On a des gueules d'émeutiers. On a des gueules de djihadistes. On a des gueules de brigands, délinquants, grands bandits. Donc, si on se met à écrire, c'est sûr que c'est vraiment nos vies qu'on écrit. Ça ne peut être que nos vies.[2]

We look like rioters. We look like jihadists. We look like robbers, delinquents, bandits. So, if we start writing, it's surely our lives that we are writing. It can only be our lives.

In addition to robbers and bandits, she invokes two particular archetypes of violence: radical Islamic terrorism and urban riots. These archetypes powerfully converge in the memory of the 2005 *banlieue* uprisings, sparked by the fatal electrocution of teenagers Zyed Benna and Bouna Traoré after they fled

[2] "Rencontre avec la rappeuse Casey," 46:37.

a police check and hid in an electricity substation. As Étienne Balibar argues, the *jeune de banlieue* figure took on a larger-than-life role in the sensationalized media coverage and law-and-order political rhetorical that ensued, becoming simultaneously synonymous with delinquency, drugs, sexual violence, disintegrating family structures, failed discipline in public schools, and ethno-religious difference.[3] National television coverage implicitly framed the riots through the lens of Islam by referring to the supposedly organized nature of the "urban terrorism."[4] The jihadist figure that Casey cites further invokes the deadly terrorist attacks of 2015, both those in early January against *Charlie Hebdo*'s editorial offices and the Hyper Cacher store, as well as those of November 13 targeting the Bataclan, Stade de France, and multiple Parisian bistros.

Through the rioter and the jihadist tropes, Casey spells out what happens for rappers whose alterity proves incommensurable with authorial vision; artistic detachment denied, autobiographical testimony becomes the only possible mode of interpretation, just as the direct transferability of symbolic violence to material destruction becomes the music's immanent effect. The presumed lack of aesthetic ambition in this image of rappers who just start writing, seemingly without meaningful reflection, invokes not only a lack of creative project but a deeper sense of myopic irresponsibility. The specter of the 2005 riots once again weighs heavily here, as contemporaneous media and political rhetoric portrayed the uprisings as a spectacular failure of French rap's responsibility. As the publicly visible face of the fantasized *banlieue* youth figure, rappers were the ideal culprits that needed to answer for the social upheaval.[5]

The understanding of rap's responsibility to not only represent *banlieue* youth but also to carry their guilt in disruptions of public order took hold in the genre's media coverage of the early 1990s, and has since stretched over a long campaign of political and legal condemnations. The most prominent early legal cases against French rappers occurred in 1995, when police officers pressed charges against NTM for insults directed toward them during a live performance of the song "Police." That same year, police unions and the Minister of the Interior pursued Ministère A.M.E.R for slander and apologia for murder in promotional interviews for their song "Sacrifice de

[3] Étienne Balibar, "Uprisings in the *Banlieues*," *Constellations* 14, no. 1 (2007): 64.

[4] Jayson Harsin, "Cultural Racist Frames in TF1's French *Banlieue* Riots Coverage," *French Politics, Culture & Society* 33, no. 3 (2005): 58.

[5] Marie Sonnette-Manouguian, "Qu'est-ce qu'on attend pour foutre le feu: le rap sur le banc des accusés," in *Une esthétique de l'outrage?*, ed. Jean-Marc Lachaud and Olivier Neveux (L'Harmattan, 2012), 273–284.

poulets."[6] These cases would serve as precursors for a series of political and legal denunciations that, beginning in the early 2000s, routinely pulled rap back into the arena of public debate. Over the course of these denunciatory campaigns, the lyrics themselves, regarded as texts, became the predominant object of debate over rap's nefarious impact on its vulnerable listeners, as well as its responsibility for violence and hatred toward the Republic.[7] Studies of National Assembly and Senate debates attest to recurrent, institutionalized efforts to delegitimize rap both culturally and politically,[8] at times explicitly distancing rap "texts" from art, *chanson*, or literature to advocate for repressive measures.[9] Attacking lyrics as injurious or inciteful statements drew battlelines around competing notions of rap's potential to realize real-world effects and the distinction—or lack thereof—between rap's aestheticized representations on the one hand and the social realities of its creative context on the other. A closer look at key moments in the penalization of French rap will tease out the theoretical stakes surrounding performativity, referentiality, and responsibility.

Performativity, Representation, and the Racialization of Poetic License

A watershed moment in rap's political delegitimization occurred in March 2006, when 152 National Assembly deputies, led by François Grosdidier of the right-wing UMP party, proposed a law to crack down on the musical genre's supposed abuses of freedom of expression. In the immediate aftermath of the 2005 uprisings, Grosdidier had already denounced rap as the catalyst that not only conditioned the violence and destruction but also sparked the rioters to act. The bill, which ultimately would not pass, featured isolated excerpts of lyrics from seven rap artists and (some already-disbanded) groups: 113, Sniper, Salif, Ministère A.M.E.R, Smala, Expression Direkt, Fabe, Ménage à 3, and Booba's former duo, Lunatic. The bill claimed that the calls to racist

[6] NTM were sentenced to three months in prison, a fine, and a six-month ban on exercising their profession, reduced in appeal to a two-month suspended prison sentence and a fine. Kenzy and Stomy Bugsy of Ministère A.M.E.R were sentenced to fines. See André J.M. Prévos, "Hip-Hop, Rap, and Repression in France and in the United States," *Popular Music and Society* 22, no. 2 (1998): 67–84.

[7] In the United States, Erik Nielson and Andrea L. Dennis have unveiled systemic recourse to rap lyrics as evidence in criminal trials. In the French context explored here, lyrics or other discourse from rappers in the exercise of their artistic profession are the criminalized acts, with the Republic and its public servants as the purported victims. See *Rap on Trial: Race, Lyrics, and Guilt in America* (The New Press, 2019).

[8] Karim Hammou, *Une histoire du rap*, 251.

[9] Question by Senator Nathalie Goulet, posed to the Minister of the Interior Manuel Valls, January 17, 2013, quoted in Marie Sonnette-Manouguian, "Des manières critiques de faire du rap: pratiques artistiques, pratiques politiques" (PhD diss., Université Sorbonne Nouvelle, 2013), 523.

hatred and violence in these lyrics held dire consequences for unmoored young people in crisis, as they could at best legitimize incivility, or, at worst, encourage terrorism.[10] To combat these risks, the deputies argued for the need to overcome two "taboos" hampering adequate application of the 1881 law on freedom of the press: failure to acknowledge minority-on-majority racism and reliance upon poetic license to exonerate rap lyrics from such racial hatred. The bill thus invests in the performativity of rap lyrics as speech acts. It shifts from an understanding of the music's effects as perlocutionary, to use linguist J.L. Austin's term for speech that inevitably provokes consequences, to illocutionary, in that they enact harm in the very moment of their utterance.[11] Close reading the bill will shed light on the slippages between discursive performativity and musical performance that underpin its logic, the shared potential of both political rhetoric and rap to forge in-groups and out-groups, and the impact of that potential on the relationship between the Republic, rappers, and listeners.

The conceptual link between rap's violent effects, credulous audience, and inherent lack of aesthetic complexity hinges upon an explicitly racialized "them vs. us" binary in the 2006 bill. The text condemns the cited rappers for "unambiguously inciting racism, hatred, and violence in their songs," before noting that these incitements no longer uniquely target French nationals as a judicial category, but also white people, defined by purely racial criteria.[12] Presented under the guise of minority-on-majority racism, the deputies mirror the same slippage they cite in rap lyrics, confounding "anti-white racism" with discrimination toward French nationals, and thus reinforcing a perception of France as a predominantly white nation. As the authors of these discriminatory acts, the cited rappers are implicitly positioned as un-French and non-white, and explicitly defined by their animosity toward the Republic. The "them vs. us" dynamic strikes a central nerve regarding rap's effects upon its presumed audience of racialized *banlieue* youth, a group seen as particularly vulnerable to naive, literal interpretations and predisposed to ideological hostility toward the nation and its white majority.

This narrow view, however, does not correspond to the dynamics of inclusion and exclusion rappers fold into their lyrics. French rappers often create

[10] Proposition de loi tendant à renforcer le contrôle des provocations à la discrimination, à la haine ou à la violence, no. 2957, 12th legislature (2006).

[11] J.L. Austin, *How to Do Things with Words* (Harvard University Press, 1962), 52.

[12] "*De nombreux autres chanteurs ou groupes de musique incitent sans ambiguïté au racisme, à la haine et à la violence dans leurs chansons. On notera que ces incitations ne sont plus uniquement orientées contre les français ('céfrancs' ou 'gouers') définis par un critère juridique mais aussi contre les blancs ('faces de craies' 'gringos,' 'navets,' 'toubabs,' 'babtous'...) répondant à un critère purement racial.*" Proposition de loi no. 2957, 12th legislature (2006).

an in-group with listeners by speaking to collective experiences, making shared moral appeals, and designating an out-group toward whom they direct insults or accusations of injustice.[13] Rappers lyrically transmit their first-person truth, which listeners will ideally adapt to their own experiences, creating shared truth and a theoretically infinite in-group. As this chapter's case studies will show, the tension between desire to speak to universal issues of injustice on the one hand, and confinement to transparent, personal testimony on the other hand, factors integrally in rap's penalization.

To illustrate French rap's racialized, ideological opposition to French nation and its white majority, the deputies include parenthetical citations of various slang terms and borrowed words from Spanish and African languages that rappers wield as injurious speech: "*céfrancs*"; "*gouers*"; "*faces de craies*"; "*gringos*"; "*navets*"; "*toubabs*"; "*babtous*." The cumulative effect frames the supposed insult behind these terms as self-evident and allows the deputies, on behalf of white French nationals, to identify as the subjects interpellated, and therefore harmed, by these names. Here, the bill shifts from a view of rap's performativity as inevitably provoking violence to enacting harm through the very pronunciation of its lyrics. In their writings on hate speech and injurious rhetoric, Judith Butler cites a similar collapse of speech into conduct in conservative attacks against US gangsta rap. In such attacks, representation becomes unequivocal, inherent injury, and thus allows detractors to dissimulate the role of structural inequalities and localize the cause of urban violence in the music itself.[14] Butler insists that no speech act necessarily has to perform injury, that the time between speech or representation and its impact creates space to resignify and rework discourse's impact. Even for illocutionary speech acts that enact effects in the very moment of their utterance, such as a judge delivering a sentence, it is never a question of a single moment, but rather a ritualized exercise of convention.[15] Grosdidier's reliance on citation in the bill seeks to historicize a tradition of anti-white racism in French rap, all while occulting his own recourse to the ritualized power of legislative rhetoric to try to redefine the boundaries of racist, injurious speech.

In addition to its assemblage of rap lyrics, the bill comments at length the music video for Monsieur R's "FranSSe." In so doing, it betrays the discrepancy between performative power—the capacity for lyrics to produce material effects—and the symbolic, staged nature of musical performance. For the

[13] Anthony Pecqueux, *Voix du rap*, 173; Marie Sonnette-Manouguian, "Des mises en scène du 'nous' contre le 'eux' dans le rap français," *Sociologie de l'art* 23/24, no. 1 (2015): 153–177.

[14] Judith Butler, *Excitable Speech: A Politics of the Performative*, Routledge Classics ed. (Routledge, 2021), 23.

[15] Ibid., 15.

deputies, the weight of Monsieur R's insult toward the French state (which the song associates with the Third Reich and the collaborationist Vichy regime) lies in its vulgar allegories of sexual humiliation.[16] The bill identifies the two female, "European," pornography actresses in the video as embodiments of the French Republic, whose degradation is amplified during the chorus: "*La France est une garce, n'oublie pas de la baiser jusqu'à l'épuiser, comme une salope il faut la traiter, mec!*"[17] Referring to the two shirtless Black men in baggy army pants that nod their heads to the beat and gaze upon the actresses with an air of satisfaction, the text racializes sexual aggression toward an ethnically European France in a familiar register: "young urban caricatures address unambiguous gestures towards two women meant to represent France and its citizens."[18] The opposition between the white women and the "young urban caricatures" capitalizes on heightened connotations of sexual threat surrounding racialized *banlieue* youth in the aftermath of the 2005 riots. The deputies therefore project violent deviance onto Monsieur R's performance by reading it through the overdetermined *jeune de banlieue* trope. The choice of the word "caricature" is critical, in that it unwittingly acknowledges an element of excess and fantasy that distances the music video from reality. The bill thus hints at a flaw in its logic; the performance is too over-the-top to truly be life-like, yet will nonetheless be subject to face-value interpretations that locate its meaning in events and social realities external to the music.

Coherence with French rap's archetypal, *jeune de banlieue* image maintains a complex role within conferrals and denials of poetic license. In 2009, feminist blogs denounced the descriptions of violence toward women in the rapper Orelsan's song "Sale Pute," which he had first published to Myspace in the form of a music video in 2006. The video structures "Sale Pute" as a rage-filled e-mail from an intoxicated man, played by Orelsan, to his girlfriend upon discovering her infidelity. While feminist critiques initially benefited from political support, elected officials abandoned the cause once national media reframed the debate around freedom of expression.[19] Journalists and politicians aided this reframing by situating "Sale Pute" within the string of legal cases and polemics over French rap. These links created space for Orelsan to accuse his opponents of racist and classist discrimination toward rap.

[16] Kathryn Kleppinger, "When Parallels Collide: Social Commentary and Satire in French Rap Before and After *Charlie Hebdo*," *Contemporary French Civilization* 41, no. 2 (2016): 204.

[17] "France is a bitch, don't forget to screw her until she's worn out. You've got to treat her like a slut, man!"

[18] "*De jeunes caricatures urbaines adressent aux deux femmes censées représenter la France et ses citoyens des gestes sans ambiguïté*," Proposition de loi no. 2957, 12th legislature (2006).

[19] For a detailed discussion of the "Orelsan Affair," see Karim Hammou, "Du web au prétoire. Comment l'affaire Orelsan est devenue une question de droit," ed. Arnaud Montas *Droit(s) et Hip-hop* (Mare & Martin, 2020).

Orelsan's "atypical" profile as a white, middle-class rapper from Normandy was also key in this shift, as he played up his distance from rap's heterosexist stereotype to deny that he could ever plausibly act on the brutal fantasies in his lyrics.[20] Orelsan's 2016 acquittal in appeal (following an initial condemnation after feminist associations pursued a case for insult and provocation of violence toward women) paradoxically elides and reinforces his singularity. Establishing strong jurisprudence in rap's defense, the court argued that rap's style could be considered "by nature brutal, provocative, vulgar, even violent since it wants to appear as the reflection of a disillusioned and rebellious generation."[21] Yet, the decision also universalized Orelsan's music, inscribing it within wider creative expressions and positioning him as the voice of "disenchanted youth" beyond particularities of race and class, as acquittals of other rappers had specified.[22]

Referencing this decision and Sniper's acquittal in 2005 (discussed later in this chapter), Anna Arzoumanov argues that rap's stylistic particularities serve as a "legal shield" against condemnation.[23] Emmanuelle Carinos Vasquez challenges the idea that style protects rappers, since many innocent verdicts or overturned sentences occur more often due to legal technicalities than to the performances' formal qualities. Instead, rap's aesthetic particularities function as an aggravating circumstance, allowing politicians, police unions, and other plaintiffs to make individual rappers emblematic of a pervasive anti-France ideology in the musical genre.[24] In the recent trials of Jo le Phéno and Nick Conrad (the former for provocation to commit an attempt on the life of, and public insult toward, the national police, and the latter for provocation to crime), the prosecutors and judges relied upon the politically engaged, vehement nature of their music videos to justify realist interpretations.[25] In both trials, if the rappers were deemed to not have personal experience of the police violence and social injustices they denounced, the prosecution invalidated the music's political statement. However, if the performances were read as eyewitness testimony, this invalidated any sense

[20] Ibid., 93.

[21] "*Le rap pouvant être ressenti par certains comme étant un mode d'expression par nature brutal, provocateur, vulgaire voire violent puisqu'il se veut le reflet d'une génération désabusée et révoltée*," Cour d'appel de Versailles, February 18, 2016, 15/02687.

[22] Emmanuelle Carinos Vasquez, "Le son qui tue: dénoncer, justifier, performer la violence dans le rap français (2000–2024)" (PhD diss., Université Paris 8, 2024), 232.

[23] Anna Arzoumanov, "Le style peut-il être un bouclier juridique? Réflexions sur l'argument du style dans les procès contemporains," *Romantic Review* 109 (2019): 31–52.

[24] Emmanuelle Carinos Vasquez, "Fuck le 17! Rap français et forces de l'ordre," ed. Arnaud Montas *Droit(s) et Hip-hop* (Mare & Martin, 2020).

[25] Emmanuelle Carinos Vasquez, "Le rap au prétoire: luttes politico-judiciaires autour de deux clips de rap (Jo le Phéno et Nick Conrad)," *Biens symboliques* 10 (2022): https://journals.openedition.org/bssg/1025.

of artistic detachment.[26] This Catch-22 relies upon aesthetic realism to deny critical distance, while limiting rap's possibilities for denunciation to first-hand accounts, and thereby denying its right to universal moral and political claims.

Legal and sociological studies have demonstrated the role stylistic analyses, political ideology, and racializing rhetoric play in trials and parliamentary debates targeting French rappers. This chapter now turns to how rappers have drawn key issues of performativity, representation, referentiality, and responsibility into their music, either as aestheticized responses to their own legal cases or through fictional confrontations with the justice system. I am interested in how fundamental questions of aesthetic realism, lived experience, and artistic detachment play out in rap performances themselves, where the available tools differ than those admissible in a court of law, and where rappers can explore their relationships to their detractors in more nuanced ways than from the witness stand.

While I frame condemnations of rap's literal, transparent violence as the flipside to literary consecration, it is important to note that France does have a long history of legal proceedings against authors. The history of literary trials in France places those against rappers in a lineage of public debate over poetic license and artists' moral responsibilities, as well as in a broader tradition of developing aesthetic strategies to circumvent, respond to, or capitalize on legal proceedings.[27] However, these parallels are not without limitations, as appeals to this history of literary trials by rappers' defense lawyers often fall flat,[28] and both political discourse and jurisprudence stress rap's stylistic singularities. Furthermore, while trials against literary works have turned away from an emphasis on the nation and its political regimes toward broader moral and ethical questions,[29] French rap's penalization remains rooted in the relationship between the Republic's institutions and its marginalized citizens. The secular sacralization of literature in France may now look past this legal history to use the author as a measuring stick of aesthetic value for other creative forms, but the performances analyzed in this chapter will show how, not unlike their literary counterparts, rappers draw the legalized terms of debate into their

[26] Opposing lawyers even cited Orelsan as a benchmark for "magnificent" artistic detachment against which Nick Conrad fell far short, Emmanuelle Carinos Vasquez, "Le son qui tue," 263.

[27] Gisèle Sapiro, *La responsabilité de l'écrivain. Littérature, droit et morale en France (XIXe – XXIe siècle)* (Éditions du Seuil, 2011), 10–11; See also Helen Craske, *Complicity*.

[28] In this regard, Orelsan is once again an exception, as his defenders in public debate over "Sale Pute" were more successful in imposing literary comparisons. See Anne-Charlotte Husson, "Genre et violence verbale: l'exemple de 'l'affaire Orelsan,'" *Pratiques* 163–164 (2014): https://journals.openedition.org/pratiques/2315; Karim Hammou, "Du web au prétoire."

[29] Gisèle Sapiro, "La responsabilité pénale de l'écrivain au prisme des procès littéraires (France, XIXe – XXe siècles)," *Histoire de la justice* 23, no. 1 (2013): 269.

creative processes. In so doing, rappers negotiate their own understandings of their craft and role in society, as well as the moral imperatives that role may or may not imply.

Musically responding to penalization is a natural strategy for rappers, and one that aligns with the broader notion of catharsis through art. Addressing lived experiences with political and legal condemnations performs authenticity, particularly for rappers seen as politically engaged, whose audiences expect them to double down on denunciations of injustice despite the risks. Responding through music also allows rappers to provide audiences with personal narratives of debates confined to the courtroom or to the National Assembly, then sensationalized in the media. Through music, rappers can free themselves from the tightly controlled speech of the courtroom and return to the aesthetic codes they master. The techniques that rappers use to stage encounters with the justice system shed light on the ritualized aspects of the courtroom and political theater, whose power, far from being self-evident, stems from reiterative exercises of authority. Against these conventions, rap performances create their own historicized, citational power by forging a community of condemned rappers, intertextual allusions, and rallying cries inspired by the routinized attacks against them.

The songs and music videos analyzed in this chapter recite, resignify, or indeed recommit to targeted lyrics. Given its emphasis on the legal sphere, this chapter perhaps best encapsulates tensions between complicity's connotations of shared responsibility in moral or criminal wrongdoing on the one hand, and a more neutral sense of entanglement on the other hand. Far from intended to reproduce the genre's penalization, complicity here refers to the ways these performances create room to reappropriate and rework the political and legal discourse that delimits French rap's representational space. Complicity also encompasses the ways making music within the parameters of courtroom terminology, explicitly engaging with plaintiffs' names or likenesses, or repurposing legal arguments risk locking rappers into a reactive stance, limiting the subject positions they can perform, and chipping away at the distinction between lyrics and other forms of speech. The following close readings examine how Tandem, La Rumeur, Sniper, and Youssoupha navigate these aesthetic, political, and professional stakes.

Theatrical Truth-Telling in Tandem's "Le Jugement"

On their 2005 album, *C'est toujours pour ceux qui savent*, the duo Tandem, comprised of Aubervilliers rappers Mac Tyer and Mac Kregor, crafted an epic trilogy recounting the fictional incarceration, tumultuous reinsertion into society, and subsequent trial of Mac Tyer for the attempted murder of his counterpart. The accompanying music videos, directed by Nicolas Benamou and Jean-Frédéric Barre, present as a cinematographic saga with end credits attributing the original screenplay to Tandem. After the first installment, "Un jour comme un autre," which recounts the hardships of incarceration,[30] the second episode, "Frères ennemis," traces Mac Tyer's failed reinsertion and return to bad habits after a stalled rap career. Upon discovery that Mac Kregor has robbed him of the production funds for his next album, Mac Tyer confronts him, Glock in hand. The heated clash takes a turn for the worst when the police arrive. The second act closes with an exterior shot of the studio's windows, lit up with the flash of a gun firing.

The trilogy's dramatic final act, "Le Jugement," sees a host of guest rappers (Diam's, Kery James, Faf Larage, Kazkami, Lino, and Tunisiano), in the roles of judge, prosecutor, police commissioner, and eyewitnesses. The distribution of roles allows the rappers to play with the courtroom's highly codified language and behavioral norms. It also creates a closed, performative space in which they can exploit discrepancies between their artistic and civil identities, as well as level accusations toward the Republic's institutions through different distancing techniques than the condemned songs of many of their peers. Though Mac Tyer did encounter the carceral system in his youth, the triptych goes beyond biographical dramatization, using its overt theatricality to probe the parameters of the ideal culprit trope, the justice system's ritualized power, and the tension between personal testimony and universal moral truths in rap. "Le Jugement" thus offers unique perspective on the pressing issues of referentiality, biographical transparency, and artistic detachment that fuel rap's penalization.

The beat for "Le Jugement," produced by Jo le Balafré, begins with faint, high-pitched violins that reinforce the episode's function as the trilogy's melodramatic culmination. Fresh off the gold certification of her second album *Brut de femme* (2003) and 2004 *Victoire de la musique* for best rap album, Diam's adopts the role of the judge. Donning bright red robes and looking sternly down from the podium, she addresses the accused through both his civilian identity—with the family name censored by a beep—and artistic alias, introducing a tenuous distinction between the man and the rapper. Diam's specifies Mac Tyer's birthdate and place, as well as the birthplace of the victim, yet refers to Mac Kregor solely through his stage name, keeping the violent

[30] Booba, discussed in Chapter 1, makes an appearance as an inmate in the neighboring cell.

offense squarely in the performance's fictionalized realm. When it is the defendant's turn to address the court, the beat drops with an emphatic drumroll. Mac Tyer accuses the police of firing the shot and implores Diam's to demand an investigation.

The judge, however, shuts down Mac Tyer's speech as inherently false, with internal rhymes and assonance giving her dismissal a sense of blunt, eloquent authority: "*Monsieur, arrêtez d'induire en erreur les enquêteurs.*"[31] The song slips into a back-and-forth dynamic with Diam's trading bars with the prosecutor, Faf Larage, who rises in objection. The dynamic, in which both rappers hyper-articulate their flow, ceremoniously invalidates Mac Tyer's claim and reinforces their power as judge and prosecutor to control the terms of the debate. The physicality that Diam's and Faf Larage bring to their roles exaggerates this prejudiced complicity and frames the performance as an absurd sweep through the motions before arriving at an inevitable verdict.[32] As judge, Diam's faithfully corresponds to feminine allegories of Lady Justice in the judicial system—a trope often reproduced in French rap. For his part, Marseille native Faf Larage (and brother of IAM's Shurik'n) was no stranger at the time to caricaturing the justice system. His 2003 parody album with the rapper Eben of the group 2Neg, *Flic$ & Hor$ La Loi*, ironized the adventures of corrupt cops. Throughout "Le Jugement," Faf Larage dramatically points to the witnesses as he raises objections and yawns during the defense's closing remarks, while Diam's restacks her court documents and either contemplatively folds her hands or props up her chin in bemused skepticism, depending on whether the testimony supports the defense or the prosecution (see Figure 2.1).

Both rappers' gestures create distancing effects, constantly reminding the audience that they are caricaturing the ways such legal figures perform authority. Their unsubtlety aligns them with the other court figures, whose facial expressions betray an orchestrated bias. Diam's turns in either exasperation or knowing satisfaction toward her two fellow judges, played by white, male actors. Her colleagues in turn either nod in approval or roll their eyes as they verify the testimony against the official records. The court reporter casts a sidewise glance and purses her lips during witness testimony for the defense, and the bailiff contemptuously stares into the back of Mac Tyer's head. The video accentuates these moments with quick cuts to close-up shots, creating

[31] "Sir, stop misleading the investigators."

[32] Mac Tyer, "Tandem: Le Jugement," YouTube Video, 7:16, February 23, 2011, https://www.youtube.com/watch?v=_o9PUU1Yx9w.

Fig. 2.1 Still from the music video "Le Jugement"

shared knowledge with the audience that we are witnessing a staged miscarriage of justice.

The judge and prosecutor's commitment to formality and to court rituals also plays out in their repeated interjections policing other characters' language. This meta-commentary creates slippages between the proceedings' codified form and the substance of the narrative the judges and prosecution seek to control. After defense attorney Kery James drudges up past accusations of corruption, the police commissioner, played by Kazkami, slips into a heated, accelerated flow that emphasizes the alliteration in "p": "*C'est mon procès qu'on traite ou quoi?/J'vois pas pourquoi on secoue mon passé.*"[33] Diam's sternly calls him to order: "*Et Monsieur le commissaire, veuillez garder votre calme, éviter tout écart/Je vous rappelle vous êtes à la barre.*"[34] The judge's exasperated authority, marked by the elongated stress she puts on the assonance in "a," keeps the commissioner in check. Diam's reinforces norms of emotional restraint and polite speech but also signals that he may be drifting from the established script.

When the victim, Mac Kregor, takes the stand, he frankly expresses frustration with the police commissioner's mischaracterizations of him as an illicit drug user. In addition to his vexed tone, Mac Kregor employs informal slang for cops (*flicaillon*) and stressed, one-syllable end rhymes—"*Madame la*

[33] "Is this my trial or what?/I don't see why we're digging up my past."

[34] "And Mr. Commissioner, please keep your calm, avoid any deviations. I'll remind you you're on the stand."

présidente pour être franc, ça fait une heure que je suis assis dans le box/J'écoute les conneries de l'autre flicaillon qui veut me faire passer pour un tox."[35] The rapper confirms the defendant's claims that he was not the one who opened fire. Faf Larage rises in protest and sarcastically reproaches the victim, feigning marvel at Mac Kregor's "eloquence," before reminding him, "*Mais nous ne sommes pas au théâtre et à la barre faut être fiable.*"[36] The lyric evokes a historic opposition between theater and the law, in which theater's ostensible artifice and staging reinforce the law's prerogative over evidentiary truth, all while occulting the highly ritualized, often dramatized performance of the law in a courtroom.[37]

The tension between trustworthiness, truth, and performance comes to a head with the final witness for the defense. Testifying under his real first name, Bachir, Tunisiano of the group Sniper (whose own legal battles will be explored later in this chapter), begins his verse claiming to have seen and heard everything. His act of witnessing becomes the focal point of contention over his testimony's evidentiary value. Faf Larage doubts Tunisiano's ability to have truly witnessed the events from the closet in which he was hiding, while Tunisiano reasserts the inherent veracity of his sight and hearing. The rapper's cyclical repetition of "I saw" and "I heard" rhythmically anchors the verse, as well as emphatically contrasts proof in the senses with the policemen's falsehoods and conspiracy.

The music video dramatizes these scenes in cinematic, black-and-white flashbacks, sharing the rapper's first-hand account with the audience, yet also implicitly acknowledging the evidentiary gap between eyewitness testimony and its inherent vulnerabilities on the one hand, and the supposedly self-evident documentary value of photographs or video on the other. Faf Larage exploits this gap, playing up his meticulously documented case, holding up the defendant's firearm in a sealed evidence bag, and distributing blown-up photographs to the jury. The prosecutor presents the facts of the case as a "simple," "routine" narrative, of "*une histoire de ghetto de plus qui vire au drame.*"[38] He invokes the *banlieue*'s stereotyped image with turns of phrase that mimic nightly news' sensationalized language. He portrays the witnesses for the defense as clichés of this universe, and thus as undeserving of the jury's faith: "*Ils jouent à l'arme à feu, drogue et j'en passe/ C'est pourquoi leurs récits*

[35] "Madam President, to be frank, I've been sitting in the dock for an hour/I'm listening to the nonsense of that copper who wants to pass me off as a junkie."

[36] "But we're not at the theater, and on the witness stand you need to be trustworthy."

[37] Julie Stone Peters, "Legal Performance Good and Bad," *Law, Culture and the Humanities*, no. 4 (2008): 179–200.

[38] "Another ghetto story that takes a dramatic turn."

ne sont pas dignes de foi."[39] Faf Larage opts for the language of play to describe the group's illicit actions, underscoring their reckless ignorance of the consequences.

The closing remarks oppose what the court may deem admissible evidence with the felt social and moral truths that many rappers convey in their music. In his role as Mac Tyer's attorney, Kery James adopts the tone of an orator, posing philosophical, existential questions to the jury rather than relating the brute facts of the case. The casting choice taps into Kery James' posture, flow, and preferred themes as a rapper known for his stressed enunciation, lyrical rebuttals of political discourse, and moral questions. Kery James cites the Republic's motto—*liberté, égalité, fraternité*—and rhetorically inquires as to why no one in "our" housing projects still believes in those principles. He invokes glaring differences in quality of life between the capital's wealthy neighborhoods and its *banlieues*, before imploring the jury—and by extension, the listeners—to refuse complicity in further injustice: "*Il faut l'avouer n'accentuons pas les injustices/Au nom d'la fraternité, refusons d'être complice.*"[40] The rapper rhetorically expands his address beyond the physical members of the jury, creating a potentially infinite collective of those who recognize the stakes of the case for the whole of French society. Kery James accumulates such questions that place the moral burden on the listeners: "*Alors qui va-t-on condamner/Le vrai coupable, ou ce Noir au lourd passé?*"[41] With the court's impending deliberation, his questions take on urgency and suspense, but also stretch beyond the parameters of the fictional case at hand to encompass a more universal sense of moral truth.

In his final pleas for justice and clemency, Mac Tyer reaffirms his version of events. He cites personal growth since his prior convictions, which he attributes to rap: "*j'ai la musique pour évacuer ma rage de vivre/C'est ma psychanalyse, celle qui m'analyse quand je vais mal.*"[42] The rapper's flow stresses the assonance in "a" and elongates "*mal*" to accentuate the emotion of his appeal. He claims to be nothing more than the seemingly perfect culprit, attesting to the power of the role the prosecutor, and society at large, designate him. These protests do not suffice, however, as Diam's coldly reads out the unanimous guilty verdict and condemns him to a five-year prison sentence. Mac Tyer passionately objects, but his appeals prove futile as the performance ends with a tragic sense of injustice. The ending reinforces the music

[39] "They play with guns, drugs, and so on/That's why their stories aren't worthy of belief."

[40] "One has to admit it, let's not accentuate injustices/In the name of fraternity, let's refuse to be complicit."

[41] "So, who will we condemn/the true guilty party, or this Black man with a heavy past?"

[42] "I have music to release my lust for life/It's my psychoanalysis, that which analyzes me when I'm not doing well."

video's theatricality and situates it within the courtroom drama tradition in film and television, which often uses the verdict's affective weight to culminate its narratives.

As in all courts of law, the trial that Tandem stages is a highly ritualized performance. Crucially, however, "Le Jugement" stylizes its proceedings through the rappers' signature flows and artistic postures. Tandem and their collaborators therefore insist upon aesthetic form and the rich, rhythmic qualities of their words—elements consistently absent from efforts to penalize rap for its lyrical content. Underscoring the fictionalized ritual of their musical performance allows Tandem to exploit courtroom dynamics, level accusations of police misconduct, and critique the state's moral failings, all while strategically sidestepping the issues of aesthetic realism, external referents, and first-hand testimony that criminalize the performances of many of their peers.

Power and Performativity in La Rumeur's *Regain de tension*

In addition to performance's salient theatricality, the fact that Tandem were not facing any charges for their music grants "Le Jugement" a further degree of separation through which to explore these dynamics. This was not the case for many other French rappers throughout the 2000s, including La Rumeur. Over the course of eight years, the group, comprised of Ekoué, Hamé, Philippe le Bavar, and Mourad, as well as DJs Soul G and Kool M, faced a protracted legal battle targeting not the content of their lyrics but that of a promotional magazine designed to accompany the release of the album, *L'ombre sur la mesure*. In this magazine, Hamé wrote in an article entitled "Insécurité sous la plume d'un barbare," "*Les rapports du ministère de l'Intérieur ne feront jamais état des centaines de nos frères abattus par les forces de police sans qu'aucun des assassins n'ait été inquiété.*"[43] On behalf of the national police, then-Interior Minister Nicolas Sarkozy brought charges against then-president of the record label EMI, Emmanuel de Buretel, and Hamé for defamation and complicity in defamation, respectively.[44]

[43] "The Ministry of the Interior's reports will never mention the hundreds of our brothers slaughtered by police forces without a single assassin being troubled." Hamé, "Insécurité sous la plume d'un barbare," *La Rumeur magazine*, no. 1 (2002).

[44] As publisher and promoter, the record label is legally considered the principal author of defamatory material.

Across the trials, the debate frequently returned to the term "our brothers."[45] When the judge asked Hamé to specify whom this term designates, the rapper responded that it is an everyday term of affection for "a brotherhood with which one can find common scars and hopes," beyond any distinction based on skin color or religion.[46] During the second appeal in 2008, a linguist and expert witness for the defense returned to this expression, deeming "brother" a term of solidarity that reunited, "all the oppressed people against a 'them' that in the context of the article refers to capitalist forces."[47] Despite the rapper's open-ended understanding of brotherhood, the courts repeatedly substituted *jeunes de banlieue* for "our brothers," depicting Hamé as the spokesperson for a racialized, working-class youth at odds with the Republic.

Although Hamé stood trial for an article published as a paratextual element of the group's album, the court proceedings themselves often sought to establish coherence between the article and La Rumeur's music.[48] The specific nature of the text had key implications for the rapper's defense strategy, as he likened his article to the pamphlet literary tradition, yet emphasized the specifics of rap as a mode of expression necessitating radical terms.[49] The defense further chose not to mobilize the jurisprudence of literary trials, particularly that of Baudelaire, to argue for a symbolic interpretation of the article. Instead, La Rumeur doubled down on the historical truth of Hamé's text and their musical approach to politically engaged themes. As Ekoué laid out, hiding behind freedom of expression would implicitly admit that the group's claims were wrong, whereas they were "imbued with an effective veracity" that historians and even police officers corroborated throughout the trials in their capacity as expert witnesses.[50]

Hamé's definitive acquittal would eventually come down to a legal technicality, the court deciding that the most appropriate charge would have been public insult (*injure*), rather than the charge of defamation sought by the prosecution.[51] The distinction lies in whether the text concerns a precise event or

[45] Even though Hamé, whose real name is Mohamed Bourokba, was found not guilty during the initial trial, the state appealed twice, and the court of cassation intervened twice, before the appellate course of Versailles issued a fourth and definitive acquittal in June 2010.

[46] "*Une fratrie avec laquelle on peut se trouver des cicatrices et des espoirs en commun.*" The group had published extensive summaries of the court proceedings, as well as interviews with Hamé, on their website. The dossier has since been removed. See Karim Hammou, "Quand la Rumeur Pointe Les Violences Policières," *Sur un son rap*, July 26, 2010, https://surunsonrap.hypotheses.org/1452.

[47] "*Tous les opprimés face à un 'eux' qui renvoie dans le contexte de l'article à ce qu'on peut appeler les forces capitalistes.*"

[48] Karim Hammou, *Une histoire du rap*, 252.

[49] Karim Hammou, "Quand la Rumeur."

[50] "*Empreints d'une véracité effective.*" See Thomas Blondeau, "La Rumeur, 'au-delà de l'acharnement,'" *Le Monde Diplomatique*, September 30, 2008, https://www.monde-diplomatique.fr/carnet/2008-09-30-La-Rumeur.

[51] Emmanuelle Carinos-Vasquez, "Fuck le 17!"

fact that harms the reputation of the national police (defamation), or whether its scope is more general (insult). La Rumeur's legal battle thus showcases the confrontation between the particular and the universal in the reduction of rappers to spokespeople for racialized, working-class young men, the subsequent restriction of their lyrics to first-hand testimony, and the burden of proof such restrictions place on their truth claims.

In the midst of the polemic, La Rumeur released their 2004 album, *Regain de tension*, which Ekoué referred to as a work of "self-defense."[52] At the core of La Rumeur's opus is a reflection on the state's punitive power, with many tracks taking up the language of police procedures, courtroom rituals, and acts of legislation, but also reflecting on the power of words. *Regain de tension* draws upon the centrality of written documentation, as well as upon judicial and political jargon, to reflect on the competing textual analyses at play in their confrontation with the state. As the specialist rap media *L'Abcdrduson* spelled out, the album's function as an outlet for rage amidst the trial poses an inherent risk of "locking themselves in the martyr role, of delighting in accentuating their identity traits to the point of being nothing more than vulgar caricatures."[53] While the critic found that the album generally avoids falling into this trap, the review nevertheless foregrounds the stakes of rap's response to penalization. Such responses require a tightrope act between harnessing the legal sphere's codes and conflating musical performance with the courtroom, between aesthetic realism and inhabiting the caricatural role outlined in the opposition's script, and between evacuating the psychological weight of lived experience and further eroding the perceived transparency between rap and the real that makes it susceptible to legal attack.

The song "Inscrivez greffier" engages with the value of material documents in the legal sphere, using metaphors and intertextuality to weave the most objected-to language of Hamé's article into the lyrics. The title instructs a court reporter to begin transcribing, framing the performance as official testimony. The track, produced by Soul G, begins with muffled scratches and a high-pitched droning that resemble the sound of a printer or mechanical recording device. Stating his identity for the record, Hamé introduces himself both in racialized terms and as if he were at physical document: "*Je suis un Arabe non daté, extrait d'une longue plaie grattée.*"[54] The rapper describes

[52] Patrick Caffin, "La Rumeur: le groupe de rap qui dérange," *Le Parisien*, November 12, 2004, https://www.leparisien.fr/oise-60/la-rumeur-le-groupe-rap-qui-derange-12-11-2004-2005448201.php.

[53] "*Tout particulièrement, le risque artistique de s'enfermer dans un rôle de martyr, de se plaire à accentuer les traits de leur identité jusqu'à n'être plus que de vulgaires caricatures.*" Reivax, "Chronique: La Rumeur, Regain de tension," *Abcdrduson*, November 14, 2004, https://www.abcdrduson.com/chroniques/regain-de-tension/.

[54] "I'm an undated Arab/Official copy (or excerpt) of a long scratched-at wound."

himself as undated—lacking crucial criteria for admissibility in bureaucratic spheres—but an official record of a long scratched-at, wound. His undated nature takes on a sense of timelessness, an embodied archive of past experiences impossible to mark with one single date. The wound may invoke the group's battle in court, but within the context of the album's thematic emphasis on colonialism, slavery, and economic domination, it takes on deeper roots in historical traumas. From the first line, Hamé's verse strikes at the parameters of representability and the quest for an identifiable event that would both narrow his words' referential scope and enhance their vulnerability to prosecution.

Hamé cycles back through this formula throughout the song, altering the descriptor through which he introduces himself, but remaining within legal vocabulary. He refers in the second instance to his initial reprimand and reprieve, while the third iteration returns to inadmissibility as he describes having been voted null and void. Over the wailing sound effects of sirens, the chorus confronts the administrative authority of record-keeping with a tone of defiance: "*Inscrivez greffier, le prévenu n'exprime aucun regret! Veuillez verser au dossier, à charge pour dommages et intérêts, article 25 bis alinéa premier.*"[55] After instructing the court reporter to officially record his lack of regret, the chorus cites the now-defunct 1945 ordinance allowing for the deportation of a foreign national if deemed a pressing necessity for public or state security. In invoking this ordinance, Hamé returns to the protracted courtroom debates opposing his "brothers" to the Republic's community of citizens. Adopting the tone of a legislative decree, the rapper accentuates the supposed threat to the nation in his article and pushes his detractors' desires to the extreme, enacting his own removal from the Republic.

Hamé further interlaces carceral and weaponized imagery with his extended metaphor of documentation. In so doing, he interjects intertextual references to themes of violent revolt in the *chanson française*: "*Dans le Paris des muselières, je marche l'arme légère/Un pied-de-biche en bandoulière.*"[56] Hamé folds an allusion to Léo Ferré's 1980 song, "La violence et l'ennui," repackaging the singer-songwriter's original lyrics, "*Dans le Paris des chiens, je vais l'âme légère.*"[57] Whereas Ferré moves with ease about the dog-eat-dog streets of Paris, Hamé reveals a more combative demeanor, choosing a light weapon to a light heart. The intertextual relationship to Ferré invites further

[55] "Record, court clerk, the defendant expresses no regret! Please add to the case file, liable for damages, Article 25b, first paragraph!"

[56] "In the Paris of muzzles, I walk with a light weapon/A crowbar over the shoulder."

[57] "In the Paris of dogs I go with a gentle soul."

parallels between the two songs' shared ambition as harbingers of uprisings to come.

Ferré begins with an anaphoric structure that repeats "nous"—forging an inclusive collectivity much like Hamé's article—that envelops those on society's margins: "*Nous, des marges, nous, des routes, nous, des bordels intelligents.*"[58] His lyrics further resonate with Hamé's decried text in their use of familial terms. While Hamé refers to fallen brothers, Ferré addresses his ode to "sister violence," of whom his collective "we" are the children. The singer-songwriter reserves fraternal bonds for his fellow revolutionaries, hoping for a different fate than the violently squashed insurrection of the 1871 Paris Commune: "*À ne jamais vouloir crever comme crevèrent les Communards/mes frères.*"[59] "Inscrivez greffier" echoes this sentiment of a suspended uprising, as Hamé concludes the song with a bridge that, similarly to Ferré, creates a rallying cry: "*Nous sommes des foules à marcher les deux pieds couverts d'ampoules.*"[60] From within this tirelessly marching crowd, Hamé ponders: "*Jusqu'à quand, combien de temps le ghetto restera-t-il aussi patient?*"[61] His musing rings out with ominous promise for those in positions of power, against whom the ghetto will one day turn.

Far from just a cursory reference, the link to Ferré frames La Rumeur's ability to forge, speak for, and aestheticize the violent impulses of a broad coalition of the marginalized against a familiar barometer for authorial ownership—the *chanson française*. The allusion echoes Médine's self-granted parallels to literary and *chanson* figures, explored in the previous chapter as a means of challenging the unequal distribution of poetic license. Hamé's interwoven reference also sheds light on the tendency to romanticize and dilute many *chanson* legends' radical politics. "Inscrivez greffier" therefore seeks to enrich the resonance of political critique in La Rumeur's music far beyond the reductive scope of the legal arguments against them.

In addition to grappling with the breadth and narrative position of Hamé's embattled text, La Rumeur's album meditates on the performative power of words in the penultimate song, "Maître mot, mots du maître"—Watchword, words of the master (also the French honorific title for lawyers). Once again rapped solely by Hamé, the song commits to nebulous shifts between the two components of a linguistic sign: the signifier, the material form of the spoken or written word, and the signified, the mental concept to which that

58 "Us, the margins, us, the routes, us, the intelligent messes."
59 "Never wanting to die as died the Communards/My brothers."
60 "We're mobs marching, both feet covered with blisters."
61 "Until when, for how long will the ghetto remain so patient?"

physical form refers. Hamé dedicates the song's two verses to the power of two institutions: the media and the police.[62] Most lines therein begin with "*ces mots*" (these words). The anaphora both reinforces the words' symbolic weight and occults their actual form and meaning. It is not a question of specific acts of language or what they signify, but rather the effects they perform. The chorus features a series of chiasmi, creating mirror-like reflections between word order ("*orde des mots*") and the words of an order ("*mots de l'ordre*"). The internal rhyme of the chorus's final line blurs the divide, "*ordre des mots dressés pour mordre*,"[63] giving semantics a biting, harmful potential.

Hamé personifies "these words" as the acting subject of his rhymes. In the second verse, the words take on a capacity for physical violence. Hamé locates them within a gun barrel, precariously contained by the safety, but still ready to hunt him down: "*Ces mots dans le barillet des sécurités/Qui retrouvent ma trace et ouvrent la chasse.*"[64] He paints a vivid picture of words unscrupulously operating beyond the confines of the law and goes further to place them at the scene of the 1998 murder of 17-year-old Algerian student Habib Ould Mohamed by police in Toulouse[65]: "*Ces mots qui regardent ailleurs quand Habib est tué à terre/Le 9 bis pour tout drap mortuaire.*"[66] Here, Hamé dangerously flirts with the lack of precise referent at the center of his case, enveloping an identifiable victim of police violence into his lyrics, but withholding murderous capacity from the words, according them weaponized inaction instead. The officers left Habib Ould Mohamed to die in the street.

In his reading of La Rumeur's music and Hamé's article, Taïeb Berrada argues that rumor, understood not as a falsehood but as a means of disseminating not-yet-verified information, reflects the way the group inhabits political and media discourse to circulate critique.[67] In "Maître Mot, mots du maître," Hamé's lyrics immerse themselves deeper in linguistic signs to muddle less the claim's verifiability than the ability to identify its referents. As "these words" take on the capacity for physical violence, tension builds

[62] Before the case brought by Sarkozy, the radio station Skyrock also attempted to press charges, this time for Ekoué's article in the same promotional magazine, in which he advised the staff to "no longer step out without your bulletproof vests." The complaint did not amount to any legal proceedings, but Sarkozy's came swiftly afterward, suggesting complicity between the aggrieved parties in the eyes of the rappers and many fans.

[63] "Order of words trained to bite."

[64] "These words in the cylinder of safety catches/That find my trace and open the hunt."

[65] Amnesty International, "France: Fatal Shooting by Police Officer of 17-Years-Old Habib Ould Mohamed," April 21, 1999, https://www.amnesty.org/en/documents/eur21/004/1999/en/.

[66] "These words that look away when Habib is killed on the ground/9bis for any funeral shroud."

[67] Taïeb Berrada, "La Rumeur et son rap: emploi de la rumeur comme fonction discursive contestataire," *Contemporary French Civilization* 37, no. 1 (2012): 64.

between their function as a floating stand-in and the increasingly salient mental image of the police that they invoke. The words hint at their metonymic function, but Hamé refuses to ever let these two sides of the coin culminate into an explicit communicative sign, nor to name the actors who commit violence with impunity. In so doing, he skirts the demand for referentiality and identifiable, scrutable targets and events that the courts require of his accusations.

At the end of the second verse, the rapper employs the amorphous vehicle "these words" to stand in for his own subject position and for the much-debated identifiers for the communities for whom he speaks. Here, words take on the full weight of their performative capacity, as they rejoin physical blows and racial profiling to shackle themselves to Hamé's body, rein him in, and infuse his very sense of self: "*Ces mots, ces coups, ces coupables désignés, ces Mohamed/Ces moricauds, ces mauvaises bêtes à mauvaise peau/Ces mots mors que je porte si bien qu'ils collent à mon ADN/Ces mots que je porte si loin qu'ils en deviennent des chaînes.*"[68] The accumulated signifiers gain traction to depict racist discourse's punitive power to designate society's ideal culprit and motivate violent repression. Hamé transforms these words and the ideologies they convey into a snaffle bit between his teeth and chains, materializing their constraining function. "*Ces mots mors*" bears phonetic similarity to "*Ces mots maures*," playing off the French for "Moorish" to further accentuate words' racializing potential.

The catch-all "these words" demarcates within the realm of discourse the conflict opposing La Rumeur and their communities to oppressive institutions and ideologies. The way Hamé maintains a tenuous relationship between signifier and signified works around the issues of referentiality at stake in his legal battle, but also allows him to flesh out the imbalance of power between his words and the institution he stands accused of defaming. In "Inscrivez greffier" and "Maître mot, mots du maître," stylistic devices foreground the material, embodied, and affective traces left by encounters with the state, racializing discourses, and colonial histories. In this sense, the music draws upon forms of knowledge and ways of transmitting experience that would be discredited in the courtroom. La Rumeur thus aestheticizes the legal criteria of their case, steeping them in metaphors that center the group's vulnerability to weaponized state power, all while sharpening the music's critical edge.

[68] "These words, these blows, these ideal culprits, These Mohameds/These dark-skinned people (using a racist term in French), these bad beasts with bad skin/These word-bits that I wear so well they stick to my DNA/These words that I carry for so long that they become chains."

Self-Fulfilling Prophecies in Sniper's "La France, itinéraire d'une polémique"

While La Rumeur opted to intertwine the parameters of their case with judicial metaphors, intertextual references, and performative metonyms, another one of Sarkozy's targets, the group Sniper, chose a more explicit, retrospective mode to narrate their experience. Sniper was formed in the Val d'Oise region outside of Paris by rappers Tunisiano, Aketo, and Blacko, along with DJ Boudj. After the commercial success of the group's first album, 2001's *Du rire aux larmes*, and 2003 follow-up, *Gravé dans la roche*, right-wing politicians sought the government's attention regarding certain lyrics, including those of "Jeteur de pierres" about Palestinian resistance to Israeli occupation, and "La France." Several excerpts of the latter, notably, "*On n'est pas dupes/en plus on est tous chauds, pour mission exterminer les ministres et les fachos*,"[69] were deemed violent toward the state, its institutions, and its values.[70] National Assembly deputies made use of parliamentary questions to solicit Sarkozy's official stance on the issue. Sarkozy's response cited the racist, antisemitic, and injurious nature of Sniper's lyrics, heading up what Karim Hammou has called a "nationalist moral crusade."[71]

The Minister of the Interior, however, only retained the motive of inciting harm and murder of police officers and state representatives in pressing charges after a live performance of "La France" in Rouen. The group was found innocent in the first instance, and the verdict was upheld in appeal. The polemic notably marked an early, but failed, attempt by far-right militants *Jeunesse identitaire* and the AGRIF (General Alliance Against Racism and for Respect for French and Christian Identity) to legitimize "anti-white racism," as the courts dismissed this argument.[72] The "Sniper affair" nevertheless demonstrated the force of orchestrated efforts to condemn rap at various levels—from far-right activists who protested concerts, garnered online traction, and harnessed the voices of national representatives, to the political theater of parliamentary questions and the media spotlight that prolonged the controversy's shelf-life.

Sniper addressed these interlocking efforts in their 2006 song, "La France, itinéraire d'une polémique." The group makes use of lyrical rewrites, shifts in

[69] "We're not duped, what's more we're all riled up, the mission: exterminate ministers and fascists."
[70] Jacques Myard, "Question écrite no. 2618," *Journal officiel*, September 16, 2002; Nadine Morano, "Question au gouvernement no. 897," *Journal officiel*, November 6, 2003.
[71] Karim Hammou, *Une histoire du rap en France*, 255.
[72] Emmanuelle Carinos Vasquez, "'Anti-White Racism' and 'Anti-France Hatred': Prosecution of Rap Music and the Paradox of Racist Use of Anti-Racist Legislation in France (2003–2019)," *POMEPS Studies* 52 (2024).

musical tone, and alternative media contexts to reframe the trial. Through these various shifts, the clarity of hindsight structures the performance, injecting dramatic irony and unheeded warnings. Tunisiano weaves a web that draws in the archetypal players—*Jeunesse identitaire*, national politicians, and the mainstream media—and recounts the consequences of their conspiring with resignation and resentment. "La France, itinéraire d'une polémique" takes on elements of tragedy to present Sniper's legal confrontations with the state as marked by missed opportunities and unjust misunderstandings. The song's dramatic structure contrasts with the elements of "farce" Sniper attributes to the campaign against them. This theatrical grammar reinforces the moral of the story: competing, self-fulfilling prophecies involving rap, marginalized communities, and the Republic have costly consequences. Playing up the role of ignored prophets, Sniper emphasizes that the state ultimately pays the price for its willful misinterpretations of rap's recourse to catharsis.

Sniper outsources the pedagogical demonstration of the political sphere's self-inflicted wounds to a sympathetic media figure, music journalist Olivier Cachin. The intro, interludes, and outro frame Tunisiano's verses as a tell-all interview and response to the pressing question: "Is rap a threat to society?" The journalist's emphatic tone parodies the pearl-clutching coverage of rap and *banlieue* unrest typical of television news and talk shows.[73] Within this staging, Cachin plays a role akin to the Greek chorus in theater, commenting upon Tunisiano's verses, drawing out key conclusions for the listeners, and prompting the rapper to pursue his narrative. His meta-commentary incites Tunisiano to plainly map out the collaboration between far-right militants, National Assembly member Nadine Morano, and Nicolas Sarkozy, to ensure audience comprehension. After Tunisiano reconstitutes this networked action, Cachin hammers home the farce: "*On pensait ce traitement de choc réservé à des terroristes, alors que vous êtes des artistes en colère, le monde à l'envers!*"[74] Through his journalistic credibility in the music scene, Cachin not only reinforces Sniper's position as the righteous party, but legitimizes their status as artists to underscore the absurdity of the state conflating them with terrorists.

The song thus recounts the controversy as a tragicomedy of errors, featuring misattributed social roles and misplaced projections of threat. In his introduction, Cachin presents the cast of characters: "certain political figures" and their "unexpected allies." While, in the recorded song, the "unexpected

[73] As discussed in the Introduction, Cachin frequently intervened in such televised debates.

[74] "We thought this shock treatment was reserved for terrorists, whereas you are angry artists, the world's upside-down!"

allies" remain a suggestive entity, the music video paints a clearer picture.[75] The video opens with a close-up of a poster that reads, "No to Anti-French Racism!" displayed on a wall next to framed military medals. We catch a glimpse of Tunisiano, head bowed, lurking in the darkness beside a dartboard with a picture of Sniper across the bullseye. As the camera pans over the wall decorations, including pamphlets about rap and fascist paraphernalia, a white man walks across the room to scrutinize a computer monitor displaying online chatrooms, blogs, and images of Sniper. The video puts Tunisiano behind enemy lines, in the position to unearth the real, shadowy threat to society: a digitally organized network of far-right militants with a dogged focus on rap's purported hatred of French citizens.

The caricatural, plotting mastermind in his lair reinforces the song's portrayal of Morano and Sarkozy's disingenuous myopia in looking past such blatant menace to see this figure as a useful ally. References in Tunisiano's lyrics spell out this hypocrisy, opposing the figurative nature of his threatening words toward government ministers with assassination attempts by these same far-right networks, such as the 2002 Bastille Day plot against then-President Jacques Chirac. The far-right archetype provides a foil through which Sniper refutes the performative nature of their lyrics and insists upon the separation between words and actions. Figuratively throwing his hands in the air, Tunisiano adopts a tone of resignation and bewilderment toward the inanity of the farce: "*Ils s'acharnent, ils insistent, mais que dire, que faire?/Nous sommes traités de racistes par les gosses à Hitler.*"[76]

As the title indicates, the song is a self-referential, before-and-after treatment of the controversy surrounding "La France." Sniper opposes the two songs in musical atmosphere, emotion, and lyrical structure. The beat for "La France, itinéraire d'une polémique," composed by Grégory Kasparian and Yann Barbarot, opens with a somber, pensive piano melody overlaid with violins and a slow-tempo kick drum and snare. For the chorus, Tunisiano is joined by the singer Cici (uncredited on the recorded track), whose soprano underlies the rapper's own vocal delivery to add to the aggrieved tone. The lyrics remold the chorus of "La France," in which Sniper's detractors found the most flagrant evidence of the group's anti-France ideology:

> *La France est une garce et on s'est fait trahir/Le système, voilà ce qui nous pousse à les haïr/La haine, c'est ce qui rend nos propros vulgaires/On nique la France sous*

[75] "Sniper—La France, itinéraire d'une polémique (Clip officiel)," YouTube video, 6:48, January 3, 2013, https://www.youtube.com/watch?v=C1mSAMhYLHY.

[76] "They hound, insist, but what to say, what to do? We're called racists by the Hitler Youth."

> *une tendance de musique populaire/On est d'accord et on se moque des répressions/ On se fout de la République et de la liberté d'expression/Faudrait changer les lois et pouvoir voir/Bientôt à l'Élysée des Arabes et des Noirs au pouvoir.*[77]

For "La France, itinéraire d'une polémique," Sniper makes significant alterations, yet couches the perceived insult in rhymes and indirect phrasing instead of renouncing their claims:

> *La France est une farce et on s'est fait trahir/Tu sais, ils ont tenté de nous salir/Oui moi j'ai parlé de garce, notamment de la France/Ils m'interdisent de l'dire en face, mais t'inquiète, je le pense/Accusé d'inciter à prendre les armes/Mais ce texte n'était qu'un signal d'alarme/Messieurs, comprenez le sens de notre discours/Ne pas confondre un appel au meurtre et un appel au secours.*[78]

The updated version euphemizes the original's gendered and sexualized language; "*garce*" becomes "*farce*" and the bold declaration of intent to "*nique*" France dissipates. These efforts, Cici's vocals, and the presence of a woman in the music video (presumed to be the singer) listening to the track on a Walkman and singing along, signal a desire to defuse the heterosexist connotations of the original's perceived violence toward the Republic.

The delivery sharply contrasts that of "La France," to which group member Blacko's reggae-inspired flow lends a more tauntingly defiant tone. The original chorus both foretells and flaunts the risks of backlash the group may face for their lyrical jabs. This reinforces the reinterpretation's prophetic tone, but also sharply accentuates its revised mood. Tunisiano does not, however, convey contrition, but instead twists the chorus' phrasing to reaffirm his view of France as a bitch. The direct address to "gentlemen," presumably the politicians targeting his group, shifts the sense of inevitability; in continuing to mistake the lyrics for a call to murder instead of a call for help, the Republic and its political class will pay the greater price.

Tunisiano's final verse culminates with the clearest counterargument against misinterpretations of Sniper's lyrics. He returns to the discrepancy between words and acts, this time re-signifying the harshness of his speech as

[77] "France is a bitch and we've been betrayed/The system, voilà what pushes us to hate them/Hate, it's what makes our remarks vulgar/We fuck France in the fashion of popular music/We're in agreement and we don't care about repression/We don't give a shit about the Republic and freedom of expression/Would need to change the laws and be able to see/Soon at the Elysée Arabs and Black people in power."

[78] "France is a farce and we've been betrayed/You know, they tried to smear us/Yeah, I spoke about a bitch, notably about France/They forbid me from saying it to their face, but don't worry, I'm thinking it/ Accused of incitement to take up arms/But that text was nothing but a warning signal/Gentlemen, understand the meaning of our speech/Don't conflate a call to murder and a call for help."

cathartic release and a necessary alternative to committing the kind of destructive acts he stood accused of inciting. The rapper suggests that the issue is that rappers use their own coded language instead of choosing a vocabulary that would be inauthentic to them. While the choice of harsh words is intentional, it is not to enact riotous destruction, but to draw attention to their distress: "*Au lieu d'aller foutre la de-mer, il préfère prendre un stylo/Il est choquant mais, il n'a d'autre solution/Il emploie des mots violents afin d'attirer l'attention.*"[79] Tunisiano reinforces the boundaries of his representational space around the role of spokesperson for the disenchanted, framing himself as the unheeded prophet of bubbling unrest. The song thus highlights the paradox of rap's responsibility—that, in rappers' view, they speak *from* the perspective of *banlieue* youth, but, for the media and political spheres, they assume responsibility *for* the *banlieue* as a homogenous entity.[80] Although the 2005 uprisings remain unacknowledged in the lyrics, they were the inescapable context of the appeal, with the definitive verdict delivered on December 14, 2005, less than two months after the riots began. The implied knowledge of those events molds the song around the media and political classes' refusal to hear the alarm signal in the lyrics. Faced with the interpretation of their music as performative acts that inevitably bring about the unrest they aestheticize, Sniper levels their own accusations of self-fulfilling prophecies, in which aligning with proponents of racist exclusion to penalize rap's cathartic function sees politicians feed the very rebellion they project onto the musical genre.

Sniper's revisions of "La France" mark the starkest example of blurring the boundaries between the dock and the recording booth. Many of the lyrical alterations in "La France, itinéraire d'une polémique" cite trial arguments for the group's defense. The last line of the chorus, "*Ne pas confondre un appel au meurtre et un appel au secours*" is quoted from the book, *Le rap ou la fureur de dire*, by academics Georges Lapassade and Philippe Rousselot.[81] Press coverage of the trials indicates that the group used the quote to defend their lyrics' violent phrasing.[82] Parts of Tunisiano's testimony also echo in the lyrics, as the rapper described how the song reflects, "a cry of anger, the statement of a young person from the suburbs who feels poorly integrated, who lets off steam by writing like a boxer hits the sandbag to release stress."[83] As with the

[79] "Instead of stirring up shit, he prefers to take up a pen/It's shocking, but he has no other solution/He uses violent words to get attention."

[80] Karim Hammou, *Une histoire du rap*, 83.

[81] Georges Lapassade and Philippe Rousselot, *Le Rap ou la fureur de dire* (Éditions Talmart, 1990), 123.

[82] "Le procureur demande la relaxe des rappeurs de Sniper," *Agence France Presse*, May 25, 2005.

[83] "*Un cri de colère, le constat d'un jeune de banlieue qui se sent mal intégré, qui se défoule en écrivant comme un boxeur qui frappe le sac de sable pour évacuer son stress*," Ibid.

final verse's rhetorical question—"*Monsieur le Ministre/Oui, nos paroles vous déplaisent/Mais que dire de celles de la Marseillaise?*"[84]—Tunisiano invoked "La Marseillaise" in court as a counterexample to demonstrate that the national anthem's bloody imagery has never pushed him to violence. The group's lawyer, Maître Dominique Tricaud, also called Olivier Cachin as a witness. There is thus a tenuous boundary between the journalist's expository role in the musical performance and his place on the stand. On the one hand, the near-verbatim use of defense arguments in "La France, itinéraire d'une polémique" draws those points out of the courtroom to circulate them in a debate over rap's *raison d'être* performed through the music. It also brings key players formally unrepresented in the plaintiffs, such as *Jeunesse identitaire*, out of the shadows—quite literally in the music video—materializing the defense's countercharge of far-right instrumentalization. On the other hand, such citations hold Sniper in a defensive position, prolonging the dynamics of the trial and tightening their posture around the tragic role of unheeded martyrs, where some listeners might expect a more frontal counterattack and unequivocal commitment to the original's lyrics and defiant tone toward the risk of repression.

Historicizing Rap's Moral Imperatives in Youssoupha's "Menace de mort"

Sniper uses hindsight, shared knowledge of external events, reworkings of their original lyrics, and transposed legal arguments to insist upon the separation of speech and acts. They root their artistic vocation in rap's potential for catharsis and role as canary in the coal mine of social unrest. The group's recourse to tragedy, dramatic irony, and moralistic commentary shifts responsibility to Sarkozy and his allies for their failures to correctly interpret their lyrics, framing the politicians as the architects of their own lost grip on public order. Five years later, the rapper Youssoupha echoes Sniper's efforts to negotiate rap's ethos in the face of repressive social realities. For his part, Youssoupha expands the parameters of his performance to create a community of embattled rappers, historicizing the genre's penalization. This collective meditation on rap's artistic and moral imperatives came in the form of the 2011 single, "Menace de mort," for which Youssoupha released the music video on the first day of his trial for public insult and defamation of the polemical media pundit Éric Zemmour.

[84] "Mister Minister/Yes our words are displeasing to you/But what to say about those of the Marseillaise?"

Dubbed the "philosopher of French rap" and self-styled as a lyricist ("Prim's Parolier"), Youssoupha is a Kinshasa-born rapper who immigrated as a child to the Parisian suburbs.[85] In addition to his lyrical prowess and eclectic musical influences including pop, rock, gospel, and Congolese rumba, Youssoupha is known for socially conscious themes. His music touches upon social issues in France, Black identity, and the African diaspora, particularly on 2015's gold-certified *NGRTD* (in reference to the Negritude movement) and 2012's platinum-certified *Noir Désir*, which features "Menace de mort." In his 2009 song "À force de le dire," devoted to the media's demonizing treatment of *banlieue* youth, Youssoupha explicitly called out Zemmour: "*À force de juger nos gueules, les gens le savent/ Qu'à la télé souvent les chroniqueurs diabolisent les banlieusards/Chaque fois qu'ça pète on dit que c'est nous/J'mets un billet sur la tête de celui qui fera taire ce con d'Éric Zemmour.*"[86] Perceiving the lyrics as a death threat, Zemmour pressed charges against Youssoupha and EMI Musique France for public insult and defamation. In October 2011, the court sentenced both the rapper and his label to fines and the repayment of Zemmour's legal fees. Youssoupha made a successful appeal the following year, with the court recognizing rap as an artistic style that allows possible recourse to a certain dose of exaggeration, and subsequently deciding that the lyrics in question did not exceed the limits of freedom of artistic expression.[87] The trials and appellate judge's reasoning centered the debate on questions of rap's stylistic specificities, supposedly inherent excess, and the accepted limits of poetic license.

Youssoupha's treatment of his legal battle confronts these same issues, but expands their scope beyond his own personal case to echo the longer history of rap's penalization. The music video, directed by Seb Cha, begins with the off-air symbol plastered across a television screen. After a burst of static, the muffled string instruments of the beat, produced by Soulchildren, come in. The screen tunes to television news archives of the trials and political debates involving NTM, Ministère A.M.E.R, Monsieur R, Sniper, and La Rumeur. The camera gradually pans out to reveal an old-fashioned television set. Another staticky interlude transitions to a television appearance by Zemmour, in which the pundit cites Youssoupha's lyrics and categorizes them as a death threat.[88]

[85] Youssoupha is the son of Congolese rumba singer Tabu Ley Rochereau, making him the uncle of Belgian rapper Shay (Chapter 4). He now resides in Abidjan, Ivory Coast.

[86] "By judging our mugs, people know that on TV the commentators demonize people from the suburbs/Every time things pop off they say it's us/I offer money to the one who will silence that moron Éric Zemmour."

[87] "Éric Zemmour perd son procès en appel contre le rappeur Youssoupha," *Le Monde*, June 28, 2012, https://www.lemonde.fr/societe/article/2012/06/28/eric-zemmour-perd-son-proces-en-appel-contre-le-rappeur-youssoupha_1726665_3224.html.

[88] Youssoupha, "Menace de Mort," YouTube Video, 5:02, September 15, 2011, https://www.youtube.com/watch?v=Arve4ZB8jog.

Sound effects of shattering glass erupt over the violin, and Youssoupha begins his verse acknowledging the gravity of Zemmour's allegations, yet giving them a banal air as something to deal with "as usual" ("*comme d'hab*"). He reframes them as a customary response to rap's hardcore nature and ability to offend—a unique gift in the music scene now that he finds rock emasculated: "*Pas d'menace de mort, le rap ne sort pas de douilles/Mais, c'est le seul son hardcore depuis qu'le rock n'a plus de couilles.*"[89] Youssoupha denies Zemmour's interpretation of his lyrics and employs ammunition imagery to oppose rap and lethal violence. He thus invokes an element of rap's self-defense that has run throughout this chapter: the distinction between speech and acts.

The rapper returns to his accuser in an interlude that features a televised snippet of Zemmour's infamous attack on rap music as an "illiterate subculture." Including the clip reframes both "Menace de mort" and "À force de le dire" as retaliations to the pundit's initial provocation. While the latter attacks over the airwaves, Youssoupha presents himself as the type to react over BPMs. To echo the clip of Zemmour in the video's introduction, in which he insists upon citing the rapper's lyrics verbatim, as if the death threat therein were self-evident, the lyrics of "À force de le dire" appear in tiny print, with the debated punchline highlighted in red. The lyrics spill over the bottom of the frame, drowning out the isolated line at the center of Zemmour's case. The frame shifts downward to show the verses in their entirety, as Youssoupha calls out the "tens of thousands of accusatory words" targeting fellow rappers. The shifted positions between accuser and accused mirror a similar flip in the target of a death threat at the end of the first verse. After denying Zemmour's claim to victimhood, Youssoupha reappropriates the charge to portray his own freedom of expression as the intended victim of a contracted killing.

Youssoupha's reference to an archive of ten thousand accusatory words against rappers gestures back toward the montage of television clips that open the music video. He creates an in-group of rappers whose freedom of expression has been similarly threatened in the courtroom or in the hemisphere of the National Assembly. In the first verse, Youssoupha weaves the stage names of his peers together to create a lineup of "ideal guilty parties": "*Coupables idéals, MC mercenaires/La Rumeur dit qu'les NTM sont les Sniper de la morale comme Monsieur R.*"[90] The video edits portraits of the rappers into a police lineup and transforms that image into a sort of "Most Wanted" poster plastered

[89] "No death threat, rap doesn't come out of bullet casings/But it's the only hardcore sound since rock music no longer has balls."

[90] "Ideal guilty parties, Mercenary MCs/The Rumor says that the NTM are the Snipers of morality like Monsieur R."

on billboards and building façades. In a gesture that reproduces Orelsan's distinct place within French rap's penalization, Youssoupha shouts out the Normand rapper, but omits him from the corpus of "ideal culprits": "*Pas facile d'ignorer ça, pas facile d'opérer seul/À la place de Orelsan, moi c'est clair que j'aurais l'seum.*"[91]

The song's outro gives voice to this collective. Against a courtroom backdrop, Youssoupha raps: "*Bien sûr qu'il y a d'la rage dans nos propos/Mais comment rester sage vu l'image de la vie que l'on nous propose?/J'ai plaidé légitime défense dans ma déposition/Qui peut prétendre faire du rap sans prendre position?*"[92] Transposing his claim to self-defense from his deposition to his musical performance, Youssoupha cites a classic, oft-recycled lyric from the duo Ärsenik's[93] 1998 song "Boxe avec les mots"—"*qui peut prétendre faire du rap sans prendre position?*" The outro repeats these lyrics multiple times, with Sniper, Monsieur R, and La Rumeur taking turns lending vocals to them. Sharing the mic, Youssoupha creates an echo effect that reverberates through French rap history and bolsters the links between the cases.

The outro's polyphony creates a united front against the state representatives and media figures seeking to penalize rap and limit its freedom of expression. While the ostensible strategy is to plead self-defense, the rappers also recognize the rage in their lyrics as their sole option, considering the image of life that's offered to them. The music video's collage aesthetic accompanies the rappers' rhetorical questions with montages of decontextualized media clips illustrating the image of the world that would generate such ire. The clips range from scenes of police brutality, famine, protests, and hate groups such as the Ku Klux Klan to global and domestic political figures including Nicolas Sarkozy, Dominique Strauss-Kahn, and Muammar Gaddafi. The range of geopolitical, historical, and popular culture referents gives a scattered effect, but together invoke a life plagued by looming senses of terror, corruption, and injustice.

Beyond the legal jargon of pleas, the rallying cry of "Menace de mort" seeks to justify artistic expressions of rage in a referential relationship to the dominant media narratives of social realities, "the *image* of life we're offered." This imbrication of rap and mainstream media forms will be explored in Chapter 5. In Youssoupha's video, televisual archives both visualize and mediate the link between rap and the dire state of global affairs, compelling rappers to take

[91] "Not easy to ignore that, not easy to operate alone/In Orelsan's place, it's clear that I'd be pissed."

[92] "Of course there's rage in our words/But how to remain well-behaved in light of the image of life that we're offered?/I plead self-defense in my deposition/Who can claim to rap without taking a stance?"

[93] Lino, mentioned earlier for his collaboration with Tandem, forms one half of Ärsenik, alongside his late brother Calbo.

strong moral and political stances. The montage follows the song's generalizing efforts to build upon Youssoupha's musical reaction to Zemmour's attacks on rappers and *banlieue* communities, historicizing political and legal campaigns against French rappers, and citing that history to ground rap's unequivocal duty to take a stance. Youssoupha thus builds a community and a common defense of rap's freedom of expression that hinges upon a complex relationship to symbolic violence, referentiality, and shared exposure to legal and political repression.

* * *

Tandem, La Rumeur, Sniper, and Youssoupha show how French rappers have channeled rap's penalization into their music, either in addressing their own experiences with the justice system or by theatrically experimenting with the accepted parameters for accusations, testimony, and moral appeals in rap. These performances each work within the key terms of the debate—the performative power of words, rap's referential relationship to external social realities, and the political and legal system's ritualized power. Their stylistic exercises and efforts to delineate their own vision of rap's moral and artistic imperatives thus maintain complicit entanglement with the mechanisms of the musical genre's penalization. Under the threat of political repression, legal action, and lost revenue or professional opportunities, the stakes are high for reflexive play with identifiable referents to public figures and institutions, as well as for aestheticized testimonies of lived experiences with state violence and denunciations of injustice. The stakes are also high for the postures of rappers whose audience may expect them to emphatically recommit to the lyrics and stances that sparked legal attacks despite the risks. As Youssoupha's community of embattled rappers shows, there is solidarity and strength to be found in the tradition of taking principled stances in the face of the genre's penalization, especially when the forces behind such a campaign find power in the reiterative nature of their attacks.

These first two chapters have taken the form of a double-edged sword carving out French rap's representational space. The ostensibly legitimizing edge selectively invests in rappers' writing talent and assimilability within established scripts of virtuosity. The penalizing edge takes up rap lyrics as performative speech acts capable of enacting harm toward the Republic. These two edges wield ambivalent effects for rappers' places within highbrow national culture on the one hand and within the French rap scene on the other. Functioning as a gauge of respectability, the literary risks devaluing rap's own aesthetic codes, while efforts to penalize rap may feed its oppositional, politicized image. Rappers' perceived racial differences have played a critical role in both conventions of reception. The performances explored thus far have demonstrated keen awareness of the role marginalization plays in either bringing them into the fold of France's literary tradition or denying their claims to poetic license. The following chapter will directly engage with the interwoven threads of racial alterity in the previous two, turning the mirror back toward the racializing gaze.

Chapter 3
Drawing in the Gaze
Reflexivity and the Performativity of Race in French Rap

In his 2015 music video "Speaker Corner," Médine walks through the streets carrying a megaphone and a stepstool.[1] He crosses paths with inhabitants that are gagged by the red, white, and blue sash of French elected officials (see Fig. 3.1).

Fig. 3.1 Still from the music video "Speaker Corner"

French uses the same word for "voices" and "votes" in elections (*voix*), and the music video visualizes this polysemy as a transaction. The regalia of government officials—to whom citizens give their "voices" in exchange for representation—silences the inhabitants as they go about their daily lives. Médine's lyrics pursue this crisis of representation, evoking disconnect between grand narratives and state symbols on the one hand, and citizens' daily lives on the other: "*Ici République et Nation c'est que des stations de métro/Encore une phrase qui devrait remplir la gueule de Finkielkraut.*"[2] The

[1] Médine, "Speaker Corner (Official Video)," YouTube Video, 4:33, May 14, 2015, https://www.youtube.com/watch?v=i_FCAOM8GG8.

[2] "Here Republic and Nation are only metro stations/Another phrase that should fill up Finkielkraut's mouth."

Reflexivity in French Rap. Emily Q. Shuman, Oxford University Press. © Oxford University Press 2026.
DOI: 10.1093/9780197781609.003.0004

first line suggests that Republic and Nation signify first and foremost as the names of Parisian public transport stations, rather than as grand political ideals. The second preempts criticism from Médine's detractors, such as the polemical philosopher and conservative pundit Alain Finkielkraut. The rapper anticipates that his lyrics will fuel public debates over his allegiance to France.[3] Aware of the risk, Médine forges ahead with the strategies of provocation that have been a staple in his creative process since the beginning of his career: "*10 ans plus tard, j'amène mon message par les voies de la provoc.*"'[4]

The rapper's use of *ici* (here) remains ambiguous, as it could evoke the subject position from which he is rapping, a specific place where France's political ideals fail to find meaning, or indeed the French nation as a whole. Tension between particularizing and more expansive interpretations underlies "Speaker Corner." In the music video, directed by Florin Defrance, the rapper performs to a crowd in a public square from atop the stepstool. The mix of low-rise and high-rise apartment buildings in the backdrop could prompt viewers to pinpoint "here" as a working-class, industrial environment in Médine's native Le Havre. Yet the visual of Médine rapping through a megaphone to a growing crowd might also suggest that the setting primarily serves to materialize an accessible public sphere in which citizens can make themselves heard. This ideal public sphere aligns with the crowd's signs demanding freedom of expression.

The song's succinct chorus, however, implies limits to this universal message: "*Ce que je suis parle tellement fort, qu'on en oubliera ce que je dis/Ce que l'on est parle tellement fort, qu'on en oubliera ce que l'on dit.*"[5] The shift from the first to third person exemplifies rap's technique of co-enunciation, whereby rappers invite listeners to identify with and reappropriate their personal narratives.[6] Médine alternates between two referents for the pronoun *on*: an inclusive entity that refers to the crowd rapping along with him and a loosely defined third party that disregards the former's voices and overinvests significance in their identities. The chorus evokes processes of essentialization that rigidly determine what certain individuals or groups inherently represent in the social imaginary. Following the lyrics, such face-value interpretations drown out the nuances and limit the resonance of what Médine and his crowd have to say.

[3] Médine released the music video for "Speaker Corner" on May 14, 2015. An earlier single off the same album, "Don't Laïk," which will feature in Chapter 5, had ignited polemics in January of the same year, in a tense political moment after the Charlie Hebdo terrorist attacks.

[4] "10 years later I'm bringing my message by way of provocation."

[5] "What I am speaks so loudly that they'll forget what I say/What we are speaks so loudly that they'll forget what we say."

[6] Anthony Pecqueux, *Voix du rap*, 173.

I begin this chapter with Médine's "Speaker Corner" because its chorus crystallizes the stakes of projecting political frames of interpretation onto rappers and their music. The song echoes the restrictive, penalizing views of French rap's representativeness and capacity for aesthetic ambiguity discussed in the previous chapter. That chapter's case studies grappled with mechanisms of delegitimization that reify a racialized "us vs. them" dynamic between France's community of citizens and rappers. This dynamic frames rap lyrics as performative speech acts capable of enacting material violence toward the Republic. However, the spirit of Médine's chorus, "*Ce que l'on est parle tellement fort*," can extend to both bad faith critics that ascribe extremist ideologies to the rapper's music *and* to the expectation, often from more sympathetic observers, that rap music serve first and foremost the function of racial representation. "Speaker Corner" thus signals the move I wish to make away from critical investments in rap solely as a mirror held up to the Republic, reflecting the nation's ideological paradoxes by its very existence in the cultural landscape. The presumption that rappers and their music inherently do this kind of representational and political work risks glossing over the ways rap's stylistic intricacies produce knowledge about how race circulates and finds meaning in France. This chapter thus explores how French rappers engage the racializing gaze, envelop it in their aesthetic techniques, and tease out its potential role in interpretations of their performances.

Performativity and the Perceptual Process of Racialization

Whether through media coverage seeking out the visible face of the presumed authors of riots or political initiatives aiming to promote social integration in the *banlieues*, French rap's role has traditionally been framed as representing the under-represented—or even the un-representable—in French society. Alongside media reception, early scholarship on French rap privileged the *banlieue* as a euphemistic signifier for the music's multiracial practitioners. For commentators from within the Hexagon, the *banlieue*'s ability to evoke a spatialized foreignness has provided a means to engage racialized difference without naming it explicitly. French cultural studies scholars, often working from anglophone academic contexts, value rap's ability to give visibility to the racialized *banlieue* inhabitants whose particularities France's colorblind, abstract mode of citizenship politically invalidates. This field of study's emphatic arguments that racialized creatives belong in the community of citizens implicitly reinforce an imbalanced burden of proof, whereby minorities must perpetually defend their Frenchness, while the normative whiteness of national identity remains unscrutinized.[7] Critical efforts to posit French rappers' presence in the public sphere as inherent challenges to narrow parameters of political and media representation align with this pattern.

Visual studies scholar and curator Nicole R. Fleetwood cites a similar phenomenon in which critics ask a tremendous amount of Black American popular culture, expecting it to intervene and effect measurable change in deep-seated, complex social issues. These expectations stem from "the desire to have the cultural product solve the very problem that it represents: *that seeing black is always a problem in a visual field that structures the troubling presence of blackness.*"[8] French rappers regarded as members of "visible minorities" (following the language of public policy and anti-racist activism in France) contend with this sort of representational task. This task expects rap to rework a universalist public sphere that disavows the very perceptibility of racialized differences, yet simultaneously sees those differences as something to be made abstract and invisible.[9] French cultural studies thus show a desire for rappers to solve, through visibility, the very logics of national belonging that posit visibility as a problem. Cultural criticism that mobilizes rap to probe universalism's blind spots therefore reproduces the political model's ocular grammar. It frames racial difference as something self-evidently intelligible and meaningful in the visual field in order for rappers' visibility to expose colorblind ideology's flaws. While shedding invaluable light on systemic discrimination and failures of political representation, this line of scholarship ultimately relies upon the naturalized ways of seeing that racialize rappers.[10] With this paradox of visibility and representation in mind, I move away from an understanding of race as something that rap reflects, and move toward an understanding of racialization as a social, perceptual process that rap's aesthetic techniques can shape.[11]

Previous analyses rest primarily on close readings of rap lyrics as cultural texts that, in acknowledging the rapper's racial identities or in critiquing inequalities in French society, disrupt the normative script of citizenship. As such, in a move not unlike the penalizing efforts of the previous chapter

[7] Katelyn E. Knox, *Race on Display*, 17–18.

[8] Nicole R. Fleetwood, *Troubling Vision: Performance, Visuality, and Blackness* (University of Chicago Press, 2011), 3. Emphasis in the original.

[9] See Didier and Éric Fassin, eds., *De la question sociale à la question raciale? Représenter la société française* (La Découverte: 2006).

[10] Cécile Bishop makes this compelling point in the context of photography, "Photography, Race and Invisibility," *photographies* 11, nos. 2–3 (2018): 193–213.

[11] Cécile Bishop and Zoë Roth, "Introduction: Race and the Aesthetic in French and Francophone Cultures," *L'Esprit Créateur* 59, no. 2 (2019): 3.

(albeit with very different objectives and effects), this method portrays rap as performative speech acts that, through their very enunciation, alter political ideologies and discursive formations. This chapter relies on a different understanding of performativity, informed by Judith Butler's theorization of the concept regarding gender as "the repeated stylization of the body, a set of repeated acts within a highly rigid regulatory frame that congeal over time to produce the appearance of substance, of a natural sort of being."[12] Inscribing racial performativity in the processes of making social meaning of bodies, E. Patrick Johnson interrogates how subjects collectively "cite, conceal, limit, expand, and give power to the elusive signifier called blackness."[13] While the regulatory regimes of race and gender have histories, codes, and manifestations that intersect in vastly different ways for different people, their naturalization similarly depends on the interaction between the ways bodies present and move in space and normative ways of decoding those embodied acts.

My understanding of racial performativity stems from Frantz Fanon's crucial text, *Black Skin, White Masks*. Fanon describes therein a scene of interpellation, in which a white child spots him on a train and cries out to his mother, "Mama, see the Negro! I'm frightened!"[14] Fanon's visceral depictions of the crushingly objectifying power of the racializing gaze, as well as its psychosomatic impact on the way he experiences his own selfhood and body, have been foundational for critical race theory. Fleetwood's reading of Fanon focuses on the scene of interpellation as the "construction of an audience and performer of difference."[15] This relationship is key to her theorization of deciphering blackness as a performative act, "predicated on a knowable, visible, and performing subject" of racialized difference.[16]

The Fanonian understanding of blackness as something that circulates in the perceptual field elucidates the relationship between race as a social power dynamic and sensorial experiences of racialized artistic expressions. Practices of listening and deciphering how musical genres like rap sonically encode ideas of racial authenticity contribute to the social construction of race.[17] In a similar vein, looking at works by Black artists exposes the pieces to the racializing gaze's power to seal them within their representational space.[18] In this social act, Darby English argues that naturalized assumptions about the

[12] Judith Butler, *Gender Trouble: Feminism and the Subversion of Identity* (Routledge, 1990), 33.
[13] E. Patrick Johnson, *Appropriating Blackness: Performance and the Politics of Authenticity* (Duke University Press, 2003), 2.
[14] Frantz Fanon, *Black Skin, White Masks*, trans. Charles Lam Markmann (Pluto Press, 1967), 112.
[15] Nicole R. Fleetwood, *Troubling Vision*, 28.
[16] Ibid., 6.
[17] Loren Kajikawa, *Sounding Race in Rap Songs* (University of California Press, 2015), 9.
[18] Darby English, *How to See a Work of Art*, 31.

work Black artists do stem less from the artwork itself than from pre-existing sociological knowledge, creating a dynamic in which "conception too often replaces perception, in effect suspending the aesthetic life of the object and replacing it with a predetermined social one."[19] Understanding racialization as perceptual acts of decoding and interpreting requires a move beyond investment in rappers' visibility as if that visibility were a given or a uniform and inherently politically significant experience. To prioritize French rap's aesthetic lives, I emphasize the space in which performances' formal qualities offer themselves up for audience interpretations and the negotiation of racial meaning.

In this chapter, performances by Médine, Abd al Malik, and Casey reflect the active relationship between the audience and performers of difference. Through stylistic devices, music video staging, and vocal techniques, they draw the racializing gaze into the performance and make apparent the kinds of interpretative work racialization requires of the audience. Each posits racial difference as something that circulates and hangs in suspension, never fully resting on the rapper, the protagonists of their music videos, or the performance itself. Médine, Abd al Malik, and Casey thus destabilize the naturalized assumption, key to French rap's representational space, that they inherently portray racial difference. The rappers reflexively intertwine performances of difference with experimentations with rap's codes and conventions: in-group dynamics for Médine, ego trip for Abd al Malik, and narrative positioning for Casey. Their stylistic exercises each outline different stakes for the audience's role both in negotiating the meaning of the performance and in the process of racialization.

These three performances foreground complicity's dual significations of folded together and ethical implication. On the one hand, in drawing in the gaze, Médine, Abd al Malik, and Casey entangle aesthetic form with perceptual mechanisms of racialization. On the other, they make the racializing gaze's presence, and potential complicity with it, the crux of their performances. As Katelyn E. Knox argues, working within and countering the racializing gaze allows francophone cultural producers to negotiate the "complex risks and stakes of self-representation," as well as their own complicity in a cultural marketplace that makes a spectacle of racial minorities.[20] The following chapter will take up how French rappers self-consciously explore the relationship between race and the commodifying logics of the cultural industries. In this chapter, rappers navigate the power and vulnerability

[19] Ibid., 34.
[20] Katelyn E. Knox, *Race on Display*, 8.

in aestheticizing mechanisms of Othering. As a white scholar, my work in this chapter also prompts reflexivity and recognition of potential complicity with the racializing gaze in analyzing these performances. With awareness of, but desire not to center my positionality, the following close readings emphasize the performances' affordances and the types of interpretative work they set up, without foreclosing the inherent openness of their reception. In exploring how rappers reflexively work within racializing logics, I am not arguing that they are responsible for their racialization, but rather that they harness complicity as a tool for their stylistic exercises and self-positioning. Médine, Abd al Malik, and Casey thus root the force of their aesthetic techniques, anti-racist stances, and connections to their listeners in their exposure to the alienating power of the racializing gaze.

"Code Barbe": Fluidity and Fetishization of Racialized Markers

I first return to an earlier performance by Médine, 2008's "Code Barbe," in which he plays with the fetishization of the beard as a racialized marker of Muslim religiosity. The racialization of Islam across Europe and the United States combines ideas about culture, physical appearance, and intimate religious conviction to read Muslim-ness on people's bodies. This combination of registers fuels an understanding of Islamophobia as processes of Othering based on signs of a real or supposed belonging to the Muslim faith.[21] In the post-9/11 era, visible religious signifiers interact with gender in the racialization of Islam to frame Muslim men as threats to national security and Muslim women who wear the hijab as threats to "Western" cultural values such as gender equality.[22] Within these gendered mechanisms of racialization, the beard proves a particularly potent, yet ambiguous marker. Islamophobic logics ascribe radicality and violent threat to the beard.[23] Facial hair may also double or project epidermalized logics of racialization onto Muslim men, as white converts who grow their beards attest to being read as Arab or Black.[24]

[21] Abdellali Hajjat and Marwan Mohammed, *Islamophobie: Comment les élites françaises fabriquent le problème musulman* (La Découverte, 2013), 20.

[22] Saher Selod, "Citizenship Denied: The Racialization of Muslim American Men and Women post-9/11," *Critical Sociology* 41, no. 1 (2015): 78; Joan Wallach Scott, *The Politics of the Veil* (Princeton University Press, 2007).

[23] See Juliette Galonnier, "Barbes et foulards: les marqueurs genrés de l'islamophobie," in *Genre et islamophobie. Discriminations, préjugés et représentations en Europe*, ed. Éléonore Lépinard, Oriane Sarrasin, and Lavinia Gianettoni (ENS Éditions, 2021).

[24] Ibid.

In "Code Barbe," Médine's wordplay and the accompanying music video's imagery highlight the beard's malleability as a signifier. The lyrics constantly prompt the audience to reconcile between what the beard tangibly is and what it is projected to be.

The lyrics follow a methodical structure that privileges the nondescript feminine subject pronoun, *elle*, to enumerate various cultural connotations of the beard (a feminine noun in French). The multitude of meanings listed in the verses gives a sense of expansiveness to the common signifier, *elle*. Shying away from directly stating the common noun he refers to, Médine invites listeners to undertake interpretive work and constantly bring these various significations back to the same referent—the beard. The tension between the repeated feminine subject pronoun and a marker associated with masculinity accentuates the need for semantic negotiation. The lyrics confront the beard's polysemy with the specificity of different proper nouns, namedropping cultural figures that range from US rappers Rick Ross and Freeway to Abraham Lincoln. The multitude of references circulating within "Code Barbe" blur the line between simple connotation and the process of metonymy by which a form of bodily stylization such as facial hair comes to stand in for the entire person.

The beat, crafted once again by Médine's loyal collaborator Proof, encompasses the song's sly subterfuge vis-à-vis essentialized markers, as well as the very real threat of surveillance and repression toward Muslims.[25] Proof layers violins over a constant clicking to create the suspenseful effect of time ticking away, reminiscent of spy films. When the beat drops, Proof accentuates the sense of urgency by incorporating high-pitched, rapidly alternating piano notes and an emphatic, resonating electric guitar. The beat's thrill-chasing tone stresses both Médine's wily, ironic twists on the beard's metonymic function, as well as the sense of tracking in the title's play-on-words. The title evokes the term *code barre*, or barcode, implying a functional similarity between the beard and the digital form that consolidates all of a given product's defining, traceable information. Just as scanning a barcode instantly reveals all the identifying details it contains, Islamophobic logics expect the beard to encapsulate the subjectivity, faith, and biographical details of the person who wears it. Médine further visualizes the phonetic slippage through the T-shirt he and the extras wear in the music video, which features a large barcode with "Code Barbe" printed underneath.[26]

[25] For more on how Muslim cultural production across the West, particularly hip-hop, takes on issues of surveillance and discrimination, as well as how cultural diplomacy tries to harness hip-hop's power, see Hisham Aidi, *Rebel Music: Race, Empire, and the New Muslim Youth Culture* (Pantheon Books, 2014).

[26] Médine, "Code Barbe (Official Clip)," YouTube Video, 4:00, https://www.youtube.com/watch?v=RFTrvbY8Bt8.

The barcode as a visual referent draws upon processes of commodification and the circulation of goods in the globalized economy. "Code Barbe" underscores the currency that racialized markers of Muslim religiosity have gained in the globalized context of the ongoing War on Terror, and even the profits the specter of Islamic terrorism produces for the security and surveillance industries.[27] Médine reinforces the dimension of tracking: "*Elle est détestée outre-Atlantique/et les seules puces qui la démangent sont électroniques.*"[28] Playing with the homonym *puce* that can signify either electronic chip or flea, Médine suggests that any infiltrations of his facial hair would more likely come from government intelligence agencies than from pests. The specter of surveillance underscores racialization's dependence on a knowable, intelligible subject. The barcode pushes this fantasy even further by imagining instantaneous, categorical knowledge about a person from the first scanning glance.

Alexis Delahaye's direction of the music video plays with the trustworthiness of the information the beard supposedly communicates. The imagery probes the beard's authenticity when it becomes attached to certain people's faces. The video features a bearded, middle-aged man standing on the sidewalk, dressed in a white djellaba and a matching skullcap that prime viewers to read him as a Muslim inhabitant of the neighborhood. A group of young children quickly run up to the man and rip off his beard, revealing the facial hair to be a simple adhesive. As the man turns to shout in protest at the fleeing children, viewers can catch a glimpse through the thin fabric of the djellaba of the word "police" written on the back of the T-shirt layered underneath. As this scene plays out, Médine invokes a popular caution as to the unreliability of appearances: "*si l'habit ne fait pas le moine, elle ne fera pas l'imam, non!*"[29] The undercover officer's flimsy adhesive underscores a sense of inauthenticity, as well as the insufficiency of perception and outward appearance. The tacked-on beard plays with the ability of racist stereotypes to latch onto and over-determine the signification of bodily signs by introducing a sense of movement and detachability that recurs throughout the performance. In this instance, the police's fetishization of the beard as a stand-in for religiosity proves futile. The undercover officer relies too heavily on this bodily stylization as a means of blending in and passing undetected in a racialized religious community. Paradoxically, the capillary signifier that prompts hyper-vigilance from law enforcement and intelligence services is repurposed here as a tool

[27] See Thomas Deltombe, *L'islam imaginaire: la construction médiatique de l'islamophobie en France, 1975–2005* (La Découverte, 2005).

[28] "It's hated across the Atlantic/and the only chips that make it itch are electronic."

[29] "If clothes don't make the man (literally: if robes don't make the monk), it won't make the imam!"

for that very surveillance. However, the video suggests that the beard alone is a hollow form incapable of fooling even young children.

The policeman's failed disguise foreshadows productive tensions in the video between authenticity and inauthenticity, between textural complexity and streamlined form, and between the stickiness and fluidity of racialized markers. The chorus creates slippage between the beard and racialized markers of blackness: "*J'avance, une coupe afro sous la mâchoire/Silhouette sur le pochoir/Fourrure de panthère couleur bon-char.*"[30] Médine likens the beard growing on his chin to an Afro hairstyle in an image that evokes discrimination toward the appearance and texture of Black hair. The reference to panther fur echoes the album's title, *Arabian Panther*, in reworking the iconic symbol of Black Liberation movements in the United States to correspond to the rapper's own racialized identity. The beat dramatically accentuates the chorus' rallying cry and defiant drive onward with sounds of a choir vocalizing. The choir's punctuating "ah" gives Médine's federating efforts an epic tone, all while fueling tension with his ironic smoke-and-mirrors approach to essentializing categories. The playful aspect of this approach emerges through his reformulation of a canonical Black Power slogan—"*Barbe is beautiful!*"

Despite the unifying focus on hair and texture, the stencil imagery in the chorus ("*silhouette sur le pochoir*") emphasizes the outline of racialized signifiers and the perceptual processes that fill them in with excessive significations. The music video pursues this juxtaposition between rich texture and simplified form with frequent cuts to extras or fellow rappers making cameo appearances, including Mac Tyer (Chapter 2) and Keny Arkana (Chapter 5). Each person meets the camera's gaze and ties a bandana imprinted with the outline of a beard over their face (see Fig. 3.2).

The bandana plays up the outlaw connotations of the beard as a means of escaping detection and disguising one's appearance: "*Elle est bien souvent de façon falche dans les braquages.*"[31] The design is a nod to the Guy Fawkes mask worn by the anarchist hacker collective Anonymous, and thus reinforces associations with the fringes of society, as well as the performance's aesthetics of subversion. The connotations of anonymity that shape these liminal figures, however, diverge from the over-investment in the beard's surface value as a marker of religious difference. Whereas the fabric suggests dissimulation, the outline of the beard imprinted onto it mirrors the process of distilling a person's subjectivity, values, and experiences into one visible referent.

30 "I advance, an afro on my chin/Silhouette on the stencil/Panther fur the color of coal."
31 "It's often fake during robberies."

Fig. 3.2 Still from the music video for "Code Barbe"

The bandana's circulation throughout the music video visualizes solidarity, defiance, and provocation in the face of French society's paranoid distrust of Muslim men. Despite its connotations of disguise, the bandana does not have an entirely homogenizing effect. In function of their skin tone, the extras and invited rappers don either a white or black version of the facial covering. The bandana's metonymic function thus expands its ability to project racialized difference onto its surface. This gesture aligns with Médine's efforts in the chorus to conceptually and politically link struggles against Islamophobia with those against anti-Black racism. The use of a split-screen to place all the rappers side-by-side visualizes the previously discussed ideal of co-enunciation in rap, in which artists rally their listeners around denunciations of injustice, creating a new collective entity, "us."[32] The image prompts the audience to position themselves in regard to the united collective placed before them. The scene further illustrates what Karim Hammou calls "minority universalism," in French rap, or inclusive gestures through which a minority condition—here essentialization targeting Muslim men—becomes something that ties people together, regardless of their different social positions.[33]

[32] Marie Sonnette-Manouguian, "Des mises en scène du 'nous' contre le 'eux,'" 175.

[33] Karim Hammou, "Das Gedächtnis der Vielheit. Minderheitsuniversalismus im französischen Rap," trans. Gesa zur Nieden, *Die Tonkunst*, no. 4 (2020): 380–392.

The beard's appropriable form further troubles the gendered racialization of Muslims in France, as both men and women tie on the bandanas. Médine's lyrics reflect the narrow repertoires of gender at play in the racialization of Islam by framing the possibility of a beard on a body that presents as feminine as a source of exoticizing fascination: "*Et portée par une femme elle devient phénomène de foire.*"[34] The music video reproduces this supposed incongruence, at times doubling the fetishized signs of religiosity on one person, as is the case with a woman who also wears the hijab. This act of doubling touches upon the "excessiveness" of Muslim modesty in the normative French imaginary, and the veil's troublesome nature therein as a sign that simultaneously reveals too much about private religious devotion and too little of women's bodies.[35] The bandana also forges a link between two feminine figures diametrically opposed in French political discourse—the uncovered woman and the woman who wears the hijab. The outline of the beard disrupts the gendered and sexualized mechanisms that pit these two figures against one another, specifically their degree of availability to the eroticizing male gaze.[36] The music video troubles the reliance on gender normativity in the racialization of Islam. Through the bandana, "Code Barbe" points to how Islamophobic representations isolate specific visual markers of religiosity, hollow them out, and reinvest them with excessive signification.

However, the bandana attests to its own failure to truly stand in for what it is meant to represent. While it succeeds in its optical illusion of giving the wearer the bare form of a beard, its smooth linen texture and neat outline stand in stark contrast to actual facial hair. The imagery and sound effects play up this contrast by staging Médine inside a barbershop. The camera repeatedly pans down to follow tufts of hair as they fall to the floor. Halfway through the video, the beat fades out and is replaced by the scraping of a straightedge razor on Médine's skin and the subtle resistance as the blade meets his facial hair. The interlude heightens focus on the beard's materiality, particularly its coarse texture. This focus points to the perceptual work behind the racialization of the beard, inviting viewers to constantly negotiate between what the bandana is intended to represent in the visual field and its inevitable failure to truly pass. Médine exploits this failure when he dons the bandana alongside his peers. The gesture creates a doubling effect that negates the bandana's ability to dissimulate, as the imprinted image reproduces the facial hair that the fabric covers up. On Médine's face in

[34] "And on a woman it becomes a circus attraction."
[35] Joan Wallach Scott, *The Politics of the Veil*, 152.
[36] Nacira Guénif-Souilamas and Éric Macé, *Les féministes et le garçon arabe* (Éditions de l'aube, 2004), 98.

particular, the beard's doubling presents the fetishized form as an excessive sign that surpasses mere facial hair.

The bandana's abstracted form allows the beard to circulate freely through the music video, passing from person to person. Its transferal simulates the accumulated currency of the Muslim internal enemy figure[37] in media and political discourses. The video's dynamic movement stresses the internal enemy figure's malleability that allows for its recitation and reinvention. The tension between fluidity and fixation in "Code Barbe" further underscores the constant interpretative work propping up the beard as a racialized signifier. A sense of irresolvability therefore lies at the heart of the performance. The visual language through which "Code Barbe" denaturalizes the beard's racialization closely mirrors that which shapes its unsettling visibility. The music video creates an atmosphere of hiding in plain sight, drawing upon the same affects that nourish the beard's troubling presence in a visual field shaped by vigilance and surveillance. The ironic play of "Code Barbe" shifts from Médine's exposure to the racializing gaze to the vulnerability of the essentialized marker, revealing its insufficiencies and instabilities. Médine's performance exploits the beard's dependency as a racialized signifier on its circulation, reiterative decoding, and cumulative connotations. Harnessing these processes, the performance finds strength in numbers against Islamophobic logics.

Abd al Malik: Pushing the Visual Limits of Abstraction

Reimagining the beard as an appropriable signifier that sits on the surface of the face, Médine's "Code Barbe" highlights racialized markers' metonymic function. The rapper's lyrics and the music video's imagery invite the audience to follow movements between the beard and the connotations that over-determine it as a stand-in for racialized difference. "Code Barbe" does not solve the beard's troubling presence in the visual field, but leaves it lingering in the performance, where it can create space for demonstrations of solidarity and fantasies of evading the surveilling gaze. In his song and music video, "Allogène (j'suis un stremon)," Abd al Malik, a polyvalent Alsatian artist of Congolese origins, rejoins Médine's emphasis on materiality and bodily surface, but pushes abstraction even further, frustrating the belief that legible signs will help make meaning of the performer in the visual field. Where Médine makes the performance of difference an inclusive act, Abd al

[37] See Mathieu Rigouste, *L'ennemi intérieur. La généalogie coloniale et militaire de l'ordre sécuritaire dans la France contemporaine* (La Découverte, 2011).

Malik stages a performance of difference so absolute it risks disorienting the audience. The song's title, which signifies "non-native," invokes foreignness, whereas the subtitle, which uses the inverted syllable slang for "monster," attributes a grotesque dimension to Otherness. The music video for "Allogène," directed by Romain Cieutat, tests the expectation of what a "non-native" would resemble.[38] The performance imagines a body thoroughly abstracted from particularities and posits this pure abstraction as unsettling for the racializing gaze. As such, Abd al Malik throws into relief the fact that the figures of the monster, the non-native, or the Other depend on a certain degree of compatibility with pre-existing categories in order to find meaning.

The move from Médine to Abd al Malik follows an existing trend in scholarship on race, religion, and subjectivity in French rap. Scholars compare Abd al Malik and Médine as practicing Muslims in their approaches to religiosity, universalism, and *laïcité*, France's particular brand of secularism. Such comparisons juxtapose Médine's rancorous critique of these ideologies as inherently discriminatory to Abd al Malik's firmer commitment to the French Republican model.[39] In Abd al Malik's view, systematic discriminations are signs that Republican universalism's ambitions have not yet fully come to fruition.[40] His approach has been met with institutional consecration, including four *Victoires de la musique*, of which three are in the "Urban Music Album of the Year" category and, in 2008, France's prestigious *Chevalier dans l'ordre des Arts et des Lettres*.

I nuance the diametric opposition of Médine and Abd al Malik in their respective degrees of adherence to universalist ideals. I instead highlight common ground and divergences in how they formally experiment with the intelligibility of racialized difference. "Allogène" invites a shift in focus from Abd al Malik's discourse regarding Republican ideology and toward how he incorporates abstraction and universalism at the level of aesthetic form to undermine racialization as a sensorial regime.[41] In the analysis that

[38] Abd al Malik, "Allogène (j'suis un stremon)," YouTube Video, 3:04, September 22, 2015, https://www.youtube.com/watch?v=MSHcJgup4Z4.

[39] Hisham Aidi, *Rebel Music*, 168, Apple Books.

[40] Jeanette S. Jouili, "Rapping the Republic: Utopia, Critique, and Muslim Role Models in Secular France," *French Politics, Culture & Society* 31, no. 2 (2013): 58–80; Olivier Bourderionnet, "A 'Picture-Perfect' Banlieue Artist: Abd al Malik or the Perils of a Conciliatory Rap Discourse," *French Cultural Studies* 22, no. 2 (2011): 151–161.

[41] For Katelyn E. Knox, through sight and sound, Abd al Malik's performances ask the audience to witness a "*décalage* between colorblind universalist rhetoric and difference-conscious lived experiences." "Abd al Malik's 'Meta-French' Perspective: An Audiovisual Approach to French Universalism and Difference Consciousness," *L'Esprit Créateur* 59, no. 2 (2019): 120.

follows, I keep discursive constructions of Frenchness at a distance to show how "Allogène" immerses the audience in a perceptual field that sonically and visually pushes abstraction to an alienating extreme. This implicated position confronts the audience with their roles in making meaning of difference.[42]

The music video features a dancing protagonist draped entirely in black clothing with a blue scarf wrapped around their head. During the first thirty seconds, the camera films the figure primarily from behind or the side, making their stylization the primary means of socially situating them. The all-black outfit of a mid-waist leather trench, hooded sweatshirt, brimmed hat, and sneakers featuring an amalgamation of brand logos fits hip-hop's streetwear aesthetic. The protagonist thus sartorially invokes the *banlieue* youth figure—connotations that the video amplifies through the backdrop of gray-scaled housing projects and parking garages. Whereas the *jeune de banlieue* is typically imagined as a masculine figure, the scarf's placement around the protagonist's head troubles this gendered reading by inviting associations with the hijab.

Abd al Malik's digitized voice repeats, "*J'suis un stremon*," mobilizing the categories of non-native and monster while the music video offers up real-world referents to xenophobic anxieties in France. The opening of the song's only verse frames this act of Othering as restricting and potentially perilous: "*Grandir dans un monde où l'altérité est assassine.*"[43] In emphasizing the deadly consequences of being perceived as different, Abd al Malik subtly places the audience before the ethical implications of attributing alterity to the video's protagonist. The lyrics extend these implications as the rapper problematizes his own identity at the intersection of nationality, race, and religion: "*J'suis né dans le pays de la guillotine/Muslim et noir de peau qu'est-ce qui me détermine*?"[44] The interrogative form draws categorizing frames into the performance and leaves them hanging before the audience.

As the verse begins, the figure raises their head to meet the camera's gaze, engaging viewers and revealing a bodily surface comprised of constantly shifting, neon-colored patterns (see Fig. 3.3).

[42] This analysis is adapted from previously published material; see Emily Q. Shuman, "'Tout de noir vêtu': Skin and Surface in the Rap of Abd al Malik," *French Cultural Studies* 29, no. 3 (2018): 209–217.

[43] "Growing up in a world where alterity is deadly."

[44] "Born in the country of the guillotine/Muslim and black-skinned, what determines me?"

Fig. 3.3 Still from the music video "Allogène (j'suis un stremon)"

The protagonist's futuristic bodily surface joins the music video's cold, depopulated, urban décor in creating a dystopian atmosphere. The beat, produced by renowned electronic music DJ and producer Laurent Garnier, contributes a robotic tone, which Abd al Malik's lyrics echo in describing a Matrix-like reign of machines. The film reference adds a technological form of monstrosity, in which artificial intelligence can both optimize and ultimately threaten human consciousness. The sonic connection to French Touch draws a parallel between the music video's robotic anonymity and the masked electronic music duo Daft Punk. The collaboration with Garnier thus places Abd al Malik's performance within a broader, yet distinctly French musical tradition of technological innovation. The protagonist of "Allogène" visually embodies high-tech cravings for perfection and control in pushing the desire for an abstract subject to the limits of illegibility.

The protagonist's confrontation with the camera challenges reliance on the body as the site on which difference is read and reimagines it as a surface on which to experiment with the very limits of the visibility of difference. Returning to the scene of interpellation in *Black Skin, White Masks*, Fanon describes his bodily awareness collapsing under the weight of the racist stereotypes and the history of his ancestors that the white gaze projects onto the surface of his body. Fanon vividly depicts this objectifying moment as a detachment, an excision, and a hemorrhage curdling black blood onto his skin.[45] In "Allogène," however, the glossy surface devoid of facial features renders a mutual gaze impossible, both depriving viewers of the ability to fully schematize the protagonist

45 Frantz Fanon, *Black Skin, White Masks*, 112.

and simultaneously preventing the protagonist from interiorizing and constructing themself through the Other's eyes. The dynamic flow of saturated colors on the protagonist's body further disrupts the racializing gaze's congealing effects and brings to the forefront naturalized expectations that vision reliably perceive difference.

These aesthetic techniques situate the music video within a broader tradition of visual practices challenging the historical relationship between image technologies and investments in the intelligibility of race. Uses of photography by colonial officials and enslavers relied heavily upon the ability of both the photographic surface and the surface of the Black people's bodies to offer legible information and continuity with social reality.[46] In her study of African diasporic image-making practices, Krista A. Thompson reads the use of saturated light, reflective surfaces, and "bling-bling" hip-hop aesthetics as critical meditations on the refusal to see Black people's human, emotional interiority that historically enabled circulations of blackness as commodity.[47] In Abd al Malik's "Allogène," the opaque bodily surface pushes the use of shine even further. The reflective gloss renders the body's exterior undecipherable, underscoring how the markers of difference on which processes of Othering rely must nevertheless be somewhat familiar in order to find meaning. The uncategorizable surface resonates with one of Abd al Malik's stated influences, Martinican novelist, poet, and philosopher Édouard Glissant.[48] Glissant demanded the "right to opacity" in the face of Western thought's requirement for difference to be transparent and knowable.[49] In his view, the coexistence of opacities, or humanities with their own unattainable, inner complexities, would be the "real foundation of Relation."[50] The protagonist's ever-shifting bodily surface in "Allogène" thus troubles the visual field to echo this call for a way of relating to one another that refutes transparent reduction to naturalized categories.

The music video for "Allogène" further draws upon its architectural décor in its experimentation with surfaces and abstraction. The editing consistently shifts between shots of the protagonist and the austere facades behind them. The neon patterns on the protagonist's screen-like bodily surface cite the rigid geometric lines of the Brutalist architecture. The figure's popping, a hip-hop dance style involving contracting and de-contracting one's muscles to the rhythm of the beat, imitates the angular Modernist buildings. In her study

[46] Alessandra Raengo, *On the Sleeve of the Visual: Race as Face Value* (Dartmouth College Press, 2013), 28.

[47] Krista A. Thompson, *Shine: The Visual Economy of Light in African Diasporic Aesthetic Practice* (Duke University Press, 2015).

[48] In the track, "Daniel Darc," off the same album, Abd al Malik raps, "Terre, feu, vent, j'ai l'flow d'Édouard Glissant" (Earth, fire, wind, I've got the flow of Édouard Glissant.), Glissant also influenced Abd al Malik's hybrid CD-poetry volume, *Le Jeune Noir à l'épée* (Flammarion, 2019).

[49] Édouard Glissant, *Poetics of Relation*, trans. Betsy Wing (The University of Michigan Press, 1997), 189.

[50] Ibid., 190.

of Josephine Baker, Anne Anlin Cheng argues that by constantly layering textures and glowing light onto her body, Baker played with Modernism's fetishization of black skin as the epitome of the aesthetic movement's ideal of sleek, pure surfaces.[51] For Cheng, this insistence on the body's abstraction in Baker's work, particularly as a means of frustrating audience's expectations to see her flesh, exposes the paradox at the heart of racial identification: the affirmation of physical difference as something material and tangible when in reality it is deeply metaphysical and abstract.[52]

Abd al Malik's "Allogène" uses surface to similarly frustrate the expectation of bare skin as a signifier of difference. The protagonist gradually sheds their scarf and clothing, shrugging off the familiarity of these markers to further reveal the brightly colored surface underneath. Each article of clothing removed confronts the audience with another, even more abstract layer. The performance ultimately leaves the "naked" figure in a barren no-man's-land with the rubble of the concrete buildings flying around them (see Fig. 3.4). The image reinforces the metaphorical intertwining of the body and architectural façade, likening the act of stripping off one's distinctive markers to that of demolition.

In these final scenes, the beat shifts in tone, layering a more hopeful, orchestral melody over the hi-hats and kick drum. The figure gazes out onto the horizon, adding an element of expansiveness to the music's upbeat shift.

Fig. 3.4 Still from the music video "Allogène (j'suis un stremon)"

[51] Anne Anlin Cheng, *Second Skin: Josephine Baker and the Modern Surface* (Oxford University Press, 2011), 20.

[52] Ibid., 64.

Despite this sonic tone of resolution, the video's final moments remain ambiguous. Shedding layers makes the protagonist's corporeal surface harder on the eye. Their saturated, technicolor silhouette stands in stark contrast to the gray wasteland where they find peace far from the buildings or their inhabitants. The abstracted surface therefore reinforces a sense of isolated individuality. The rubble reproduces this abstraction, stripping down the buildings' identifiable, architectural form until nothing but the building blocks remain. Defying gravity, the floating streams of concrete follow the protagonist toward the horizon's edge. Pure abstraction thus distances the protagonist from their social world, rather than allowing them to dwell in it, leaving open the question of what a society where relation is founded on opacity would truly look like.

Through experimentations with surfaces, colors, and abstraction, Abd al Malik's "Allogène" destabilizes reliance on bodily surfaces as sites of legible difference. The performance confronts the processes through which "non-native" becomes a meaningful category. In presenting a form that unsettles the visual field and resists categorization, "Allogène" highlights how mechanisms of Othering depend on familiar, pre-established schemas. At the end of his verse, Abd al Malik seemingly nods to the role such expectations play in the performance. As the beat transitions to the hopeful melody, the lyrics fade out in an echo that parallels the song's opening: "*Lyricalement, j'suis un stremon.*" Engaging in rap's fundamental ego trip style, Abd al Malik reaffirms his talents as a rapper. Modifying the original repetition to refer to his lyrical abilities, he seemingly calls out the audience as if to say, "what did you think I meant by *stremon*?"

This chapter's move from Médine to Abd al Malik nuances the critical dichotomy between them along the lines of their relationships to Republican universalism. Drawing in the racializing gaze, "Code Barbe" and "Allogène (j'suis un stremon)" find common ground in their emphasis on indecipherability as a means of teasing out the audience's interpretative work. In Abd al Malik's "Allogène," the late addition of "lyrically" to qualify his monstrosity abruptly shifts the performance from an exploration of alterity to a classic ego trip. Any assumptions as to what "non-native" signifies are left suspended, and the stakes of the audience's role in deciphering difference become more explicit in retrospect. For Médine's part, the bandana's fetishized form rallies the audience to participate in the playful exhaustion of the beard as a malleable signifier. The intricacies of these stakes are lost, and indeed risk interpretative failure, if the audience restricts each rapper's representational space to read Abd al Malik's performance only through the prism of abstract universalism, and Médine's through particularism.

Casey: Undermining Colonial Discourse from Within

The 2010 song "Créature ratée," by Casey, the rapper of Martinican origins whose perspicacious commentary on rap's representational space set up the two previous chapters, plunges listeners into the co-construction of the "failed creature." Like Médine and Abd al Malik, Casey instills her performance with a sense of movement. Her lyrics create room for racializing descriptors to circulate and bounce off one another, eventually taking the forms of two opposing figures: the colonizer and the colonized person. While Médine and Abd al Malik accentuate abstraction and indecipherability, "Créature ratée" takes on the presumption of epistemological authority and historicity in colonial discourse. In this sense, Casey disentangles the ways the racializing gaze pulls from and collapses historical repertoires of racist tropes in the act of essentialization. As Fanon writes of this collapse: "I was battered down by tom-toms, cannibalism, intellectual deficiency, fetichism, racial defects, slave-ships, and above all else, above all: 'Sho' good eatin.'"[53]

Whereas Abd al Malik rhetorically challenges his audience to define his identity and intimates the consequences of attributing alterity, Casey raises more distinct ethical stakes for her audience. Rapping from the narrative position of the colonizer, Casey requires active interpretative work of her listeners to situate themselves vis-à-vis the lyrical content. While, for some listeners, familiarity with the rapper's posture and critiques of France's colonial past and postcolonial present facilitates this act of decoding, "Créature ratée" uses stylistic devices in the lyrics, elements of the beat, Casey's flow, and filming techniques in the music video to prompt the audience to actively negotiate between the said and the unsaid of the performance.[54] "Créature ratée" tightly weaves together the perceptual process of racialization with divergences from the conventions of the rapper–audience relationship. In making the audience aware of the interpretive work they perform in experiencing the song and music video, "Créature ratée" also throws into relief the interpretative work behind processes of racialization.

[53] Frantz Fanon, *Black Skin, White Masks*, 112. In the original French, Fanon references the slogan, "*Y a bon banania.*" Advertisements for the chocolate drink Banania long used racist caricatures of colonized African conscripts for the French army.

[54] For more on these themes in Casey's music, see Virginie Brinker, "Actualité de la pensée de Frantz Fanon dans le rap de Casey," *Mouvements* 96, no. 4 (2018): 36–42; Amine Baouche, "*Négrographèse: être noir•e, s'écrire noir•e. L'écriture de la 'race' chez Casey,*" *Itinéraires. Littérature, textes, cultures* 2021–2 (2022), https://doi.org/10.4000/itineraires.11324.

From the first verse, Casey creates an imaginary space in which two figures circulate and take shape.[55] The first line, "*Blanc ingénieur, noir ingénu,*"[56] operates along a paronomasia that underscores the phonetic similarity between *ingénieur* and *ingénu.* The caesura reinforces the racialized opposition that associates whiteness with technical expertise and blackness with childlike credulousness.[57] Casey structures the first verse along these antonymic, fragmented descriptors that hang in the air without a stable referent and find meaning uniquely in their contrast. The lyrics thus invite listeners to follow a distribution of value that fluctuates between two extremes. The "*inventeur cravaté*" and the "*créature ratée*"[58] take form through mirror-like oppositions, culminating in the figures of the colonizer and the colonized. The oppositions slip into the register of French colonialism's civilizing and enslaving missions, juxtaposing the "civilizer's" pillage of the land with the "motor" whose forced labor makes it profitable. A further contrast between the refined taste of literature and poetry and the frenzied noise of drums seeks to naturalize this division of labor: "*Amateur de belles lettres, de poésies/Frappeur de tambour avec fracas et frénésie.*"[59] The opposition recalls Jacques Rancière's "distribution of the sensible," the political and aesthetic process that determines what is visible or invisible, or what is speech or noise in a given social order.[60] "Créature ratée" reifies this distribution along binaries, using rhyme to posit "*poésie*" and "*frénésie*" as antipodes, while harnessing alliteration in "fr" to mimic the drum rhythm the colonizer figure deems cacophonous. Casey's lyrics thus aestheticize the hierarchical differentiation through which racialization finds its strength.

Near the end of the verse, the lyrics move from detached fragments to totalizing descriptions, in which the use of third-person, possessive adjectives indicates that the narration collapses into the colonizer's gaze. Citing various institutions, Casey uses the first-person plural to situate her narrative voice in racial superiority to the object of the gaze: "*Que disent la science et la messe/Toutes les grandes puissances du monde et la presse/Que cette noirceur en présence dans la pièce/Nous est inférieur comme la chienne et l'ânesse.*"[61] The alliteration in "s" creates the effect of science, religion, the world's great powers,

[55] This analysis is adapted from previously published material, Emily Q. Shuman, "Esthétique et performativité de la race dans 'Créature ratée' de Casey," *Itinéraires: Littérature, textes, cultures* 2020-3 (2021), https://doi.org/10.4000/itineraires.8805.

[56] "White engineer/Naive Black person."

[57] Pap Ndiaye, *La Condition noire*, 217.

[58] "The prized inventor" and the "failed creature."

[59] "Admirer of literature, of poetry/One who hits a drum with commotion and frenzy."

[60] Jacques Rancière, *Le partage du sensible: esthétique et politique* (La Fabrique, 2000), 14.

[61] "What do science, mass, all the great world powers and the press say/That this blackness present in the room/Is inferior to us like female dogs and donkeys."

and the press building upon one another's claims to authority and knowledge in an effort to assert blackness' inferiority and animality. Gazing upon the colonized figure, the rapper's narrative voice invests the colonizer with emotions such as distress and fear, while leaving the colonized person's lived experience unspoken: "*les os glacés, placés devant ce corps sans grâce.*"[62] Through this point of view, the bodily descriptions take the form of self-evident, naturalized observations. As these assessments accumulate, the colonized person materializes through the colonizer's objectifying gaze.

While the lyrics themselves lack temporal markers, the representations call upon a longer, colonial history of scrutinizing racialized people's bodies in search of supporting evidence for racial hierarchies. The lyric, "*ses fesses sont une énorme masse*,"[63] invokes the famed and exploited silhouette of Sarah Baartman, a woman born in South Africa who was displayed as an exoticized spectacle in exhibitions around Europe in the early 19th century under the moniker "Hottentot Venus." In Paris, scientists took advantage of Baartman to produce and circulate pseudo-scientific theories of racial hierarchies based on supposed correlations between physiognomy, intelligence, and social roles.[64] After her death, the French zoologist Georges Cuvier made a cast of Baartman's body and preserved her brain and sex organs, which were in turn exhibited by several Parisian museums until the mid-1970s, and only repatriated to South Africa in the early 2000s.[65] Casey's lyrics pursue the focus on anatomical descriptions, amassing the supposedly visible manifestations of difference upon which racial discourse depends to secure its meaning.

Casey's choice to narrate from the colonizer's perspective deviates from the beaten pathway through which rappers use their personal voice, beliefs, and experiences to invite their listeners to form a collective rooted in shared moral truths and in opposition to the injustices caused by a third party. Casey plays with pronouns, imperative forms, and direct address to prime listeners to attribute irony to her narration and to underscore that what is at stake is complicity in the colonizer's system of representation. This style of address that places listeners before the ethical implications of their interpretation is common in her music. Casey often maintains ambiguity and allows for

62 "Chilled to the bone placed before this graceless body."

63 "Her buttocks are an enormous mass."

64 Robin Mitchell, *Vénus Noire: Black Women and Colonial Fantasies in Nineteenth-Century France* (University of Georgia Press, 2020), 36. For more on the legacy of such representations of Baartman on narratives of Black female sexuality in France, see T. Denean Sharpley-Whiting, *Black Venus: Sexualized Savages, Primal Fears, and Primitive Narratives in French* (Duke University Press, 1999).

65 Gilles Boëtsch and Pascal Blanchard, "The Hottentot Venus: Birth of a 'Freak' (1815)," in *Human Zoos: Science and Spectacle in the Age of Colonial Empires*, ed. Pascal Blanchard et al. (Liverpool University Press, 2008), 69.

multiple reactions, even at the risk of damaging the relationship of trust between herself and her audience.[66] In "Créature ratée's" first verse, she uses the first-person plural imperative to propose that the collective entity "we" teach "them" to pray to Jesus Christ and sort sugarcane with a smile. The imperative highlights listeners' role as the addressees of the colonizer's efforts to promote slavery and the civilizing mission. The recruiting gesture—and the discomfort or disgust it may provoke—primes listeners to locate a gap between the narrative voice and Casey's own position, and inverse the lyrics' significations in order to pursue identification with her.

The rapper does not let up with these efforts to draw listeners toward her narrative position. In the second verse, Casey calls out to "clients," staging the dehumanizing, commodified spectacles of slave auctions or 19th-century human zoos: "*Chers clients, clientes, ne vous arrêtez pas à cette laideur criante/ Les jungles de l'Afrique, lointaines et luxuriantes/nous offrent des spécimens de différentes variantes.*"[67] The lyrics seek to stir up the exoticized desire, fascination, fear, and disgust that human zoos capitalized on in offering up "specimens" of foreign lands for public, ethnological observation.[68] The address of "clients" draws attention toward listeners' implication in following the lyrics' dichotomies and observational gaze to make racial meaning of the colonized figure.

The beat's sonic effects and Casey's flow heighten the stakes of detecting irony. These elements play between tension as listeners are drawn into violent acts and descriptions, and false release as they are left before the ramifications of those scenes. The beat, crafted by Laloo, creates a hypnotizing mood by overlaying low-pitched piano notes, staccato violins, and high-pitched synth sounds that imitate an electric guitar. The deep piano notes at the end of each line serve as menacing punctuation, whereas the strings add a sense of anxiety. The monotonous notes build pressure that reaches its apex when the high-pitched, tweaked guitar enters during the chorus. Casey's flow plays with this rising tension and release: "*Parfois le sauvage plonge dans la démence/En rage, peut réduire un humain en miette/Mais le passage du fouet le ramène au silence.*"[69] The enjambment between "*démence*" and "*en rage*" gives a sense of lost control in the supposed danger the enslaved person presents. The last line sounds like a decrescendo, a pressure release, whereas

[66] Karim Hammou, "Das Gedächtnis der Vielheit," 391.

[67] "Dear clients, do not get caught up on this flagrant ugliness/The jungles of Africa, distant and luxurious/Offer to us specimens of different varieties."

[68] Pascal Blanchard et al., "Human Zoos: The Greatest Exotic Shows in the West," in *Human Zoos*, 3.

[69] "Sometimes the savage plunges into insanity/In rage, can reduce a human to crumbs/But the crack of the whip brings him back to silence."

semantically it depicts an act of cruelty. Casey's flow creates an effect of meiosis, a figure of speech that minimizes, or even repackages a violent act in a reassuring tone. As she pronounces "silence," the music briefly cuts out. The pause opens space to bring in what remains unsaid in the lyrics: the experience of the person on the receiving end of the violence. Casey's use of the imperative once again positions listeners as the potential addressees, and thus, as witnesses to the act of cruelty. Left before that complicit position, detecting the gap between the said and unsaid becomes essential to attributing biting irony to the verse and realigning with Casey in opposition to her own narrative voice.

While these call-outs in the verses routinely threaten to draw listeners back into complicity as the addressees with whom the colonizer shares their exoticizing gaze, the chorus excludes listeners from a possible community with the colonizer through the address: "*toi, ton identité, c'est d'être la créature ratée.*"[70] In turning the dehumanizing speech onto the listeners, Casey further destabilizes their position in the song, from the potential figure to whom the colonizer details their racist representations, to the potential object of them. The language risks offense, but can also invoke mutual understanding, empathy, or identification with the experiences and emotions of the colonized figure left unsaid in the lyrics. Among the possible responses, the direct address seeks to stamp out the possibility of passive listening, for to brush off the insult and recognize the Other as the addressee would mean complicity in colonial discourse's representational power. In all cases, the call-out requires an active rejection of the colonizer's desired power to determine someone's essence and worth—one's own or anyone else's—in order to preserve a relationship of trust with the rapper.

Live performances of the song underscore the stakes of rejecting the colonizer's representational authority by directly implicating Casey's subjectivity. At the 2017 Montreux Jazz Festival, the rapper replaced the "you" of the chorus with "me," and pointed to herself: "*moi, mon identité, c'est d'être la créature ratée.*" This slippage in pronouns directly brings the rapper's experience of racialization into the performance. Casey has spoken about how the specific history of colonialism and slavery in the French Antilles has forged her hybrid identity, in that she has in her veins, "as much blood from the slave as blood from the colonizer."[71] Designating herself as the chorus' failed creature, Casey makes explicit an unsaid element of the lyrics: that

[70] "You, your identity, is to be the failed creature."

[71] "*J'ai autant le sang de l'esclave que le sang du colon dans les veines.*" "Rencontre avec la rappeuse Casey," 5:59.

the racist representations target her as well. The "me" of the chorus creates insurmountable tension in the song's narrative structure. Through this tension, Casey draws out the ambivalences that Homi K. Bhabha pinpoints in the civilizing mission's paradoxical desire for mimicry from colonized subjects, despite the colonial system deriving its power from racialized hierarchies.[72] Narratively inhabiting colonial discourse, the rapper disrupts the authority of its representations from within and exposes it as "capable only of ironizing itself."[73]

Whereas the lyrics and Casey's flow accentuate the stakes of audience interpretation by intertwining the perceptual work of racialization with the listening experience, the music video, directed by Chris Macari, foregrounds the ethical implications of the gaze.[74] The video deepens the confrontation between the said and the unsaid by visualizing the experiences of colonized people that the lyrics omit. The filming and editing techniques play with the audience's potential complicity in the objectifying gaze, all while exacerbating the friction in the rapper's narrative position. From the first few seconds, Macari's video plunges into the performative space of *quimbois*, practices in the French Antilles that mix sorcery, magic, African religiosity, and some elements of Catholicism. *Quimbois* has a rich history of resistance to slavery and evangelizing projects under French colonial rule.[75] However, there is an ambivalence to it as something that can curse and inflict harm, or heal and protect from evil.[76]

The camera follows a ritual in which the *séancier*, or *quimboiseur* rapidly shakes his head while the other participants hold candles in a circle around him. Macari mixes panoramic shots that give the feeling of being caught up in the ritual with observational high-angled and low-angled shots. The oscillation between observation and participation, the black-and-white style, and the visual effects of scratches on the film reel echo the genre of ethnographic films. This filmic tradition has encountered many critiques for its exoticism, the most scathing coming from Senegalese filmmaker Ousmane Sembène toward Jean Rouch, founding figure of *cinéma verité*: "*tu nous regardes comme des insectes*" (You watch us like insects).[77]

[72] Homi K. Bhabha, *The Location of Culture* (Routledge, 1994), 122.
[73] Ibid., 124.
[74] CASEY Anfalsh, "Créature ratée (Clip Officiel)," YouTube Video, 4:38, January 17, 2020, https://www.youtube.com/watch?v=Fa7nN1YXQv0.
[75] Anny Dominique Curtius and Simonne Henry-Valmore, "Quimbois," in *The Encyclopedia of Caribbean Religions*, vol. 2, ed. P. Taylor et al. (The University of Illinois Press, 2013), 738.
[76] Ibid.
[77] Cited in Paula Amad, "Visual Riposte: Looking Back at the Return of the Gaze as Postcolonial Theory's Gift to Film Studies," *Cinema Journal* 52, no. 3 (2013): 49.

Fig. 3.5 Still from the music video "Créature ratée"

"Créature ratée" thus joins Abd al Malik's "Allogène" in exploring image technologies' role in objectifying the racialized Other. Both the *séancier* and another protagonist performing *danmyé*, a choreographed form of martial arts from Martinique, stare directly back into the camera's lens in close-up shots (see Fig. 3.5). These looks echo the "return of the gaze" trope in visual archival practices and in criticism of ethnographic films. Film scholar Paula Amad cautions against politicized interpretations that fetishize these often fleeting glances as a definitive recovery of agency for historically marginalized people and as a reversal of colonial power dynamics.[78] She nevertheless acknowledges the potential for this formal device to create a contact zone between the filmed subjects and the audience, as well as to inspire storytelling that centers the people left off the film record.[79] The music video's emphasis on the returned gaze creates this contact, making passive viewing even more morally dubious, and putting the viewers before their ethical duty to make meaning of the representations put in front of them.

The return of the gaze and the music video's staging further blur temporal distinctions between the traumas of the colonial past and the performance. Both Casey and the *séancier* appear with their faces covered in white powder. The edited transitions articulate this parallel by superimposing a close-up of the *séancier* onto the rapper's image, creating the impression

[78] Ibid., 53.
[79] Ibid., 65, 74.

Fig. 3.6 Still from the music video "Créature ratée"

that they fade into and absorb one another (see Fig. 3.6). This visual collapse attributes to Casey the *séancier*'s role of interpreting the past, present, and future.[80] The editing reinforces this role of transmitting memory with a rapid juxtaposition at the forty-second mark of a close-up of the *danmyé* practitioner's back with the famous 1863 photograph from *Harper's Weekly* of Peter (formerly identified as Gordon), an enslaved man whose back bears thick scars from being whipped. The reference to *quimbois* therefore brings spiritual effects into the performance, such as contact with those who are no longer living, which visualize the lyrics' violence. The staging bolsters the link between the rapper and the colonized figure in her lyrics, troubling her narrative position and further guiding the audience toward securing the irony of her words.

As a final rebuke to the colonizer's erasure of the colonized figure's rich history in the first verse, the beat fades out to end the song with a sample of Ti-Émile, a prominent figure of Martinican bèlè music, performing with the traditional *tibwa* instrument. The brief percussive outro, resurging from the seemingly finished song, echoes what Edwin C. Hill Jr.—reading Fanon—calls a *raté*, "a sonic symbol of slippage, excess, waste in the colonial machine."[81] The sample distills the unsaid elements floating through the performance, threatening to undermine the colonizer's discursive, sonic, and

[80] Anny Dominique Curtius and Simonne Henry-Valmore, "Quimbois," 738.

[81] Edwin C. Hill Jr., *Black Soundscapes White Stages: The Meaning of Francophone Sound in the Black Atlantic* (The Johns Hopkins University Press, 2013), 15.

visual regimes of representation. "Créature ratée" stages racialization as a sensorial process that seeks authority over what is perceptible and meaningful. By cyclically drawing listeners toward complicity with the colonial discourse she narrates, Casey heightens the stakes of attributing irony to her voice. The preservation of the rapper–audience relationship depends on rejecting the racializing gaze's authority. "Créature ratée" thus places the audience before the weaknesses of the representational regime that colonial discourse seeks to impose, undermining it from within.

* * *

This chapter demonstrated how rap performances stage the perceptual process of racialization. Médine, Abd al Malik, and Casey draw in the racializing gaze through lyrical, sonic, and visual aesthetics. Over a beat evoking surveillance, Médine's play upon the pronoun "*elle*" in "Code Barbe" circulates the beard as a malleable form that takes on different connotations depending on the wearer. Through bandanas stamped with the beard's fetishized outline, the music video reproduces this movement to reveal the racialized signifier's instability. For his part, Abd al Malik's "Allogène" uses French Touch electronic music, a vibrantly colored bodily surface, and lyrical claims to monstrosity to prompt the audience to read the performance through the lens of alterity. Casey's "Créature ratée" inhabits colonial discourse from within, exploiting tension in the beat and in her flow to undermine her own narrative position. The music video alternates between observational and situated perspectives to further trouble the exoticizing gaze upon the French Antillean practice of *quimbois* it stages.

In each performance, entangling aesthetic techniques with the racializing gaze foregrounds the interpretative work the latter requires. Potential complicity with the gaze heightens the stakes for the rapper–audience relationship and for each artist's anti-racist stance. Médine opens up the possibility for the audience to join in appropriating the beard and contest its essentialization. Abd al Malik's performance primes expectations for legible difference only to surprise them. In "Créature ratée," decoding the rapper's ethical position within her narrative becomes crucial to preserving a connection of trust. Casey's performance pushes the stakes of the audience's interpretive work the furthest by making the recognition of their perceptual role in racialization the means of avoiding a breakdown in the audience-artist relationship.

In their emphasis on assembling, circulating, and obfuscating signs of alterity, Médine, Casey, and Abd al Malik problematize racialization as an act of decoding that takes place in the space between the aesthetic elements of their performances and the audience's interpretations of them. Race is not a constant that these performances reflect, but rather something that circulates throughout them, never fully resting or latching onto the rappers or their cultural product. The songs and music videos explored in this chapter challenge the logic of visibility underpinning critical efforts to draw rap's representational space around disputing France's colorblind ideology. Holding up French rappers as self-evident indicators of universalism's blind spots reinvests in their intelligibility as racialized subjects. Médine, Abd al Malik, and Casey harness their stylistic signatures to trouble that knowability. In so doing, they produce intricate knowledge about how race has historically and continues to find meaning in France.

The following chapter will grapple with the fact that the social, perceptual construction of race is a commodified process as well. The thread of commodification was woven into the fabric of this chapter's case studies—through Médine's emphasis on barcodes and printed bandanas, through the streetwear aesthetic of Abd al Malik's protagonist, and through Casey's callouts to the clients of slave auctions and human zoos. Teasing it out further in the next chapter, I will examine how perceived alterity shapes rap's value, before exploring rappers' reflexivity toward the mechanisms that inform their music's commercial appeal. Building upon this chapter's close readings, the next will interrogate how the aesthetic qualities that perform marginality interact with those that comment upon rap's commodification.

Chapter 4
Illicit Aesthetics

Market Cravings and Rap's Stupefying Appeal

After more than four decades of French rap, cultural critics form a consensus around three main assessments: the genre, once believed to be an ephemeral trend, is here to stay; it has aesthetically flourished into multiple subgenres that refute a homogenized vision of rap; and it increasingly dominates physical and digital music sales. However, as French rap matures, some critics don rose-colored glasses that idealize the music's socially engaged past and regret its supposedly apolitical present. In 2018, Julien Baldassarra lamented in *Le Monde Diplomatique*,

> From the end of the 2000s, the genre slowly finished conforming: individualism and competition became its favorite themes. The texts became standardized based on a common denominator: money, and, more broadly, showcasing capitalist values.[1]

Baldassarra places the rap of the 2010s in strict opposition with its politically radical predecessors. His diagnosis of the contemporary rap scene zeros in on two malignant elements: the individualistic pursuit of wealth on the one hand and the reduction of artistic expression to formulaic, mass-produced entertainment on the other. In this view, the commodity's omnipresence in French rap has thoroughly stifled aesthetics.

Baldassarra is not the only critic to posit themes of material wealth and aesthetic complexity as mutually exclusive. In *Le Monde*, Stéphanie Binet cites the rapper Niska, "*du lundi au lundi, du Gucci au Fendi, on a les llé-bi*,"[2] to contrast young rappers who "write choruses with hardly two or three words

[1] "*A partir de la fin des années 2000, le genre achève lentement sa mise en conformité: l'individualisme et la compétition en sont devenus les thèmes fétiches. Les textes s'uniformisent autour d'un dénominateur commun: l'argent et, plus largement, la mise en scène des valeurs capitalistes*," Julien Baldassarra, "Rappe pour Nike!," *Le Monde Diplomatique*, October 2018, https://www.monde-diplomatique.fr/2018/10/BALDASSARRA/59127.

[2] "From Monday to Monday, from Gucci to Fendi, we've got the bills."

Reflexivity in French Rap. Emily Q. Shuman, Oxford University Press. © Oxford University Press 2026.
DOI: 10.1093/9780197781609.003.0005

and settle for narrating their daily lives" with "the old guard like Solaar who multiplied stylistic devices to take stock of the state of play in France."[3] For these critics, as market forces favor music that fetishizes monetary gain, they simultaneously snuff out rich stylistic choices. Binet reproduces the aesthetic validation of MC Solaar's writing style and measured social commentary explored in Chapter 1. In her nostalgic retrospective, Solaar's elaborate poetic devices serve a larger purpose, whereas Niska's use of repetition reflects complacent navel-gazing. Such an assessment denies the latter intentionality or any real creative ambition. The opposition between these two camps of rappers therefore relies on both aesthetic and political judgments. Following such judgments, while today's commercially oriented rappers merely settle for describing quotidian experiences, the old guard possessed the ability to reflect on their craft and develop a purposeful aesthetic—always with the noble vocation of commenting upon the state of society. This line of critique hinges upon the notion that aesthetic value is indissoluble from perceived political consciousness.

Where performances that revolve around the pursuit of commercial success perturb these sorts of politicized readings, those explored in the previous chapter would likely satisfy expectations for aesthetic sophistication and sociopolitical resonance. Chapter 3 demonstrated how Médine, Abd al Malik, and Casey imbricate rap's stylistic conventions with the process of racialization. Their performances draw in the racializing gaze in order to denaturalize the interpretative work it requires. In so doing, they trouble the notion of race as a pre-established, social reality that rap reflects. Rather, such performances underscore race as a construct that is made meaningful in the perceptual field. As a cultural product that circulates within this perceptual field, rap's lyrical, sonic, and visual aesthetics may reiterate, reshape, or indeed unsettle the performativity of race. In this chapter, I build upon those analyses to examine the relationship between aesthetic qualities that evoke racialized difference on the one hand and techniques that make apparent rap's status as a cultural commodity on the other. By extending the previous chapter's approach to performances that self-consciously comment upon their commodification, I challenge the false binary that would oppose these two sets of performances.

[3] "*Écrivent des refrains avec à peine deux ou trois mots et se contentent de narrer leur quotidien*"; "*les anciens comme Solaar [qui] multipliaient les figures de style pour dresser l'état des lieux de la France*," Stéphanie Binet, "Que raconte le rap aujourd'hui?" *Le Monde*, November 15, 2019, https://www.lemonde.fr/culture/article/2019/11/15/que-raconte-le-rap-aujourd-hui_6019347_3246.html.

Political Struggle, Aesthetics, and the Commodification of Racialized Cultural Products

Studies of popular culture have long debated commodification's potential neutralizing effects on political resistance. For Walter Benjamin, the reproducibility and mass diffusion of cultural objects such as film and photography can put spectators in a position to absorb tools of social critique through distraction and pleasure. The cultural consumer becomes a critic, even if they are not explicitly aware of the political dissection they are performing.[4] Theodor W. Adorno scathingly dismissed Benjamin's romanticized view of mass culture, arguing that highly commercialized forms, in particular popular music, were signs of complacency toward the destruction of resistance and individuality.[5] Whereas Benjamin argued that the distracting power of mass cultural forms could subtly turn spectators into social critics, Adorno contended that deconcentrated listening enables popular music to function like advertising. For him, the familiar pop song formula, much like an advertising jingle, prompts listeners to consume. This canonical opposition between popular culture as a channel for revolutionary ideals versus a vessel for conspicuous consumption informs Leftist critiques of contemporary French rap. Indeed, Baldassarra ends his text with the charge that, in promoting brands like Nike, French rap's current stars distance themselves from the pioneering generation's revolutionary spirit, and ultimately serve to placate the masses and maintain the capitalist status quo.[6]

In these sorts of critical judgments, signs of political resistance in an object of popular culture not only augment its perceived aesthetic value but also elevate it above the forces of commodification. This view echoes patterns of thinking about other popular music genres in late 20th-century France, in which themes of protest, Leftist politics, and hostility to music industry logics were key to securing authenticity.[7] The ostensible focus on rap's subversive potential overlooks the integral role that perceived contestation played in securing its market value. Karim Hammou demonstrates how three different views of French rap—as an art form, a social message from marginalized youth, and as a means for commercial radio stations to profit from a multiethnic *banlieue* image—converged in the mid-1990s to secure rap's

[4] Walter Benjamin, "The Work of Art in the Age of Mechanical Reproduction," trans. Harry Zohn, in *Illuminations*, ed. Hannah Arendt (Schocken Books, 1969).

[5] Theodor W. Adorno, "On the Fetish Character of Music and the Regression of Listening," in *The Culture Industry: Selected Essays on Mass Culture*, ed. J.M. Bernstein (Routledge, 1991), 32.

[6] Julien Baldassarra, "Rappe pour Nike!"

[7] Barbara Lebrun, *Protest Music in France: Production, Identity, and Audiences* (Ashgate, 2009), 15.

status as an "Othered cultural good."[8] The imaginary of the street served as a space of entente for both artists and industry actors; "a banner of combat for the former" and a source of "exoticist appeal" for the latter.[9] Investment in French rap's racialization as the cornerstone of its political value has therefore been crucial for its commercial development, even during the "golden age" for which many yearn. The marginalized *jeune de banlieue* figure's centrality to rap's representational space and commercialization reconfigures the relationship between aesthetics, politicization, and marketability laid out in the critiques that began this chapter. Contemporary debates over social commentary and commodification must examine how racialized difference informs the ability of popular culture objects such as rap to incite desire to consume, possess, or enjoy proximity to certain aesthetics.

The relationship between political struggle and commodification is thus far from a neat binary. The cultural industries' commercial logics nevertheless obscure, even fracture links between racialized cultural forms and social justice ideals in the pursuit of mass market appeal. This appeal relies upon consumers latching onto cultural products that stir up affective experiences of marginality, without necessarily relating those sensations to the power structures behind them. Marketing initiatives may, for instance, incorporate Black music to intertwine a range of emotional effects with the consumer experience, including sensuality, soulfulness, or rushes of adrenaline.[10] As Black cultural expressions circulate widely through the cultural industries, the ways they may have historically engaged with Black liberation politics blur, making it possible, as Harry J. Elam puts it, to "love Black cool and not Black people."[11]

As Robin D.G. Kelley incisively lays out, while the appeal of racialized aesthetics may appear disjointed from politics, it is intimately embedded in larger economic and social forces:

> [Capitalism] is also responsible for a shrinking labor market, the militarization of urban space, and the circulation of the very representations of race that generate terror in all of us at the sight of young black men and yet compels most of America to want to wear their shoes.[12]

[8] Karim Hammou, "Mainstreaming French Rap," 70.

[9] Ibid.

[10] Kennell A. Jackson, "The Shadows of Texts: Will Black Music and Singers Sell Everything on Television?" in *Black Cultural Traffic: Crossroads in Global Performance and Popular Culture*, ed. Harry J. Elam and Kennell A. Jackson (University of Michigan Press, 2005), 102–103.

[11] Harry J. Elam, "Change Clothes and Go: A Postscript to Postblackness," in *Black Cultural Traffic*, ed. Harry J. Elam and Kennell A. Jackson (University of Michigan Press, 2005), 386.

[12] Robin D.G. Kelley, "Playing for Keeps: Pleasure and Profit on the Postindustrial Playground," in *The House That Race Built: Black Americans, U.S. Terrain*, ed. Wahneema Lubiano (Pantheon, 1997), 224.

Here, Kelley touches on a crucial element that Baldassarra neglects as he chastises French artists that "rap for Nike": representations and aesthetic forms that engage with the racialized repertoire of the street, illicit activity, and socioeconomic marginalization—experiences that global capitalism has itself engendered—produce desire for certain commodities. Fetishized into footwear, consumers can purchase proximity to these representations, often while maintaining a safe distance from the criminalized activities and experiences of oppression that made them enticing in the first place. This system of value reflects a paradox—that racialized aesthetic forms become appealing and marketable as capitalist forces and systemic racism devalue the lives of racial minorities. Racialized cultural products indeed generate new consumption patterns, not through generic, advertisement-like form, but through the disjointed ways they evoke struggle, radicalness, and even danger in the eyes of certain consumers.[13]

Just as the aesthetics of racialized cultural forms contribute to the social production of race, the cultural industries play a crucial role in the making of race through their own apparatuses, production rationales, and logics.[14] This has long been the case for the music industries on both sides of the Atlantic, with commodification packaging genres such as soul and jazz as forms of stylistic and sonic intimacy with liberatory struggle.[15] Rap is far from immune to these dynamics, as the music reifies and rationalizes certain narratives of Black American life in line with market appeal, such that representations take on a life of their own, ultimately feeding off their own profitability more than real-life referentiality.[16] Within the apparent paradox of rap as commercialized resistance music, European rappers and their labels often "have it both ways"—as J. Griffith Rollefson puts it—performing provocative critique of racist tropes and colonial histories on the one hand and playing into and profiting from stereotypes on the other.[17] Portrayals of rap as resistance music too often occult this imbricated relationship between racialized aesthetics and market desires.

[13] *bell hooks: Cultural Criticism and Transformation*, directed by Sut Jhally (Media Education Foundation, 1997), 1:00:00.

[14] Anamik Saha, *Race and the Cultural Industries* (Polity Press, 2018), 11.

[15] See, e.g., Mark Anthony Neal, "Sold Out on Soul: The Corporate Annexation of Black Popular Music," *Popular Music and Society* 21, no. 3 (Fall 1997): 117–135. For the French context, see Celeste Day Moore, *Soundscapes of Liberation* (Duke University Press, 2021).

[16] Franck Freitas, "'Blackness à la demande.' Production narrative de 'l'authenticité raciale' dans l'industrie du rap américain," *Volume! La revue des musiques populaires* 8, no. 2 (2011): 116; Eric K. Watts, "An Exploration of Spectacular Consumption: Gangsta Rap as Cultural Commodity," in *That's the Joint! The Hip-Hop Studies Reader*, ed. Murray Forman and Mark Anthony Neal (Routledge, 2004), 687.

[17] J. Griffith Rollefson, *Flip the Script*, 89.

Rather than chastising commodification for impoverishing stylistic complexity, I posit a more symbiotic relationship in which aesthetic qualities and artistic postures self-consciously reflect back on French rap's status as a cultural product to be bought and sold, as well as on the mechanisms that instill it with value. This value is constantly in flux, and the performances I analyze in this chapter reflect a changing landscape in the French music industry since 2015, in which rap now holds a large share of the market. Rap's tightened grip on the industry also coincides with the 2016 decision from the SNEP (*Syndicat national de l'édition phonographique*) to factor digital streams into album certifications, making these benchmarks far more attainable for French rappers.[18] In 2017, hip-hop music—encompassing genres such as rap, R&B, and urban pop—generated at least 250 million euros through concert ticket sales, music streaming, and physical CD or vinyl sales.[19] The SNEP's 2024 annual report attests to hip-hop genres' crucial place in the French music industry's steady financial growth, as they represented 53% of the top 200 albums. A focus on recent performances gets to the heart of pressing questions about value and the cultural commodity, as rappers now create with the awareness that the genre's commercial value is more evident than ever.

In this chapter, marginalization and commodification appear as distinct, aestheticized processes in a metaphorical relationship. The performances I analyze borrow from the logics of commercial exploitation to articulate alterity and conversely employ tropes of marginalized life to give form to the music's profitability. This chapter examines the complex metaphors in performances by PNL, Alpha Wann, and Shay as conjunctures where the formal qualities that make race, class, or gender differences sonically and visually perceptible meet those that make commodity status tangible. Within these stagings of alterity, rappers' vocal efforts and embodied performances foreground the racialized and gendered forms of work that the commodification of the finished musical product might mask. One such critical intersection is the narrative of the drug trade, in which illicit activity allegorizes the racialized cultural commodity's value. Throughout the chapter, this metaphor envelops rappers' power and vulnerability in a cultural marketplace designed to capitalize on marginality. The reflexive performances of PNL, Alpha Wann, and Shay negotiate their complicity within music industry logics. On the one hand, they claim an enrapturing, profit-generating hold over the state of mind, sensorial experiences, and emotions of their listeners. On the other, in offering

[18] The thresholds are now as follows: equivalent of 50,000 units sold for gold-certified albums; 100,000 for platinum; and 500,000 for diamond.

[19] Karim Hammou and Marie Sonnette-Manouguian, "Socio-économie," 114.

themselves and their music up for consumption, they become susceptible to the clientele's appetites, which risk restricting their representational space.

PNL and the Controlled Substance of Subjectivity

The rap duo PNL's 2015 debut EP, *Que la famille*, begins with a few isolated, reverberating keyboard notes. The first track, "Je vis je visser," produced by DRMZBeatz, uses these airy, drawn-out notes to create a sense of space, as if listeners were descending into the rappers' universe from above. A distant, Auto-Tuned voice repeats "*Que la famille, que la famille*,"[20] progressively getting louder each time to enhance the impression of spiraling down toward the voice's source. When N.O.S. begins his verse, he plunges listeners head-first into the daily hustle of low-level drug dealing: "*Ouais igo à l'aller j'ai d'la monnaie, au retour le coffre est chargé comme un poney/J'écoute, je ramasse, je claque, j'y retourne, du début à la fin de l'année abonné.*"[21] N.O.S. raps in a rapid flow, reflecting the routine steps of the supply chain.

Over the course of his verse, he elongates his flow and slips into a sung delivery, culminating in the chorus, "*Je vis, je visser (j'm'ennuie), je vis, je visser (j'bibi)/Je vis, je visser (j'm'enfuis), je vis je visser.*"[22] The anaphoric structure equates the rappers' existence with the act of serving their clientele. The alternating echoes of "*j'm'ennuie, j'bibi, j'm'enfuie*" mirror the monotonous comings and goings of their day's work. The use of slang—some of which, like *igo*, is strongly associated with their native Essonne region—inscribes PNL in a particular geographic location and class background. The terminology reinforces an in-group with listeners familiar with the jargon and keeps those who would find the language enigmatic at a distance. Yet, as is the case with *j'bibi*, slang also serves a specific stylistic function, creating assonance, completing the rhyme scheme, and shaping the chorus. The lyrical structure, Auto-Tuned vocals, and ethereal beat put a fine gloss on illicit activity and effortlessly float listeners along the current of these transactions. PNL's fetishization of the informal economy brings to the surface how peripheral life becomes valuable, aesthetically palatable, and consumable through the musical product.

Through poeticization of the drug trade's mundane labor, PNL turns away from the seemingly unfiltered, realist aesthetic that critics value as an authentic portrayal of marginalization and vehicle for social commentary.

[20] "Only family."

[21] "Yeah, man, on the way there I've got cash, on the way back the trunk is loaded like a pack horse/I listen, I pick up, I close up, I return, from the start to the end of the year, subscribed."

[22] "I live, I serve (I get bored), I live, I serve (I sell)/I live, I serve (I flee), I live, I serve."

Instead, the duo, comprised of brothers Tarik (Ademo) and Nabil (N.O.S.) Andrieu, have created a visual and lyrical universe centered on mythifying their recourse to the drug trade as a means of financial stability. Indeed, the name PNL stands for "*Peace N' Lovés*," or "Peace and Money." As was the case with "Je vis je visser," PNL cushions these tales in the dreamlike beats typical of the cloud rap subgenre, keeping their otherwise gritty or risky connotations at a dazed remove. The selective personal details that Ademo and N.O.S. distill into their performances emphasize their half-Algerian, half-Corsican roots and prop up an origin story steeped in the codes of organized crime, particularly with regard to their father's criminal past.[23] References to specific biographical or emotional experiences are fleeting, and the value of this teased access is augmented by the fact that the duo refuses all interviews. They notably did not respond to any questions for a profile in the American magazine *The Fader* and sent a chimpanzee in their stead to Skyrock's radio show *Planète rap*.[24] This evasion makes it difficult to secure any referent to reality in the music. Depriving audiences of biographical information also undermines devaluating views of rap as transparent, brute reflections of lived experiences and literal calls to material violence (Chapter 2). The systems of value behind PNL's musical product depend on this overt flouting of the expectations for fleshed-out autobiography in rap.

Ademo croons in the song 91's, "*on chante en public mais nos larmes sont privées*"[25] as a reminder to listeners that the music PNL performs in public is the tip of the iceberg, and the troubled emotions that lie beneath will only manifest rarely, if at all. Moments in which the brothers reveal the depth of their emotional interiority or the reality of their past experiences are dosed out to their audience like controlled substances—creating desire and intrigue for the product and keeping listeners coming back for more. The duo's enigmatic public presence gives the impression of pure image, an impenetrable surface that at the same time packages the music as a fetishized point of access into the complex beings behind the product. This dynamic became spectacularly apparent in April 2019 when, two weeks after the release of their third studio album *Deux frères*, an enormous reproduction of the album cover appeared

[23] Their father, René Andrieu, was a figure in organized crime in the 1980s. In the 1990s, he ran a youth association in Corbeil-Essonnes, working closely with billionaire and then-mayor Serge Dassault. Dassault's political career was marked by corruption, eventually leading to a formal investigation for vote-buying and a conviction for money-laundering. Dassault appealed the latter, but died before a definitive judgment could be made. The relationship between Andrieu and Dassault soured over a financial dispute and, in 2013, Andrieu was the target of a shooting by one of Dassault's associates.

[24] "Planète rap" is a popular radio program diffused on the channel Skyrock since 1996. It has played a pivotal role in Skyrock's "first on rap music" strategy.

[25] "We sing in public but our tears are private."

on their childhood apartment building. The building, located in the Gagarine housing projects in the southeastern Parisian suburb of Ivry, was destined for demolition. The image—almost oppressive in size—dominated the landscape. The neon colors contrasted with the uniform bricks of the building behind it. The interaction between the nostalgia, love, and melancholy that circulate in the empty building and the striking promotional visual that covered its façade epitomizes PNL's modus operandi of playing with tensions between public and private and between surface and depth.

The duo's image-building recalls Marx's commodity fetishism, or the veiling and mystification of the material processes through which commodities are produced and consumed. This obfuscation gives the commodity its allure.[26] PNL's strategic withholding and unveiling of biographical details make folklore of their origin story, leaving listeners with a detached narrative of illicit drug dealing and adoration of their "Baba's" criminalized expertise. This carefully woven narrative circulates in their lyrics, spaced-out beats, and visuals, referring back to and building upon itself until it takes on a life of its own. Through the aesthetic experiences they offer, PNL stages a process of self-commodification that hollows out the low-level drug dealing of their past, freeing it of any definitive anchor in a visceral reality and instead sublimating this experience as allegory for the performative work of their music. This stylized notion of controlled circulation aligns with PNL's status as one of French rap's most commercially successful and most resolutely independent acts.[27] The duo's depiction of the parallel economy thus operates as a metaphor for their artistic work and the musical product they deliver to their fans. As with controlled substances, the conservative doses in which personal attachments and emotional displays manifest in the music generate value and sustained appeal.

The cover art for their debut EP, *Que la famille*, attests to the transactional undertones of sentimentality and the mythification of family bonds in their music (see Fig. 4.1). The cover features a human heart against a sterile, white backdrop. The organ's rich pink color dissipates into the violet of five-hundred-euro bank notes. A daguerreotype family portrait figures at the center of the heart. While we cannot discern the likenesses of the family members, we can make out, despite the deep pink stain, children dressed in white and adults in somber black. The letters "QLF" are

[26] Karl Marx, *Capital*, trans. Samuel Moore and Edward Aveling (Encyclopedia Britannica, 1955), 31.

[27] PNL operates their own independent label *QLF Records*, with distribution through Believe Music. At the time of writing, 2015's *Le Monde Chico* has been certified triple platinum, 2016's *Dans la légende* diamond, and 2019's *Deux frères* double diamond.

Fig. 4.1 Cover art for the EP *Que la famille*

etched into this sober, middle-class family cameo, which starkly contrasts the Andrieu brothers' own upbringing (their mother was absent during their childhood, and their father was often at odds with the legal system). The image accentuates the discrepancy between a very traditional notion of family and PNL's understanding of the word, which they use to describe lifelong friends, trusted collaborators, and their loyal fan base. The anonymous portrait stands in for these sentimental connections and translates them into a readily identifiable symbol. Family, in its normative, institutionalized form, sits firmly at the border between the two lifelines that keep the heart pumping: blood, the testament to genetic ties, and the pursuit of material wealth. The artwork for *Que la famille* sets the stage for a theme that pulses through PNL's oeuvre: the amalgamation of currency and intimacy.

The heart of paper money is a recurring trope in PNL's music, and many of their lyrics make intertextual ties to their first EP's artwork. To return to "Je vis je visser," the first track of *Que la famille* verbalizes the direct exchangeability between inner emotional life, commodities, and currency: "*J'veux du L, j'veux du V, j'veux du G/Pour saper mes marques dans le cœur.*"[28] Alluding to the haute couture houses Louis Vuitton and Gucci, Ademo plays with the multiple meanings of *saper* (either to dress or to diminish) and *marque* (either brand or mark) to express the desire that donning these labels will diminish the lingering traces of a painful past etched in his heart. The lines encompass a process of objectification and monetization of intimacy. These transactions reappear in PNL's 2018 single "À l'ammoniaque," in which Ademo sings with Auto-Tuned, reverberated desolation, "*J'remplace centimes par sentiments, mon cœur se transforme en billets.*"[29] While the first half of the lyric hints at potential for emotional maturation, over the course of which the pursuit of material wealth would take a backseat to sentimental investments, the second half reverses the transaction. The set-up and punchline create fluid circulation between emotions and profits, in which money can be substituted for feelings—either his own or those held for him—and in which one's emotional core possesses monetary value. In other words, Ademo sets up a relationship of equivalent value, in which both money and the promise of interiority are forms that express one another's worth.

The lyric undeniably refers back to the cover of *Que la famille*, yet it also packages PNL's subjectivities as commodity forms. The seemingly paradoxical line contributes to the song's melancholic atmosphere, while simultaneously bringing to the surface the music's status as a cultural product to be bought and sold. Over the simple flamenco guitar chords of the beat crafted by Sam H, Anaika, and IBØ, the chorus reimagines the popular musings of a love-struck person picking off flower petals. Ademo recites the French equivalent of "they love me, they love me not": "*je t'aime/à la folie/passionnément/à l'ammoniaque.*" The bittersweet adlib adds toxicity to this love, enveloping it in the universe of the drug trade, where ammonia transforms powder cocaine into crack rocks. PNL thus opts to express love through the drug's cheaper and more accessible form. As opposed to cocaine's association with energy, wealth, and partying, crack evokes a more somber reality of addiction and marginality that resonates with chorus' depiction of tainted love. Echo effects, such as the repetition of gimmicks like "*ouais, ouais, ouais*" and reverberation in the beat, create a void that adds to the depressive atmosphere.

This sonic gulf finds visual translation in the music video, directed by Kamerameha, Kim Chapiron, and Mess, which stages the two brothers in

[28] "I want some L, I want some V, I want some G/To diminish the marks on my heart."

[29] "I replace cents with sentiments, my heart transforms into bills."

Fig. 4.2 Still from the music video "À l'ammoniaque"

a post-apocalyptic, desert environment.[30] The rappers appear in the lobby of a destroyed apartment building, ready to deal to the seemingly endless line of clients that stretches out into the sand (see Fig. 4.2). Enveloped in both the visual allegory of drug dealing and the song's depressive mood, the image of exchanging coins for feelings brings to light the fact that bearing witness to the rappers' pain is a monetized experience—whether in the form of a stream or a view on YouTube. Indeed, it is the promise of access to the artists' inner selves and the hint of an emotional connection between rapper and listener that provides the pleasure of consuming the song. The heart transforms into bills in the process of commodity exchange—the music for money form.

The potential to tap into this emotional space works in tandem with the familiar narrative of illicit activity to secure the music's appeal and profitability. This critical juncture between sentimentality and the dealer figure also articulates the musical product's value along gendered lines. PNL's vocals channel serene melancholy through the use of Auto-Tune, aligning with the pitch-correcting technology's affordances of vulnerability that, in the US context, diverge from hegemonic hip-hop masculinity.[31] This emotional weight, however, often encounters more normative performances of masculine virility in PNL's work. The duo scatter boastful references to their machismo throughout their lyrics. As in the 2016 song, "DA," they often allude to their father and his gangster persona as the ideal model of masculine toughness: "*Bats les couilles qu'ces pédés m'aiment pas, pas, pas/Au fait moi j'ai les*

[30] PNL, "A l'Ammoniaque [Official Video,]" YouTube Video, 5:47, June 22, 2018, https://www.youtube.com/watch?v=Vl-GJaitlNs.

[31] Marc Lafrance, Lori Burns, and Alyssa Woods, "Doing Hip-Hop Masculinity Differently: Exploring Kanye West's 808s & Heartbreak through Word, Sound, and Image," in *The Routledge Companion to Popular Music and Gender*, ed. Stan Hawkins (Routledge, 2017).

couilles de papa, pa, pa."[32] PNL's lyrics therefore contain emotional disclosures traditionally seen as antithetical to heteronormative masculinity as well as performances of virility rooted in physicality and homophobia.

This friction between sentimentality and virility also plays out in the video for "À l'ammoniaque," in which Ademo intermittently appears shirtless to reveal a muscular torso. The complex performance of masculinity in PNL's music invokes a longer history of stereotypes about Algerian men in France. In his study of the "Arab man" figure in the post-decolonization era, Todd Shepard traces the evolution of "the erotics of Algerian difference," from fascination with the gritty virility of the anticolonial struggle, to the Sexual Revolution's turn to Algerian men as models of sexual and gender fluidity, to fears of their supposed sexual violence, to disapproval of religious orthodoxy.[33] In insisting on the narrative of the drug trade, PNL reactivates the nuanced, historical repertoire of Algerian masculinities through the most recent stereotyped North African male figure in the French social imaginary: *banlieue* youth.

The racialized dealer figure, devoid of the visceral transparency that has traditionally motivated investments in French rap, reveals itself as a fetishized shell in PNL's performances. The heavy use of reverb and ethereal beats reinforce this hollowness, all while leaving space for the music's emotional weight to resonate with listeners. The sonic qualities that betray the dealer narrative's superficiality also disseminate the rappers' melancholy, trauma, or ennui. Through their lyrical and visual imagery, PNL expresses the value of these instances of interiority by presenting sentiment and currency as exchangeable forms. Through metaphors of packaging, distribution, and sale, the brothers maintain a sense of control over the emotional exposure they distill into their music. The stylistic elements of PNL's performances make commodity status perceptible to the audience's eyes, ears, and imaginations. That these formal qualities find meaning in reference to the performances' overarching frame of peripheral life underscores how alterity informs their cultural product's value. It is through the aesthetic experiences they afford that PNL envelops their listeners and makes them complicit in their self-commodification.

Rap or the Art of Selling Oneself Like a Brick of Hashish

PNL comments on the commodity status of their work by tightly controlling and metaphorically monetizing traffic along the border between their

[32] "Don't give a fuck if these fags don't like me/In fact I have balls like my Dad."
[33] See Todd Shepard, *Sex, France, and Arab Men, 1962–1979* (University of Chicago Press, 2018).

subjectivities and the musical product. By sublimating the few personal details they unveil, the duo reveal how crucial the impression of lived experience has been to the exploitation of racialized cultural products. Whereas PNL forces a gap between themselves as performers and racialized expectations for their music in order to exploit desire for the autobiographical, Parisian rapper Alpha Wann turns these expectations into the crux of his 2018 song "Stupéfiant et noir" by likening himself to hashish. Subsuming his person within the illicit product analogy, Alpha Wann stages how the commodification of blackness promises a peripheral, even dangerous "coolness" that is appropriable and consumable through cultural forms such as rap. The "Stupéfiant et noir" music video visually entwines these processes to such an extent that the audience is pushed to reckon with the occultation of the Black person upon which the marketability of "Black cool" relies.

The black-and-white music video for "Stupéfiant et noir," directed by Scotty Simper,[34] first finds Alpha Wann nestled in the back of a truck among cardboard boxes marked with the name of his independent record label, Don Dada Records.[35] A group of men load the truck's cargo as Alpha Wann begins his verse. These images depict a particularly precarious form of employment in today's ever-expanding gig economy—delivery services—to create an ambiguous portrayal of the rapper as either a laborer toiling to maintain the supply chain or as a form of merchandise himself. The camera frames Alpha Wann, seated in the shadows, between the amputated body parts of white, plastic mannequins. The uncanny visual combines with the song's simple, hypnotic melody. The beat, produced by Hologram Lo', features a slow succession of high-pitched notes to create an eerily enticing atmosphere. In this sonic and visual environment, "Stupéfiant et noir" stages the processes of producing and selling oneself as a cultural product, as well as the forms of alienation that lie in the tensions between subject and creator on the one hand, and object and commodity on the other. As the camera follows the rapper through rows of warehouse storage, the video's initial hints of self-objectification crystallize in the chorus' poignant image: "*J'suis comme le shit: stupéfiant et noir.*"[36]

Under Simper's direction, the music video builds its visual narrative around fleshing out the comparison to hashish. In the dimly lit warehouse, we follow two simultaneous assembly lines: one producing the narcotic and the other

[34] DonDada Television, "Alpha Wann—Stupéfiant et noir," YouTube Video, 3:30, July 19, 2018, https://www.youtube.com/watch?v=2UMML7hPDec.

[35] The label has a distribution agreement with Universal Music Group France.

[36] "I'm like hashish: stupefying and black."

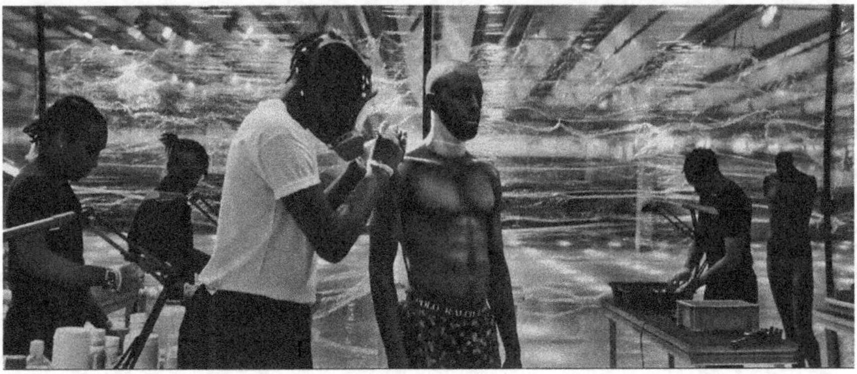

Fig. 4.3 Still from the music video "Stupéfiant et noir"

fabricating the rapper himself. While the workers cut the hashish, they dip a mask and prosthetic hands into a basin of black liquid. They then spray paint a white mannequin with this same resin to transform the plastic form into Alpha Wann's body (see Fig. 4.3). The video flashes through disordered steps in the production line, following the liquid as it percolates in a beaker, oozes into a petri dish, sloshes in a basin, and ultimately coats the plastic and coheres to form Alpha Wann's skin. Through these transmutations, the resin proves an essential ingredient in the creation of both the illicit substance and the performer. Thus, what stands in for blackness gives the commodity its tangible form.

Through viscous resin and filmy layers of spray paint, the music video gives blackness form through visual and tactile sensorial experiences. The video simultaneously follows both the material production of the rapper's blackness as the workers paint on his body and the reproduction of blackness as the liquid soaks into the masks and amputated mannequin hands. The workers involved in this step are all other Black men. As such, these scenes depict collaborative cultural and aesthetic labor behind performances of blackness, as well as the production logics of the cultural industries that rationalize those performances into knowable, reproducible forms.[37] The resin depicts blackness as the essence that transforms inanimate, white plastic into the rapper's corporeal form, and as something that can be replicated *en masse*, even tried on and worn like a mask. The emphasis on the mannequins' initial surface gives whiteness a prominent place in the visual narrative, despite its absence from Alpha Wann's lyrics. Through collaboration with Simper, the mass production of blackness that the music video stages takes on further fetishized

[37] Anamik Saha, *Race and the Cultural Industries*, 172–173.

connotations. The imagery of "Stupéfiant et noir" thus brings Alpha Wann into visibility as a racialized subject in a way that straddles the ambiguity between blackness as something perceived as integral, indissociable from a person, and as an aesthetic form that can circulate and exist apart from the physical presence of Black people.

Alpha Wann directly links his blackness to his musical talent's mind-altering effects. Allegorizing skin as drug resin implicates blackness in the logics of producing and commercializing the musical product. The connection further likens the circulation of blackness through popular culture to the heavy underground traffic of the drug trade. The metaphor throws into relief the idea of race as the essence of cultural products' authenticity and as what secures their affective potential to evoke distinctly racialized, masculine, "outlaw" notions of coolness, even as highly reproducible commodities.[38] In materializing blackness as drug resin, "Stupéfiant et noir" gives race a form steeped in connotations of illicit coolness.

This narcotic form materializes Alpha Wann's person and therefore serves as the substance that makes him his authentic self. The same liquid form preserves a trace of this authenticity as it enables the rapper's reproduction in the form of lifeless mannequins. Under the glare of a spotlight, Alpha Wann stands out amid a seemingly endless supply of clones of his likeness. The image bears a striking resemblance to scenes from HBO's science fiction series *Westworld*, in which decommissioned "hosts," or androids, are stripped of their artificial intelligence and placed in storage. The allusion, as well as the visual contrast between the light hitting the animated rapper and the shadowy replicas, hints at a gap between individual authenticity and the rapper's mass-reproduced form. This gap lays bare the cultural marketplace's promise that the reproducibility of racialized aesthetics delivers the same essence of cool, even once removed from the performer himself.

In giving commodifiable blackness narcotic form, "Stupéfiant et noir" exemplifies the performances of blackness, and Black masculinity in particular, that become appealing and marketable through rap. These performances are multivariate, reflective of what Michael P. Jeffries refers to in the context of American rap as "complex cool," which often simultaneously encompasses challenges to social injustices, appeals to collective racial identities, narratives of criminalized activity, odes to conspicuous consumption, and heterosexist attitudes.[39] In Alpha Wann's own performance

[38] Nicole R. Fleetwood, *Troubling Vision*, 152.

[39] Michael P. Jeffries, *Thug Life: Race, Gender, and the Meaning of Hip-Hop* (University of Chicago Press, 2011), 60.

of masculinity, the rapper tends to recognize vulnerability, or a failure to live up to the desirability of the dominant model of virility in US rap. For example, in "Pour celles," a track off the same album, *Une main lave l'autre*, he acknowledges that, despite his sartorial choices of Timberland boots and oversized T-shirts in his adolescence, he did not appeal to his female classmates: "*Je reste sur le bas-côté malgré ce style cain-ri/L'impression qu'elles aiment les bouffons ou les thugs.*"[40]

Despite recognition of a power imbalance between his own sexual prospects and the Black American masculine ideal, complex displays of heteronormative virility and politicized stances factor into Alpha Wann's posture in "Stupéfiant et noir." The song takes the form of an ego trip intended to show off the rapper's technical prowess. Alpha Wann goes from flexing about how women approach him at parties to echoing calls for justice for victims of police violence, such as Adama Traoré and Théo Luhaka. The rapper further differentiates the high quality of his music from the jarring "noise" of other MCs in terms that perpetuate homophobia and make light of domestic violence: "*J'oublie rien, j'ai pas Alzheimer, y'a des MC homos, c'est un tas d'zamels/ leur musique, c'est du bruit qui m'dérange comme le voisin quand il tape sa meuf.*"[41] These forms of braggadocio expand the astounding effects of Alpha Wann's talent beyond the narcotic metaphor. What is supposed to entice potential consumers is also the familiar, heteronormative performance of Black masculinity often packaged through rap music.

The commercial exploitation of racial authenticity does not leave the performer unscathed. While the illicit aesthetic rests in part on harmful norms, seeing himself become a commodifiable object exposes the rapper to alienation. Once the workers finish painting Alpha Wann's body into its recognizable form, they load him onto a conveyor belt. A sequence of flashes creates disjointed images that give the impression that his body has been deformed under the machine. Only the rapper's mouth, still rapping the lyrics but now transformed into a brick of hashish, continues down the conveyor belt (see Fig. 4.4). The visual emphasizes that an album is a form of material merchandise to be sold, but that it's also the rapper—his person, his voice, and the work of his body—that creates the music and invests it with value.

The image is striking in that it recalls Karl Marx's "impossible" figure of the talking, or in this case rapping, commodity. To illustrate objects' inherent

[40] "I stay on the side despite this American style/Impression that they like clowns or thugs."

[41] "I don't forget anything, I don't have Alzheimer's, there's homo MCs, they're a bunch of fags/Their music is noise that bothers me, like when the neighbor hits his girl."

Fig. 4.4 Still from the music video "Stupéfiant et noir"

absence of value before their exchange, Marx fabulates a commodity's self-reflection:

> Could commodities themselves speak, they would say: Our use-value may be a thing that interests men. It is no part of us as objects. What, however, does belong to us as objects, is our value. Our natural intercourse as commodities proves it. In the eyes of each other we are nothing but exchange-values.[42]

Cultural theorist Fred Moten illustrates what he considers to be Marx's oversight in portraying the commodity that speaks as a purely hypothetical figure through the transatlantic slave trade's historical exchange of human bodies as commodities. For Moten, the object (rather, the Black person treated as object) that speaks, and the sonority and grain of their voice resist dehumanization, throwing into question the kinds of exchanges and forms of value made possible in a capitalist society built on slavery:

> . . . The truth about the value of the commodity is tied precisely to the impossibility of its speaking, for if the commodity could speak it would have intrinsic value, it would be infused with a certain spirit, a certain value given not from the outside, and would, therefore, contradict the thesis on value—that it is not intrinsic—that Marx assigns it.[43]

While Marx contends that value does not belong to commodities themselves, but arises in transaction, the enslaved person's irreducible vocal production

[42] Karl Marx, *Capital*, 37.
[43] Fred Moten, *In the Break: The Aesthetics of the Black Radical Tradition* (University of Minnesota Press, 2003), 13.

shows they have value that precedes their exchange.[44] Moten traces the materiality of this voice and its cry for freedom through Black musical performances in the United States.

The fate of the rapping brick of hashish in "Stupéfiant et noir" offers a more ambivalent take on the question of inherent value and liberatory potential. The image evokes the final step of commercialization as it pushes the transformation from subject to object to the extreme. All that's left of the rapper is his mouth, the source of his vocal production. This last trace of Alpha Wann and his racialized, performative labor is the voice, which will ultimately be digitized, reproduced, and consumed through audio technologies. The paradoxical image of the rapping brick of hashish packages Alpha Wann's technical rapping ability—the quality he is most known for in the French rap scene—as the product's ultimate source of value. The visual ambiguity reinforces the lyrics' conflicting investments in commercial and aesthetic value. In the chorus, Alpha Wann asserts the quality of his album and incites the listener to purchase multiple physical copies: "*Je suis quelqu'un d'peu exemplaire/Ouais j'suis peu exemplaire/Mais l'album est frais, achète deux exemplaires.*"[45] Alpha Wann plays off of the double meaning of *exemplaire* to insist that while his own behavior is not exemplary, nor a model to copy, his album's artistic merit warrants the purchase of two copies of its commodified form.

The emphasis the rapper places on physical album sales and his idiosyncratic, embodied artistic value is crucial in light of the music's ambivalent economic status in the streaming era. In this context, where music appears as a utility always already available on platforms for the consumer's taking, Eric Drott cites a form of "non-commodity fetishism," in which the process depriving music of its value is misrecognized, leaving a view of the musical product as inherently valueless, apart from what it does to bolster the value of the platform itself.[46] While Alpha Wann's incitation to over-consume physical copies may challenge this devaluation, it contrasts with a lucid reflection on the album's commercial prospects in the second verse, "*très peu probable que je tape un platine/Faut que j'fasse un classique.*"[47] The rapper proves aware of his place in the industry as an independent artist known for technical skills that impress his peers, but remain inaccessible to a wider audience. He thus preempts a lack of commercial success in terms of sales and certifications and sets his sights on lasting aesthetic recognition.[48]

[44] Ibid., 10.

[45] "I'm someone who's not very exemplary, Yeah, I'm not very exemplary/But the album is fresh, buy two copies."

[46] Eric Drott, *Streaming Music, Streaming Capital* (Duke University Press, 2023), 96.

[47] "Very unlikely that I'll reach platinum/I've gotta make a classic."

[48] In 2022, *Une main lave l'autre* did indeed reach platinum certification, nearly four years after its release.

As the brick of hashish makes its way down the conveyor belt, "Stupéfiant et noir" manifests the tension between the defiant trace of the rapper's unique, inherent value and the forces of alienation that the market will exert on him. In conflating his musical product with his bodily form, the video exemplifies blackness' disembodied social currency in today's cultural market as an appropriable consumer experience. The final images shift to follow the hashish's perspective as it is placed in a bed of tobacco leaves. Through a cloud of smoke, the camera pans out, and we see a person smoking a blunt, marking the final erasure of the rapper's body as his object form carries out its psychoactive effects. In staging this transmutation, Alpha Wann abandons himself to the inherent risk of alienation in offering his music up for consumption, all while asserting his aesthetic, affective power over listeners. "Stupéfiant et noir" plunges the audience behind the scenes of the commodity fetishism that glosses over and naturalizes the disjuncture between the performer and their reproducible, consumable aesthetic. The performance entwines the creation of sensorial pleasure with the process of making race intelligible, thereby materializing the role of race in securing aesthetic value and insisting upon the racialized artist's place at the center of that transaction.

Gimmicks and Gendered (De)valuations in Shay's "Cocorico"

Through the central metaphor of illicit substances, both PNL and Alpha Wann imbricate their musical product's aesthetic value with the complex performances of racialized masculinities that have proven to be profitable in rap. Before diving into this chapter's final case study, dedicated to Shay, it is important to discuss the entangled relationship between the marketability of racialized masculinities and the devaluation of racialized women's labor in the rap scene, as well as the impact of that relationship on female rappers' representational space. The tropes of social contestation and subversion that became profitable for male French rappers in the second half of the 1990s distinguished themselves from styles associated with femininity and inauthenticity, such as R&B.[49] However, in the early 2000s, rappers and R&B singers often collaborated via a gendered division of labor, with female R&B artists invited to sing the choruses on rap songs. As this type of chorus satisfied the desires of major record labels and radio stations, it played a key

[49] Karim Hammou and Marie Sonnette-Manouguian, "Introduction," in *40 ans de musiques hip-hop*, 34.

role in rap's commercialization.[50] Rap's commercial success, however, did not necessarily translate into professional opportunities, or sometimes even basic credit for the R&B singers in question. In French rap music videos, certain performances of masculinity, albeit to a lesser extent than in the United States,[51] find their appeal through sexualized denigration and ill-compensated labor of racialized, female performers.[52]

Gendered and racialized mechanisms shape the representational space for female rappers in France, particularly around the expectation that they revolutionize the rules of a rap game perceived as inherently heterosexist.[53] Many female rappers active in the 1990s identified less with this ambition, seeing rap instead as a shared form of sociability with their masculine peers or as a means of resisting classist and racist discrimination. However, the longer they stayed in a professional career, the more gender factored into their artistic approach.[54] Female French artists have also navigated gendered judgments of their rapping ability from collaborators and industry professionals, such as the double bind requiring their vocal techniques to avoid being either too masculine to be authentically theirs or too feminine to be authentic to rap.[55]

The national press has typically framed female rappers in France as racialized and defeminized, in line with the *banlieue* girl media figure.[56] Diam's (Chapter 2) phenomenal commercial success in the 2000s left an enduring barometer for talent and mass market appeal, as well as a blueprint for image, since the press emphasized her "tomboy" aesthetic. Underscored androgyny symbolically distances racialized female rappers from the social privileges of the emancipated, feminine, white woman trope, but it comparatively valorizes them against the foil of the hypersexualized "bitch."[57] In the visual economy of French rap and R&B, the "bitch" figure symbolizes the exposed, sexualized bodies of Black women in rap videos. This exposure contrasts sharply with

[50] Rhoda Tchokokam, *Sensibles. Une histoire du R&B français* (Audimat Éditions, 2023), 144.

[51] Mako Fitts, "'Drop It Like It's Hot': Cultural Industry Laborers and Their Perspectives on Rap Music Video Production," *Meridians* 8, no. 1 (2008): 211–235.

[52] Anissa Rami, "Figurantes de clips: les précaires du rap français," *Médiapart* and *The Bondy Blog*, July 23, 2022, https://www.mediapart.fr/journal/france/230722/figurantes-de-clips-les-precaires-du-rap-francais.

[53] Claire Lesacher, "'Le rap est sexiste': ou quand les représentations sur le rap en France engagent une réflexion à partir de l'intrication et de la coproduction des rapports de pouvoir," in *Genre et migrations postcoloniales: lectures croisées de la norme*, ed. Yolaine Parisot and Nadia Ouabdelmoumen (Presses Universitaires de Rennes, 2013), 155–170.

[54] Karim Hammou, "'J'suis une femme d'affaires/viens m'faire le café.' L'articulation des rapports sociaux de pouvoir dans la mobilité sociale des rappeuses françaises des années 1990," *Biens symboliques/Symbolic Goods* 10 (2022), DOI: 10.4000/bssg.935.

[55] Karim Hammou, "'Une exclusion qui ne dit pas son nom?' Les rappeuses face aux appariements genrés des carrières artistiques," *Travail, genre et sociétés* 53 (2025): 55–56.

[56] Marion Dalibert, "Les masculinités ethnoracialisées des rappeur-se-s dans la presse," *Mouvements* 96, no. 4 (2018): 28.

[57] Ibid.

the modest and self-confident North African femininities performed in R&B music.[58] Such performances of Maghrebi female respectability distinguished themselves from the politicized "*beurette*" figure, often fetishized as a symbol of liberated Muslim femininity to contrast the supposed oppression of the Muslim woman who veils herself.[59]

Shay, a francophone Belgian rapper born in Brussels to a Polish father and a Congolese mother, reappropriates the "bitch" insult in her self-styled moniker and title of her first studio album, *Jolie Garce*.[60] She extends its newfound connotations of self-confidence, ambition, and beauty to her fan base, the "Jolie Garce Gang." Describing her own performances of femininity, Shay dismisses the popular conception that, opposed to the United States, female rappers in France cannot be feminine and sexual.[61] She cites her own toiling and eventual success in the French rap scene as proof.[62] In reappropriating and translating the "bad bitch" trope into French, she echoes a repertoire with which American female rappers found success in the 1990s and 2000s. Female rappers in the United States responded to the rise of gangsta rap by strategically reappropriating some of the genre's most misogynistic representations—notably the hypersexualized "bitch."[63] Though Shay acknowledges that her US counterparts inspire her, she does not wish to go as far into the hypersexualized register and detail her personal life in her music.[64] The rapper thus positions herself as an artist charting her own path amid globalized flows of racialized and gendered representations.[65]

Shay takes the value of such representations head-on in her 2019 single "Cocorico," in which she emphatically rejects the exploitative world of the traditional workforce and advocates for proper compensation. Imagining herself far from alarm clocks and commutes, Shay visually inhabits rap's

[58] See Rhoda Tchokokam, *Sensibles*.

[59] Karima Ramdani, "Bitch et beurette, quand féminité rime avec liberté. Représentation du corps féminin noir et maghrébin dans la musique rap et le R'n'B," *Volume!* 8, no. 2 (2011): 14.

[60] While Shay is a Belgian national, the shared language, as well as the concentration of record labels and a large portion of the audience in France mean that francophone Belgian rappers are systematically included under the umbrella of French rap.

[61] "SHAY: son album, le féminisme, Niska, Bruxelles, son frère . . . " *Mouv'*, Dailymotion Video, 28:21, May 14, 2019, https://www.dailymotion.com/video/x78b1q6.

[62] Shay began her career signed to Booba's Universal Music Group imprint 92i (Chapter 1), but left the label following the release of her first album. She remains signed to Capitol, under UMG.

[63] For more on the "bitch" figure in US rap, see Cheryl L. Keyes, "Empowering Self, Making Choices, Creating Spaces: Black Female Identity via Rap Music Performance," *The Journal of American Folklore* 113, no. 449 (Summer 2000): 255–269; Patricia Hill Collins, *Black Sexual Politics. African Americans, Gender, and the New Racism* (Routledge, 2005); Keivan Djavadzadeh, *Hot, Cool & Vicious. Genre, race et sexualité dans le rap états-unien* (Éditions Amsterdam, 2021), 104.

[64] "SHAY," *Mouv'*, May 14, 2019.

[65] For more on how Shay's self-presentation engages with intersectional afro-feminism, see Buata B. Malela, "Le sujet afro-féministe dans le discours de l'œuvre musicale de Shay," *Transposition. Musique et sciences sociales* 12 (2024), https://doi.org/10.4000/12fpv.

kingpin narrative that has often relied on the exploitation of Black women. "Cocorico" aesthetically places questions of worth and work at the heart of the performance, and teases out gendered assumptions behind them. The song explores these dynamics through a repetitive structure, a catchy hook, and heavy use of Auto-Tune—techniques that critics such as those cited at the beginning of this chapter would deride as cheap, unskilled, or overly commercial. The aesthetic category of the gimmick will thus be essential to my reading of Shay's performance. Literary critic Sianne Ngai defines the gimmick as "our culture's only aesthetic category evoking an abstract idea and sense of over-evaluation bound to appraisals of deficient or excessive labor encoded in form."[66] The judgment of a gimmick's poor aesthetic value simultaneously implies an assessment of the work or effort it accomplishes. Either the device tries too hard for minimal pay-off or it's seen as taking a lazy shortcut. By multiplying aesthetic elements that echo the gimmicky or the kitsch, Shay's "Cocorico" foregrounds mechanisms of devaluation at work in the cultural industries and in turn stages the value her racialized and gendered labor can generate.

The music video for "Cocorico," directed by Shay's frequent collaborator Guillaume Doubet, plunges the rapper into the gray-scaled, corporate world.[67] The camera profiles Shay in a packed elevator. The shot focuses on the rapper, whose smaller frame forces the camera to crop out the faces of the other elevator riders, reducing them to anonymous male suits. The track loops through the chorus, "*Cocorico/Se lever tôt/Prendre le métro/Ooo, ooo, ooo/Jamais*,"[68] to accentuate the setting's monotony. Stepping off the elevator, Shay confidently struts through this masculine space as the camera zooms in on the sway of her hips, framing her presence in sexualized terms. The rapper makes her way into a windowless room, where she sits facing a mustached, white, older gentleman in a drab suit. As the chorus tapers off, she allows the man to take a peek at the contents of her briefcase. The briefcase opens away from the camera, but we see his face light up with a warm, gold hue. The image cites a scene from Quentin Tarantino's *Pulp Fiction*, in which hit man Vincent Vega (John Travolta) is bathed in a similar golden light after unlocking the briefcase he and his partner Jules Winnfield (Samuel L. Jackson) have retrieved for their boss. The scene's intertextuality frames Shay's performance through a cinematic style known for its aestheticized, gratuitous, and virile violence.

[66] Sianne Ngai, *Theory of the Gimmick: Aesthetic Judgment and Capitalist Form* (Harvard University Press, 2020), 5.

[67] Shayofficiel, "Cocorico," YouTube Video, 2:51, January 11, 2019, https://www.youtube.com/watch?v=7z_38QNOgHM.

[68] "Cock-a-doodle-doo/Wake up early/Take the metro/ooo, ooo, ooo/Never."

Her assertive confidence and clear distaste for the corporate environment find power and salience through the video's allusion to canonical performances of masculine criminality.

After briefly allowing the man to marvel at its contents, Shay slams the briefcase shut. Her gesture coincides with the transition into the post-chorus, which repeats salary amounts in increasing, one-hundred-euro increments, expressing baffled scorn each time: "*Mille un, mille deux, mille trois, de quoi tu m'parles?*"[69] The camera reproduces the lyrics' call-and-response structure as it jolts back and forth from the businessman, who mouths the different increments, to Shay, who flippantly rejects his offers. The shots become increasingly wobbly as the businessman proves visibly flustered with each refusal. In contrast, the camera holds steady when filming Shay, who rolls her eyes and laughs off the meager sums he proposes. The businessman pulls at his shirt collar and frantically runs his hands through his hair as the camera pans up and down his body. Picking up on his discomfort, Shay readjusts her posture and playfully cups her breasts. The overt emphasis on her sex appeal definitively overwhelms her adversary.

Shay reminds viewers that her body's appeal is never fully divorced from appraisals of her performance's worth. Her gestures therefore create friction with the masculine framing of the scene through the reference to *Pulp Fiction*. Shay takes the virile script and bends the role to fit her femininity and sexuality. The jerky camera movements and exasperated facial expressions serve to ridicule a white, masculine figure that is normally one of power. He is even reduced to effective silence, able only to lip-sync the words produced by Shay's voice. Across the table, the rapper assumes a position of authority and appears calm, composed, and confident in her freedom to reject insulting compensation and even walk away from the negotiating table.

Shay stands up just as the gray office wall behind her topples over to reveal a green pasture. This deliberately visible transition between artificial backdrops eschews more technologically sophisticated editing techniques and gives the false impression of poor production value. Several elements of both the song and the music video infuse questions of production, work, and worth into sonic and visual form. These qualities work within the repertoire of the gimmick and the appraisals of labor, time, and value behind its connotations of fraudulence, untimeliness, and cheapness.[70] For instance, as Shay steps into the pasture, she tosses her briefcase into a pile of soil. In a choppy, stop-action

[69] "1,100 1,200, 1,300, what are you talking to me about?" (And so on and so forth up until 1,900.)
[70] Sianne Ngai, *Theory of the Gimmick*, 23.

Fig. 4.5 Still from the music video "Cocorico"

sequence, her briefcase sprouts into a head of cabbage from which a male fieldworker pulls a green, one-hundred-euro bill (see Fig. 4.5). Mimicking stop-action, a labor-intensive animation technique, the video creates a fast-forward effect that would condense, or even skip over, the rapper's toiling to bear limitless, instantaneous fruit. Through a technique that openly acknowledges its artifice, "Cocorico" stages an alternate relationship between labor and value than the reality of the modern workforce.

These formal elements bring economic anxieties into the performance and conflate them with aesthetic judgments about artistic merit and skill. The oft-repeated chorus, "*Cocorico/Se lever tôt/Prendre le métro/Ooo, ooo, ooo/Jamais*," mimics the rote, programmatic function of an alarm clock. Its lyrical and melodic simplicity, created in collaboration with the Martinican topliner and rapper Meryl,[71] all but ensures that the catchy chorus will seep into listeners' heads with relatively little effort. The nature of the chorus troubles understandings of aesthetic value by instilling doubt as to whether enjoyment of the performance stems purely from its insistent, catchy repetition. Auto-Tune also invokes questions of under- or overproduction, effort, and dematerialized labor. The distortions of Shay's voice alienate the emitted

[71] A topliner is a songwriter specializing in creating vocal melodies for a given track. One of the most sought-after topliners in French rap, Meryl also collaborated with Niska on the previously mentioned "Du lundi au lundi."

sound from the body that produces it and thwart understandings of musical talent as tied to authentic vocal production and mastered technique. The saturated vocal effect risks familiar critiques—primarily from those unfamiliar with the genre or from partisans of the aesthetic trends of rap's earlier eras—that would find the performance inauthentic and unskilled. Auto-Tune further shifts the focus to the producer's labor and technological mastery.

The use of Auto-Tune in "Cocorico" critically works within the technology's gendered connotations. In addition to the affordances of intimacy, Catherine Provenzano argues that Auto-Tune allows men in rap and contemporary R&B to "[lay] claim to the power and legitimacy of abstraction, masculinity, and technology," whereas women's vocal, emotional, and performative labor needs to be heard.[72] The heavy use of pitch-correcting technology on Shay's voice as she sings of her refusal to work for measly pay flouts expectations of audible effort in the feminine singing voice. It further lays claims to the advantages of abstraction and technological mastery associated with masculine Auto-Tuned voices. Producing Shay's voice to sound overtly manipulated also echoes trends in automation and artificial intelligence, which are coded feminine in popular cultural representations and assistant technologies (e.g., Apple's Siri and Amazon's Alexa). However, the raspy qualities of Shay's flow and the production's adjustments imitate the guttural sounds of a rooster's morning caw as she repeatedly calls out "Cocorico!" Bringing her voice closer to a symbol of masculinity (and of the French nation) disrupts the gendered connotations of the automated voice and subtly places Shay in a place of power and command typically afforded to male artists.

The beat, produced by JoATouch, Junior Alaprod, and Le Motif (who is also Shay's brother), uses a digitized banjo to create a folksy atmosphere that embellishes the video's rural setting. Combined with this soundscape, the music video's techniques of exposing the cracks of its production—the collapsing backdrop, the cabbage's rough special effects—contribute to a kitsch and tawdry aesthetic. Shay oversees the cultivation of the newly discovered cash crop as a group of Black male workers toil in the cabbage fields. The video evokes in an absurd way the adage "*les garçons naissent dans les choux et les filles dans les roses.*"[73] The unusual farm setting also deforms the saying, "money doesn't grow on trees," and therefore offers a rebuttal to those who might critique Shay's refusal to abide by the constraints of a salaried job.

The agricultural setting further references cultural adages in featuring a chicken coop in which hens lay golden eggs. A recurring figure in fables,

[72] Catherine Provenzano, "Making Voices," 74.
[73] "Boys are born in cabbage patches and girls in roses."

including one from Aesop and a variation by Jean de la Fontaine, the hen that lays golden eggs warns against impatient greed. In most iterations of the fable, the farmers slice open the hen, convinced it must have even more gold inside. Discovering that, internally, the hen is just like any other, the farmers destroy their potential for long-term wealth in the pursuit of one big payday. Keeping with its kitsch aesthetic, the music video builds upon this reference with a shot of the rapper, now dressed entirely in white, dancing as hens fly across the digitized blue sky behind her. The image echoes rudimentary desktop screensavers, aligning with the gimmick's outmoded form. To add to the performance's play upon inauthenticity, a hen unfurls its wings directly behind Shay, creating an image that mimics the backdrop of the confessional scenes in the popular French reality show *Les anges de la téléréalité* (Angels of Reality TV). Within the context of the fable, the shot solidifies the visual analogy that likens Shay to the source of golden eggs and suggests that she too is a source of unlimited value that the industry does not know how to properly exploit.

"Cocorico" incorporates adages and fables and seemingly takes them at surface value by lending them direct, transparent representations. The video once again reproduces the gimmick's form in this seemingly ready-made, contrived assemblage of cultural maxims and requiring them to work too hard to make a coherent narrative and reinforce the moral of the story.[74] "Cocorico" feigns the naïve credulity of children who are spoon-fed these didactic narratives that respectively oversimplify sexual reproduction or the complexities of labor, investment, and compensation under capitalism. Bringing these sayings to life in such a literal way forces them to over-perform their moral role and ultimately makes their "natural" order of things an easier target for ridicule. Multiplying gimmicky elements allows the music video to explore the profitability of gendered and racialized tropes and the work they do to maintain the status quo.

Beyond allusions to fables, Shay's stylization and bodily performance question the value of gendered tropes in rap's visual culture. Dressed in long, black leather gloves and a matching brassiere, Shay works within the dominatrix repertoire to assume a position of power over the male farmhands in the cabbage patch. Assuming a sexualized form of control, Shay plays with the "bitch" figure and flips the script on the exploitative representations of Black women that often dominate rap's visual culture. Indeed, Shay's watchful eye over the fields reverses the typical gender roles on music video sets. The camera switches from Shay looking up over the rim of her

[74] Sianne Ngai, *Theory of the Gimmick*, 106.

sunglasses to the male workers bending down over their hoes and popping their hips. The camera movement gives the impression that the men fall in line and dance under Shay's gaze, transforming them into traditional "video vixens."

When the harvest of one-hundred-euro banknotes comes in, Shay adopts the kingpin role. She moves through long strands of bills hung up to dry as the men wash—and quite literally launder—the money (see Fig. 4.6). Here again, the video masculinizes a common rap video trope in which women, stripped down to their undergarments to discourage theft, cut and package drugs under the surveillance of male dealers. These scenes make tangible the idea that music video's performances are generating an endless flow of cash before our very eyes. In response to the businessman's paternalism or the simplified adages evoked earlier in the video, "Cocorico" puts at its center typically masculine pursuits of wealth that are met with glorification and financial encouragement in popular culture. The video's repertoire of cinematic and popular culture references attests to Shay and Doubet's familiarity with these representations, as well as the rapper's willingness to inhabit them and make them her own. Her performance draws these racialized and gendered representations into the music video's visual economy, where the seemingly endless harvest of cash cabbages serves as a constant reminder of their commodifiable nature. Interweaving these performances with gimmicky or kitsch forms invites scrutiny of their value, productivity, and the nature of the

Fig. 4.6 Still from the music video "Cocorico"

labor that goes into their creation. It also provokes uncertainties about what happens when these representations become played out and the cycle of consumption breaks down.

"Cocorico" pushes the generation of value to a point of extreme surplus. Gathered around the table, Shay and the fieldworkers sit down to a dinner of fried chicken sandwiches for which the green bank notes serve as lettuce, garnish, and napkins. The visual of the men biting into a money sandwich and delicately patting their mouths with one-hundred-euro bills provides a ludic dead end to the circulation of currency. The video stretches the cash-cabbage trope as far as it can possibly go and touches on key worries in capitalist systems—the underuse or misuse of surplus capital. Instead of injecting the bills back into the larger economy, where they would serve to profit others, they remain in the hands of those who sowed, cultivated, and reaped them. The feast thus breaks down the cycle in which the performers and producers of racialized and gendered cultural representations consume and reinvest in their own images as authentic icons of Black culture to the profit of others.[75]

The fantasized space of the music video posits a world in which the profits of these aesthetic commodities definitively return to Shay. As Shay rotates through the ready-made, masculine kingpin archetype that has structured rap's illicit value, "Cocorico" calls to mind the fact that such tropes have always relied on an under-valued labor pool of Black women. The song and the music video absorb these questions of devaluation and worth into their lyrical, sonic, and visual form. "Cocorico" openly flirts with the gimmick and unabashedly relies on the staples of a commercial rap aesthetic—a repetitive lyrical structure, an insidiously catchy hook, and a heavily Auto-Tuned chorus. These qualities invite criticism along the lines of talent, artistic reflection, and stylistic complexity. "Cocorico" seemingly denies such criticisms any weight by overtly pursuing heavy radio airplay and mass consumption on streaming platforms.

Embracing the formula for commercial success and defending her right to enrich herself from it, Shay incites, and seems to revel in, a crisis of labor, production, and value at the heart of capitalist and patriarchal systems. The end of the music video, however, proves more ambivalent toward the likelihood of this crisis. The last seconds find Shay back in the dull office setting, fast asleep at her desk. In reframing the video as a dream sequence, the final scene injects further elements of fantasy into Shay's gimmicky pursuit of limitless financial gain. As her office worker character awakens and logs onto her outdated desktop computer, she plugs in a headset and returns to work, listening to Shay. The brief, muffled audio of the rapper's subsequent single, "Notif,"

[75] Patricia Hill Collins, "Selling Blackness in a Global Marketplace," *Ethnicities* 6, no. 3 (2006): 310.

leaves her music in an ambiguous position between pleasurable escape for her listeners and the motivational soundtrack for the very devalued, mundane labor she rejects.

In a 2024 interview, Shay contextualizes her aesthetic ambitions and quests for commercial success within audience and music industry expectations of her as the only active female rapper in France with certified albums—gold for 2016's *Jolie Garce*, and platinum for *Antidote*, the album which features "Cocorico."[76] In her solitude in this position, Shay describes the injunction that everything she put out be an instant, unequivocal success, and how that weighs upon the inherent uncertainty of releasing music and testing new styles. This pressure is both external and internal, as she feels the responsibility to do well, because if she fails, it will fuel the view that women don't belong in rap.[77] Shay's reflections on her representational space add nuance to a song like "Cocorico's" assertions of her right to chase financial gain for her performative labor. That pursuit stems from the heightened stakes for commercial success and professional vulnerabilities her position places upon her.

* * *

PNL, Alpha Wann, and Shay articulate the musical experience and the relationship between the artist and the audience through the language of transaction, circulation, and production. The drug trade metaphor lends form to the musical commodity and allows the rappers to express the value and appeal of their craft through the lens of the illicit. Through mind-altering and endlessly profitable narcotics, the rappers make claims about the aesthetic effects of their performances. This relationship moves beyond the debate between mass cultural forms as a means of priming audiences to receive political ideas and mass culture as empty promotion of conspicuous consumption. The illicit intertwines these two functions of the commodity. It evokes both the addictive consumption of the cultural product and the racialized coolness, sexual desirability, and melancholy of marginality that frame its appeal. Reflexively weaving their commentary and assertions of their music's value through this metaphor allows rappers to navigate their complicit positions within the cultural marketplace. The illicit balances rappers' power as the source of the

[76] At the time of writing, Shay's 2024 album, *Pourvu qu'il pleuve*, has been certified gold.

[77] As of 2019, Keny Arkana, discussed in Chapter 5, has reached platinum for her 2006 album *Entre ciment et belle étoile*, and gold certifications for 2008's *Désobéissance* and 2012's *Tout tourne autour du soleil.* Shay's case remains exceptional in the contemporary French rap scene for the relative rapidity with which her releases reach these benchmarks. "Shay, l'interview par Mehdi Maïzi—Le Code," YouTube Video, 39:06, January 19, 2024, https://www.youtube.com/watch?v=H6Ljp2JWUE8.

music's intoxicating effects with their exposure to the insatiable demands of the market that delimit their representational space.

This chapter's close readings challenged the romanticized view that finds stylistic sophistication only in rap that performs oppositional social positions and seemingly eschews commercial success. They demonstrated the aesthetic complexity of performances that engage with commodification and highlight their complicity with the logics of the cultural marketplace. The next chapter will pursue this line of inquiry by critically examining the frame of reception that invests in French rap's oppositionality to mainstream media. Just as rap is embedded in the capitalist cultural industries, the next chapter will demonstrate that rappers also create from a situated position within the larger media landscape. Emphasizing this complicity, I will argue that rappers aesthetically pull from the dominant media logics, thus challenging the view of rap and mainstream media as diametrically opposed in their values and working ideologies.

Chapter 5
Complicit Critiques
Rap's Immersion in the Media Landscape

The return of the critically acclaimed, commercially successful rapper Orelsan[1] in November 2021 with the single "L'odeur de l'essence" ("The odor of gasoline") generated almost instant media buzz and millions of views of the accompanying music video on YouTube. Critical reception framed "L'odeur de l'essence" as subversive social critique. In the pages of *Le Monde,* Stéphanie Binet hailed the song for bringing back an absent tone of denunciation: "the song is a sonic explosion, it takes risks where today's rap does its best to no longer denounce anything."[2] *20 Minutes* homed in on the music video's use of looped television news footage, and particularly that of the Yellow Vests protests, in their presentation of Orelsan's "long tirade" that depicts a "harsh portrait" of French society. The nightly television program *Quotidien* similarly highlighted the video's nod to the Yellow Vests as it featured the song in its pre-electoral coverage.[3] These reactions from the media focused on the rapper's references to political events and repurposing of news footage (perhaps inspired by, or directly pulled from, their own archives) as illustrations of his incisive take on France's polarized state.

Yet, these sorts of media outlets are in fact the principal antagonists of Orelsan's song. The rapper chastises their reactionary logic and responsibility in deteriorating public debate: "*Gamins d'douze ans dont les médias citent les tweets/L'intelligence fait moins vendre que la polémique*"; "*on soigne le mal par le mal et les médias s'en régalent.*"[4] This very criticism fueled media coverage

[1] As of 2023, Orelsan has won twelve *Victoires de la musique*, including the 2022 "Original Song" prize for "L'Odeur de l'essence." He is the third most consecrated artist of any genre in the history of the awards ceremony. His four studio albums have all reached at least platinum or diamond certifications.

[2] "*Le titre est une déflagration sonore, une prise de risques, là où le rap actuel s'évertue à ne plus rien dénoncer*," Stéphanie Binet, "Orelsan: 'Le monde n'a plus besoin de cynisme'," *Le Monde*, November 19, 2021, https://www.lemonde.fr/culture/article/2021/11/19/orelsan-le-monde-n-a-pas-besoin-de-plus-de-cynisme_6102677_3246.html.

[3] Quotidien, "L'odeur de l'essence": Orelsan atomise les politiques et les médias," TF1, 0:53, November 17, 2021, https://www.tf1.fr/tmc/quotidien-avec-yann-barthes/videos/lodeur-de-lessence-orelsan-atomise-les-politiques-et-les-medias-88666750.html.

[4] "The media quote tweets from 12-year-olds," "We fight fire with fire and the media eat it up."

Reflexivity in French Rap. Emily Q. Shuman, Oxford University Press. © Oxford University Press 2026.
DOI: 10.1093/9780197781609.003.0006

of the song. *Quotidien* dubbed their segment "Orelsan takes politicians and the media to pieces," whereas RTL acknowledged not only that Orelsan's punchlines hit at them directly but also that there was some truth to them.[5] The packaging of "L'odeur de l'essence" as an explosive, politicized act of denunciation rests heavily on the feedback loop in which media outlets praise and draw attention to the song precisely for its criticisms of them and for its aesthetic proximity to their own product.

The praise for Orelsan's song from the same outlets he disparages illustrates a media logic that compounds and prolongs attention to a given event or phenomenon through chains of reactions. His own performance imitates this kaleidoscopic effect. Each line of the first verse begins with an imperative to watch or listen as the rapper observes his fellow citizens succumbing to different emotions and impulses:

> *(Re-re-regarde) La nostalgie leur faire miroiter la grandeur d'une France passée qu'ils ont fantasmée/(Regarde) L'incompréhension saisir ceux qui voient leur foi dénigrée sans qu'ils aient rien d'mandé/(Regarde) La peur les persuader qu'des étrangers vont v'nir dans leurs salons pour les remplacer.*[6]

The verse's structure redirects listeners' attention to the emotion—nostalgia, incomprehension, or fear—before the social phenomenon itself. The lyrics filter awareness of xenophobia and religious discrimination through other people's affective reactions to them.

In the music video, directed by David Tomaszewski, a larger-than-life image of Orelsan's face appears on a giant panoramic screen as he instructs the viewer to watch (see Fig. 5.1).[7] The visual injects a dose of self-referentiality, as it nods to Orelsan's 2011 music video "RaelSan," also directed by Tomaszewski, in which the rapper suddenly appears on screens throughout Paris.[8] Donning a black superhero mask over his eyes, Orelsan raps in "RaelSan" to mark a new phase in his career, with several punchlines commenting on the legal battles with feminist organizations over his song

[5] Aymeric Parthonnaud and Steven Bellery, "Avec l'Odeur de l'essence', OrelSan dit leurs 4 vérités aux Français avant 2022," *RTL*, November 18, 2021, https://www.rtl.fr/culture/medias-people/avec-l-odeur-de-l-essence-orelsan-dit-leurs-4-verites-aux-francais-avant-2022-7900097594.

[6] "(Wa-wa-watch) Nostalgia lure them in with the grandeur of a past France that they fantasized about/(Watch) Incomprehension take hold of those who see their faith denigrated without them asking for anything/(Watch) Fear persuade them that foreigners are going to come into their living rooms to replace them."

[7] Orelsan, "L'odeur de l'essence," YouTube Video, 4:44, November 17, 2021, https://www.youtube.com/watch?v=zFknl7OAV0c.

[8] Orelsan, "RaelSan," YouTube Video, 3:29, August 24, 2011, https://www.youtube.com/watch?v=Qu3WOFqoQbQ.

Fig. 5.1 Still from the music video "L'Odeur de l'essence"

"Sale Pute" (Chapter 2). Where "RaelSan" pivots inward toward the white, Normand rapper's artistic trajectory, "L'odeur de l'essence" pivots outward, interspersing Orelsan's omnipresent gaze with images that illustrate the social phenomena described in the lyrics, including climate change, migration, and political polarization. The footage resembles television news or social media content and thus foregrounds the image technologies that mediate viewers' experiences of these forces. The transition between Orelsan's watchful eye and the footage creates a dystopian *mise en abyme* in which the rapper, as a Big Brother figure, watches the viewers watching the phenomena to which he directs their attention.

In this regard, "L'odeur de l'essence" stylistically mirrors the reactive logics,[9] affective economies,[10] and perceptive filters of the media it denounces. The lyrics' repetitive structure generates cyclical intensity, a sense of spiraling out of control that, rather than resolve, Orelsan brings to a fatalistic end in the song's "mic-drop" conclusion: "*On s'bat pour être à l'avant dans un avion qui va droit vers le . . . crash.*"[11] The rapper rides the turbulence of emotional reactivity, braces for impact, and prepares to go down with the aircraft. The explosive release fuels critical praise of the song's incendiary denunciations, but also primes a media system designed to absorb and refuel itself from the force of the impact. In this regard, "L'odeur de l'essence" and its reception illustrate what media scholar Yves Citton has called "mediarchy," or the power of media to constitute us as individuals and collectivities, structure our capacities for

[9] Nelly Quemener, "'Vous voulez réagir?' L'étude des controverses médiatiques au prisme des intensités affectives," *Questions de communication* 33 (2018): 23–41.
[10] Sara Ahmed, *The Cultural Politics of Emotion* (Routledge, 2004).
[11] "We fight to be at the front of a plane heading straight for a . . . crash."

attention, organize our pathways of action, and even render us reliant on media objects for critiques of this very power.[12] Orelsan's performance therefore brings forth a tension between critique, aesthetic proximity to other media forms, and compatibility with the norms of the larger media landscape.

Media, Complicity, and French Rap's Representational Space

The antagonistic role that Orelsan designates to the media faithfully corresponds to long-standing expectations of French rap. Within the genre's representational space, blaming the mainstream media and proposing counterpoints to its discourse traditionally figure among its major themes.[13] To recall Youssoupha's "Menace de mort" (Chapter 2), the rapper asserts that the moral imperative to express rage through rap stems from the mediated social realities and worldviews on offer. These understandings of rap invest heavily in the idea of the music's status as a truly alternative form of expression from the media it critiques. They implicitly rely on the presumption that rap's counternarratives are more transparent and closer to on-the-ground, lived experiences. However, the relationship between rap and media is not purely one of discrete, opposing entities. Since the early 1990s, when national television turned to them as *banlieue* spokespeople, rappers have worked within the media's projection of them, putting the categories assigned to them in productive interaction with their own lived experiences to legitimize certain stylistic devices, points of view, and themes in their music.[14] Instead of raw, uncut experiences, the materials rappers create from are rather the already mediated social realities transmitted through information technologies such as television or social media. Understanding media forms and paradigms not as purely exterior forces to be countered, but as integral aesthetic elements of rap performances, calls for a more nuanced view of rappers' relationships to the media than one of a clash between distinct, opposing systems of norms and values.

By dedicating the final chapter to the media, I come full circle on the role that the national press and television have played in delineating the

[12] Yves Citton, *Mediarchy*, trans. Andrew Brown (Polity Press, 2019), 30, 89.

[13] Jean-Marie Jacono, "Musique et politique: le cas du RAP," in *Arts, transversalités et questions politiques*, ed. Sylvie Coëllier and Louis Dieuzayde (Publications de l'Université de Provence, 2011), 204; Mathieu Marquet, "Politisation de la parole: du rap ludique au rap engagé," *Variations* 18 (2013), DOI: 10.4000/variations.645.

[14] Karim Hammou, *Une Histoire du rap en France*, 141; Karim Hammou, "Rap et banlieue: Crépuscule d'un mythe?," *Informations sociales* 190, no. 4 (2015): 80.

boundaries of rap's representational space around issues of public order and the racialized *banlieue* youth media figure. The media's treatment of rap has greatly evolved since the early 1990s. Despite lingering traces of stigmatizing stereotypes, studies of television and radio show that an unprecedented process of legitimization is underway, in which rap finally enjoys a consequential and professional media coverage commensurate with its economic power in the music industry.[15] Increased visibility expands the back-and-forth relationship between media frames and rap's aesthetic criteria. This relationship can be seen as one of increased susceptibility to the market forces weighing upon media outlets,[16] dependence on the media's modus operandi,[17] or rather uneven, multidirectional flows of production, circulation, and interpretations between media actors and forms.[18] From these various theorizations, I retain both a sense of vulnerable exposure to media logics, narratives, and aesthetic codes, as well as the potential for rappers to channel their signifying power into their artistic projects. As in the previous chapter, which highlighted the ways French rappers self-consciously negotiate their exposure to the forces of commodification at work in the cultural industries, this chapter also questions rap's autonomy, examining its immersion in the larger media landscape and the types of reflexivity that embeddedness might spark.

The media landscape is not just a question of values and logics, but also the technologies, pathways of diffusion, platforms, and algorithms that create and sustain them. In this regard, complicity represents a fundamental, and perhaps insurmountable, obstacle for activist and artistic projects that make use of the same technologies behind discriminatory regimes of representation, visibility, and surveillance.[19] Recognizing complicity as a starting point for contestation reconciles activist strategies with a highly networked world in which subjects enact opposition from within the mediated domain of images, narratives, and products that shape their senses of self, present realities, and imagined alternatives for society.[20] This understanding resonates with rap

[15] Karim Hammou et Marie Sonnette-Manouguian, "Mesurer les processus d'(il)légitimation des musiques hip-hop en France. Méthodologie et premiers résultats d'une recherche en cours sur la période 1990–2019," *Volume! La revue des musiques populaires* 17, no. 2 (2020): 124.

[16] Pierre Bourdieu, *On Television*, trans. Priscilla Parkhurst Ferguson (The New Press, 1996), 56.

[17] Stig Hjarvard, *The Mediatization of Culture and Society* (Taylor & Francis, 2013), 17.

[18] Nick Couldry, "Mediatization or Mediation? Alternative Understandings of the Emergent Space of Digital Storytelling," *New Media & Society* 10, no. 3 (2008): 380.

[19] Ulrike Lune Riboni, *Vidéoactivismes. Contestation audiovisuelle et politisation des images* (Éditions Amsterdam, 2023), 15.

[20] Naomi Mandel, "Toward a New Complicity for New Media," *Comparative Literature Studies* 56, no. 4 (2019): 705–706; Yves Citton, *Mediarchy*, 98; Ingrid Maria Hoofd, "Complicit Subversions: Cultural New Media Activism and 'High' Theory," *First Monday* 13, no. 10 (2008), https://doi.org/10.5210/fm.v13i10.2147.

performances that reappropriate or mirror television news, documentary footage, or social media aesthetics in order to assert their stylistic idiosyncrasies or understandings of rap as an artistic medium. Far from negating rap's potential for critique, this chapter examines how French rappers use aesthetic techniques to highlight their situated position within the media landscape. The following close readings will move from performances that stage media takeovers as a means of securing oppositional stances, to ones that progressively acknowledge that their aesthetic intertwinement with mediated objects leaves their reception vulnerable to dominant media narratives. Through these case studies, an increasingly reflexive, complicit relationship emerges between rap and the media landscape, in which the codes, forms, and ideologies of the latter bolster the aesthetic claims of the former, and in which critique is not inherent but situated within, exposed to, and potentially up for grabs in its media environment.

Radical Posture and Disavowed Complicity in Keny Arkana's "V pour Vérités"

In her 2011 music video, "V pour Vérités," Keny Arkana performs a hijacking of a live news broadcast.[21] Through this fantasized act of sabotage, the rapper stages a struggle for truth and audience attention between herself as spokesperson for an anti-establishment movement and the journalist. This struggle asserts the radical power of her voice, values, and the message that she brings through her music. "V pour Vérités" eschews external referents, just as Keny Arkana refuses to break character, presenting the pirated broadcast as a closed performative space and relying upon television's self-referentiality to pit her authority against that of the newscaster. The performance collapses any distinction between the rapper and the activist and thus uses television as a foil to posit her voice as a transparent, direct line to the public's ears. The self-contained, fictionalized broadcast renders the performance an instance of disavowed complicity, in which the rapper never directly acknowledges her situatedness in the media environment she challenges, yet sources her posture from the logics of television news. Keny Arkana seeks to shore up a politically resistant reading of her performance through a complicit exercise of self-referential truth claims and authority that intertwine with those of the journalist she disrupts.

[21] "Keny Arkana—V pour Vérités (Clip Officiel)," YouTube Video, 4:09, April 23, 2011, https://www.youtube.com/watch?v=eQwxh68kKYc.

The music video begins with an energetic television news theme song and a behind-the-scenes look at the producers and journalists preparing for the broadcast. A red and blue logo for "CF1 news," modeled after the French channels TF1 and CNews, appears on the screen as a white male journalist reads the day's headlines. The newscaster discusses the fictional "Movement for the Living," which leads massive, violent protests that block economic activity in major cities. Just as the journalist turns to his invited guest, a specialist on insurrectional and social movements, static appears on the screen, and Keny Arkana infiltrates the broadcast. She appears dressed in a sweatshirt and bandana from the merchandising for her activist collective, *La Rabia del Pueblo* (The People's Rage). The rapper also wears a black and white keffiyeh, a symbol of Palestinian nationalism and liberation. Through this self-presentation and staging, the French-Argentine rapper from Marseille reinforces her public image as a politically engaged artist and activist for alter-globalization, a movement for international cooperation in the face of neoliberalism's negative economic consequences.

The video cuts to a wide-angle shot that shows a group of similarly dressed activists surrounding her, in a configuration akin to coup announcements, where military or militia leaders declare a regime change in a formal press conference set-up (see Fig. 5.2). The insurrectional staging also creates an intertextual link to her fellow Marseille rappers IAM and their 1998 ode to the city's cultural autonomy, "Independenza." IAM's music video[22] and live performance at the 1999 *Victoires de la musique* took the form of press conference, with IAM clad in black balaclavas and leather jackets in the style of Corsican nationalist movements, whose waves of terror attacks known as *nuits bleues* struck both the island and mainland France in the mid-1970s, early 1980s, and early 1990s. During the live performance, masked men in army fatigues progressively joined IAM on stage, marched up the aisles of the Olympia concert hall in Paris, and tossed propaganda pamphlets into the unsuspecting audience. "V pour Vérités" echoes IAM's staged coup of the awards ceremony broadcast and their declaration of independence from the Paris-based media and cultural industries. In addition to this homage to Marseille's rap history, Keny Arkana's parasitic takeover of the airwaves reinforces her positionality as a rapper-activist and seeks to make her politically dissident voice more salient. In this regard, the music video's insurrectional aesthetic aligns with the

[22] "IAM—Independenza (Clip officiel)," YouTube Video, 3:54, June 12, 2015, https://www.youtube.com/watch?v=UPrpwzpdzWI.

Fig. 5.2 Still from the music video "V pour Vérités"

title's allusion to the 2005 film *V for Vendetta*, in which a masked anarchist takes on a neo-fascist regime with the help of an employee of the state-run television network.

Keny Arkana's posture as a counter-authority and disruptive force sets up an antithetical relationship between her narrative voice and that of the news broadcast. The track, produced by JR Pole Prod, samples the string instruments from the opening television news theme, but increases the tempo and heightens the pitch to accentuate the tone of anxiety. The rapper begins her first verse by parroting the journalist's language to directly address the television audience: "*Mesdames et messieurs, excusez pour la gêne/Coupure momentanée de votre journal télé car notre voix est HS/Besoin d'exprimer notre point de vue aux yeux du pays.*"[23] In referring to the audience as the eyes of the country, she relies on an understanding of television news as a medium for capturing the attention of the masses. The video cuts to scenes of people young and old in the intimacy of their homes, zoned out in front of their screens. They meet the interrupted broadcast with frenzied enthusiasm, surprise, or confusion. These staged reactions portray the rapper's performance as a break—either welcomed or threatening—from the programmatic norm. The music video's staging of direct communication with a diverse audience reproduces the fantasy of primetime television news as a nightly appointment for the entire nation. This fantasy finds itself at odds with the fractured,

[23] "Ladies and gentlemen, excuse me for the inconvenience/Momentary disruption of your nightly news because our voice is out of order/Need to express our point of view to the eyes of the nation."

privatized media landscape at the time of the video's release, as well as its intended site of transmission: online platforms such as YouTube. Keny Arkana's hijacker persona depends upon this idealized notion of direct mass communication to advocate for her alternative worldview and portray herself as a dangerous, disruptive force.

Keny Arkana continues to address the viewers and reassures them that she and her movement are not their enemies, but rather the system's. The video cuts to frantic scenes of the journalist and producers trying to make sense of the pirated stream, offering them up as illustrations of the system that the collective seeks to attack. The image of the powerless producers inverts a common trope in television news, in which the multiplicity of screens and behind-the-scenes glimpses orchestrate a sense of omnipotence, omnipresence, and control. The performance underscores the ways television news cites its own formal qualities—graphics, split screens, illustrative images, invited experts—as evidence of its authority and hold on the real. This formal self-referentiality bolsters the way mass media rapidly process information and transmute their stories into the accepted facts and common-sense premises of both social debate and their own future coverage.[24] The video cuts between the newscaster and the rapper as they compete for this self-fulfilling authority over the established terms of debate. The journalist's voice intervenes between each verse, apologizing to the audience and denouncing the responsible party as a terrorist organization. Keny Arkana resumes rapping each time by imitating his language, but only addressing the audience. The two voices feed off one another and rely on their competition for the airwaves to reassert their claim to the truth and to position the other as a source of disinformation.

The final verse marks the culmination of the struggle, as Keny Arkana explicitly directs the audience not to listen to the broadcaster's characterization of her as a terrorist: "*Pas de débats face aux dégâts/Le mensonge sort de la bouche des médias/Ils veulent nous bâillonner.*"[25] The rapper justifies the act of on-air sabotage as a means of refusing debate and sidestepping direct engagement with the media's lies. The broadcaster's interjections personify the threat of censorship, framing Keny Arkana's performance as an inherent act of resistance. Usurping the broadcast is therefore more about undermining the newscaster's authority and sowing doubt and distrust in his motives and those of governing institutions, than it is presenting evidence-based claims about realities beyond the airwaves.

[24] Yves Citton, *Mediarchy*, 115.
[25] "No debates in the face of damages/Lies come out of the media's mouth/They want to silence us."

Addressing the television audience, Keny Arkana implores them to be suspicious:

> *Mesdames et messieurs, ne croyez pas que les gouvernements vous protègent/Ils se préparent le terreau hors-pair du plus grand génocide/La famine dans les pays riches, répression, mais aussi/Des épidémies, peut-être pour qu'on ait peur de se rassembler/Ou juste pour biznesser un tas de vaccins empoisonnés.*[26]

The rapper's hypotheses as to hidden government plots bring her public address closer to the realm of conspiracy theories. The echo between her voice and that of the newscaster underscores commonalities between these two approaches to information, often thought to be diametrically opposed. Keny Arkana's appeals to the television audience and reassurances that she is not their enemy position her intervention as one of public service, an ideal shared with mainstream journalism. Her oppositional stance also shares with journalism the purported objectives of truth-seeking and checking the power of institutions.[27] This underlying common purpose reinforces the intertwined positions of the rapper and the newscaster within the performance. Both figures' claims to the truth are caught up in one another.

The tension between the two voices of "truth" remains within the fictionalized broadcast and staged protest footage. Unlike Orelsan's "L'odeur de l'essence," which incorporates third-party archives of identifiable, real-world events, Keny Arkana's music video remains detached from referents to a reality beyond the performance. This places her narrative in a similar cycle of self-citation as the televisual discourse she contests. In reproducing the cyclical processing of information and reiterative authority of truth claims from the television news she pirates, Keny Arkana roots the potency of her message and activist posture in the media logic of self-referentiality. Rather than break character or acknowledge this complicity, the rapper uses televisual authority to try to control for any contradiction or efforts to discredit her critique.

"V pour Vérités" thus reinforces Keny Arkana's vision of her music as a vehicle for her values and as a means of representing a broader coalition of the marginalized under global capitalist systems. In the following example, NTM stage a similar broadcast takeover and exploit television's fantasy of getting up close to the real. Unlike Keny Arkana, however, NTM infuse their act of

[26] "Ladies and gentlemen, don't believe that governments protect you/They're laying the groundwork for the unmatched, biggest genocide/Famine in rich countries, repression, but also/Epidemics, maybe out of fear that we'll gather together/Or just to make money off of a bunch of poisoned vaccines."

[27] Kris Fallon, *Where Truth Lies: Digital Culture and Documentary Media After 9/11* (University of California Press, 2019), 160.

hijacking with ironic exaggerations that play up television news' distorted depictions of rappers and the *banlieue.* These distancing techniques allow NTM to reappropriate the material means of the broadcast, situate themselves within its framing, denounce manipulative coverage of rap, and ultimately advance their own understanding of rap authenticity.

NTM: Distorted Media Frames and "On the Ground" *Banlieue* Authenticity

NTM's 1991 hit "Authentik" attests to the early importance of television in presenting rap to French audiences and in negotiating the cultural phenomenon's image and aesthetic merit for the general public. To assert their own vision of authenticity, NTM, one of French rap's trailblazing groups, work within the framing of television news and its investment in rap as synonymous with the *banlieue.* The music video for "Authentik" stages the media's intrigue toward the *banlieue* as the site of unruly energy.[28] Under Pascal Venturini's direction, the video begins with a white, male television journalist adopting the role of a foreign correspondent in NTM's territory. A series of outtakes undermine and ridicule the journalist. He struggles to say the group's name correctly and requests that the cameraman use a low-angled shot to give the segment a "rock n' roll" feel. The reference to rock music further discredits the journalist, as it underscores the extent to which he is out of touch with the "new" hip-hop phenomenon. The journalist seeks a shot that translates the edgy subversion he ascribes to rap. The exposé does not go according to plan, however, as NTM quickly ambush the reporter and confiscate his camera. JoeyStarr and Kool Shen take the means of their representation into their own hands, but crucially preserve the low-angled shot, inhabiting the deliberately exoticized framing that television news projects onto them. NTM therefore elaborate their own concept of authenticity in direct relationship to the modes of representation the mainstream media imposes.

"*Piétinant toutes critiques journalistiques,*"[29] NTM perform their rejection of this distorted image through an increasingly hostile appropriation of the camera. Kool Shen and JoeyStarr enact their lyrics with punches, kicks, and jabs directed at the lens (see Fig. 5.3).

[28] Suprême NTM, "Authentik," YouTube Video, 3:58, https://youtu.be/z_ffMoV-qpE.
[29] "Stomping on all journalistic critiques."

Fig. 5.3 Still from the music video "Authentik"

The visual aesthetics of disorder—the cracked, fragmented lens, upside-down shots—accompany sonic disruptions that make the song difficult to listen to, perhaps even incomprehensible, for the unaccustomed ear. JoeyStarr punctuates the lyrics with abrupt growls and gunshot onomatopoeias in his signature hoarse flow. The track, produced by DJ S, reinforces this energy through the sampled breakbeat of James Brown's "Funky Drummer." The beat also accentuates media fantasies of the *banlieue*'s alien Otherness through sampled guitar feedback from funk rock group ESG's "UFO." "Authentik" pushes the journalist's desired "unconventional" framing to its extreme in an effort to play up their marginality in the eyes of the general public.

Kool Shen dedicates his second verse to the media and denounces their cynical orchestration of his group's false public image—"*Écrivant, expliquant ce qu'ils veulent, ce qui les arrange*."[30] The video also features a freestyled outro in which JoeyStarr, Kool Shen, and their entourage encircle the thoroughly cracked camera lens while the rappers double down on their "radical opposition" to the media's greed, dishonesty, and incompetence: "*Généralement mal informés, ils déforment la vérité/Le business est partout et il faut vendre, voilà*

[30] "Writing, explaining what they want, what's convenient for them."

tout/Sensationnel, à la Une à la pelle!"[31] The beat punctuates this tirade with sampled vocals from Public Enemy's "Don't Believe the Hype," in which the New York natives vent their own frustration toward their falsified image in the press. Against distorted, sensationalized media narratives, NTM own their supposed position as "outsiders," precisely since they are the only ones who represent something *real.*

"Authentik" touches on the complex back-and-forth between themes imposed by television coverage of rap and the genre's internal criteria of authenticity. The performance introduces a slippage between an essentialized notion of "truth" and its aestheticized representations. The journalist emphasizes the fact that he and his crew have made the trek to the *banlieue* to meet NTM in their territory and get "on the ground" coverage in the hopes of attaining the group's true essence. Yet NTM also evoke the idea of the truth and root it in the *banlieue* as a means of dismissing the media's misconceptions. Kool Shen raps, "*la vérité habite la rue en face de chez moi.*"[32] NTM thus portray themselves through their physical proximity to "the street"—a mythicized space that embodies realness. Their self-definition of authenticity therefore relies on a similar link to the *banlieue* as that of the mainstream media's conflation of rappers and the *jeune de banlieue* figure. However, in stark opposition to the media's abstract vision of the suburbs, the rappers emphasize the street as a situated, lived reality for them. In this sense, NTM attest to the crucial role that physical places and spatial imaginaries play in shaping notions of "the real" in rap lyrics and hip-hop culture.[33] The group further introduces an important nuance missing from media discourse—the poeticized nature of their performance. JoeyStarr affirms that he is "*Authentique: oui trop typique, cette saveur aromatique/qui jamais identique reste pourtant poétique.*"[34] His authenticity therefore lies in both his ability to portray a reliable image coherent with his social world and in the possession of an idiosyncratic touch that makes him distinct. This unique essence is ultimately poetic in nature. NTM's rap is therefore anchored in the realm of representation and musical performance, capturing the spirit of the street while also aestheticizing it.

Through its editing techniques, the music video folds the journalistic fantasy of unfiltered proximity to the *banlieue* into its own aesthetic product. The opening sequence gives the impression of raw footage, complete with a series of outtakes manually separated by the journalist tapping his microphone.

[31] "Generally ill-informed, they deform the truth/Business is everywhere and you have to sell, that's it/ Sensational, headlines by the shovelful!"

[32] "The truth lives on the street facing my home."

[33] See Murray Forman, *The 'Hood Comes First*, 3, 9.

[34] "Authentic: too typical, this aromatic flavor/never identical, stays however poetic."

The music video thus stylistically differentiates itself from the polished final segment destined for television broadcast. By preserving these botched introductions, the music video portrays itself as a mistake or accident—a truer glimpse of the *banlieue* that would have ended up on the cutting room floor if the television producers had maintained control. "Authentik" nevertheless reveals editing—images of the frustrated journalist appear amid static between scenes of hip-hop dancers. This betrays its status not as footage "found" on an abandoned videotape, but as an aesthetic product destined for its own broadcast on contemporaneous music video programs, such as Olivier Cachin's *Rapline* (see Introduction and Chapter 2). The lingering traces of the frames, technology, production logics, and referentiality of television news create tension with NTM's aestheticized claims to an authentic real.

NTM's vision of their artistry finds meaning in opposition to the dominant media narrative of rap, and the video perpetually invokes this antagonistic relationship by drawing attention to the materiality of the camera lens. Performing from within the news' exoticized view of the *banlieue*, NTM embed their authenticity in television's fantasies of physical proximity to the social realities it seeks to transmit. NTM capitalize on television's importance as an informational medium to expose the public to this "truer" version of themselves. Whereas Keny Arkana fantasizes a return to broadcast television as a direct line to the public in the era of video-sharing platforms, NTM's "Authentik" engages with a context in which music videos depended on public television channels for diffusion. At this nascent stage in the group's career and in rap's implantation in France, "Authenik" probes the mutual, albeit imbalanced, dependency between rappers who turned to television for exposure, and television programs that needed rappers, often NTM themselves, to serve as the visible faces of social issues in the *banlieue* and of the "new" hip-hop cultural phenomenon. In reflexively foregrounding their complicity with the televisual broadcast, NTM both acknowledge their susceptibility to its exoticizing frames and root the force of their claims to authenticity therein.

"11 septembre": Investigation and Irresolution in the Televisual Archives

In the previous section, both Keny Arkana and NTM take hold of the means of image production and transmission to bolster their truth claims and understandings of authenticity. Their performances emphasize the power of television by drawing attention to the technological apparatuses through which it records and broadcasts its narratives, as well as the journalists who embody its narrative authority. These embodiments of the mainstream media at large feature within the performative space, which allows the rappers to harness the logics of the media they pirate—self-referential knowledge production for Keny Arkana and the fetishization of on-the-ground proximity to the real for NTM—as they formulate their critical stances. While both imagine a hostile takeover of the airwaves, NTM does so with more ironic awareness of their exposure to television's power in framing public perception of them as rappers, and with the more explicit artistic purpose of advocating for rap's aesthetic nature.

The second half of this chapter continues the narrative of progressive reflexivity toward the opportunities and risks that complicity raises for rap's media critique. It does so through performances that, rather than inhabit image and broadcast technologies, take already mediated objects as their primary source material. I contrast two performances from Médine, both of which take media jargon, tropes, and archives as creative raw materials for the rapper and his music video directors, but reflect different stylistic choices and moments in his career. As Médine experiments with new aesthetic codes and as his own place in French media debates evolves, so does his performed self-consciousness of not only the power of his critique but also of its susceptibility to polarized media narratives.

In his 2004 music video "11 septembre," Médine wades through the depths of information to offer his audience a more nuanced narrative of critical global events. During his appearance before the ENS seminar "La Plume et le bitume" (Chapter 1), Médine described the September 11, 2001, terrorist attacks as a pivotal moment in his artistic development. The attacks, the War on Terror, and the ensuing stigmatization of the Muslim community led him to conclude that rapping for the sake of rapping would not be fulfilling, that his music needed a politically engaged dimension.[35] In line with an overarching theme of his music, denouncing falsehoods diffused by mainstream media,[36] Médine's "11 septembre" seeks the remedy for polarized narratives of the attacks and their aftermath. He sifts through televisual archives, reinforcing the medium's self-referentiality, as well as its dual capacity to provoke anxiety and promise resolution. The duality of instability and resolution underlies Médine's meta-reflections on his song's place within the dominant media frames he critiques.

[35] Savoirs ENS, "La Plume et le Bitume: rencontre avec le rappeur Médine," March 28, 2017, 8:09, https://savoirs.ens.fr/expose.php?id=3114.

[36] Marie Sonnette-Manouguian, "Des Manières critiques," 180.

The album *11 Septembre (Récit du 11e jour)* opens with "Ground Zero," a four-and-a-half-minute track comprised entirely of sampled audio from news coverage of the 9/11 attacks. The orchestrated chorus of voice-overs ends with the phrase, "*Rien n'est donc résolu*" ("nothing is resolved"), foreshadowing Médine's investigative position in the album's final, eponymous song. The beginning of Médine's first verse in "11 septembre" alludes to the complementary relationship between the two tracks: "*J'recrache le drame du monde qui nous entoure/Bizarrement le vent souffle en bas des tours/L'envers du décor j'le rapporte sans détour.*"[37] Médine assigns himself the mission of bringing "behind-the-scenes" information or offering a more incisive take than that of the media discourse in the album's introduction. Alexis Delahaye's direction of the music video incorporates a range of media archives that often align with Médine's narration as he moves through histories of war and colonialism in an effort to blur the binaries of victim and aggressor and of good and evil.[38]

Beatmaker Proof loops bagpipes into the track, giving it the ceremonial air of military funerals. The mournful tone retains the ambivalences of Médine's narrative, as it could ring out for both the victims of the terror attacks and those of the US-led War on Terror. The video cuts to footage of George W. Bush just as Médine cites the former US president's characterizations of North Korea, Iran, and Iraq as "rogue states," and flips the label back onto the United States: "*C'est nous les gentils et vous l'État voyou!*"[39] The use of archival footage to support Médine's lyrics mimics a documentary style that reflexively stages the televisual production of knowledge, as well as underscores the intensely mediated nature of the War on Terror.[40] The synced lyrical and visual content reinforces Médine's narrative authority and ability to parse out evidence. Other sequences, however, are not as readily identifiable. The video intersperses scenes of war, corpses, and protests, many of which exceed the song's chronological and geographic focus on the War on Terror. These fleeting allusions create an unsettling, unresolved effect that underscores the necessity of Médine's investigative work.

The televisual frame proves essential to how the rapper positions himself as both a consumer and producer of information. In several scenes, Médine

[37] "I regurgitate the drama of the world that surrounds us/Bizarrely the wind blows below the towers/I'm reporting directly from behind the scenes."

[38] "Médine—11 Septembre (Official Clip)," YouTube Video, 6:04, March 25, 2012, https://www.youtube.com/watch?v=YYsXaQeesqI&rco=1.

[39] "We're the good guys and you're the rogue state!"

[40] Kris Fallon, *Where Truth Lies*, 20.

Fig. 5.4 Still from the music video "11 septembre"

appears in a dimly lit, windowless room with newspaper cutouts tacked to the walls. The decor visualizes the rapper's self-appointed role to investigate and expose the underside of one of the most powerful media and geopolitical narratives of the 21st century. The scene conjures up a common popular culture trope of the dedicated detective working a complex, far-reaching case, and thus invests Médine with a similar sense of authority based on extensive research and a dogged commitment to revealing the truth.[41] The video often cuts to profile shots of the rapper in front of a television screen showing only static, situating Médine on his own wavelength in the pursuit of a nuanced narrative and operating outside the typical paths of distribution as a new rapper and co-founder of the independent label, Din Records. The shadowy, isolated room also draws on the figure of the misunderstood "lone wolf" chasing conspiracies, reinforcing the marginality of his position.

Médine also appears before a wall of television sets that reproduce his image in miniature. The video layers a bright red digital clock over the frame (see Fig. 5.4). The countdown clock is reminiscent of the popular US television series *24* that narrates a day in the life of counter-terrorist agent Jack Bauer as he thwarts national security threats in "real time." The intertextual reference places Médine's "11 septembre" in a post-9/11 moment marked by the spectacular dramatization of Islamic terrorist threat in US popular culture and the routinization of an "ends justify the means" approach to counterterrorism. The reference further pulls from *24*'s relationship to time, terror, and the televisual, which immerses the audience in the experience of the Counter

[41] As discussed in Chapter 2, Sniper also made use of this trope in the music video for "La France, itinéraire d'une polémique."

Terrorism Unit analysts, weaving together myriad pieces of intelligence in the adrenaline rush of crisis and ultimately enjoying the fantasy of a timely, definitive resolution.[42] Médine's "11 septembre" places viewers in a similar position of sifting through the information the music video presents to them. This far-reaching hold on fractured social realities is both a source of anxiety and reassurance for the televisual medium, which offers itself up as the antidote to the disquiet its own representations sow.[43] Médine's narrative position relies on this duality; he both seeks to unsettle the essentialized binaries of dominant media frameworks and to offer up the televisual archives that hold the key to resolution.

However, in the song's final moments, Médine recognizes his inability to fully control the conclusions the audience will draw from his performance. He acknowledges the possibility that, in dredging up these archives, the dominant media framing of the War on Terror will overpower his own contextualization. Médine raps:

> *Et vous verrez on retiendra que ce morceau/On dira de nous que nous sommes fous dans les journaux/D'avoir écrit et fait l'apologie du crime/De se servir de la violence uniquement pour la frime/Distribue, les arguments de ma tribu/Anti-américain est l'étiquette qu'on m'attribue/Non! Le peuple américain derrière Michael Moore/Ce que nous sommes est tellement fort qu'on en oublie notre amour/Dans nos ghettos on nous applaudira/Pour avoir hurlé ce que tout le monde pense tout bas/Mais ils croiront que Ben Laden est un héros/En foulard palestinien, sur les roues de leurs motos.*[44]

The rapper preempts the risk that his performance will fuel the polarized landscape he attempts to navigate. On the one hand, supporters of the War on Terror may interpret his narrative as anti-American rhetoric. Médine suggests that this interpretation will rely on predetermined notions of what he and his community represent in the post-9/11 imaginary—"*ce que nous sommes est tellement fort qu'on en oublie notre amour.*"[45] On the other hand, ghettoized youth may latch onto his critiques of US military history and idealize the

[42] William G. Little, "24: Time, Terror, Television," *Journal of Popular Film and Television* 42, no. 1 (2014): 6–7.

[43] Samuel Weber, *Mass Mediauras: Form, Technics, Media* (Stanford University Press, 1996), 126.

[44] "You'll see, they'll only remember this song/They'll say that we're crazy in the newspapers/For having written and made an apologia for crime/For having used violence uniquely to make money/Distribute the arguments from my tract/Tag me as Anti-American/No! The American people behind Michael Moore/What we are is so strong that they forget our love/In our ghettos they'll applaud us/For having cried out what everyone thinks deep down/But they'll believe Bin Laden is a hero/In a Palestinian scarf on the wheels of their motorbikes."

[45] The line also serves as a prototype for the chorus of 2015's "Speaker Corner" (Chapter 3).

terrorist attacks. In performing his viewpoint from within televisual images, Médine roots his narrative in the medium's fundamental tension between anxiety and resolution. The rapper seemingly acknowledges, however, that the lure of resolution may ultimately overpower some listeners' tolerance for ambivalence and push them back into polarized frameworks. Médine's performance thus problematizes the slippery slope of complicity. Absorbing media objects and logics into his lyrics and music video bolsters his critique and posture as a politically engaged rapper, but leaves a porous barrier between the performance and the very tensions it dissects.

"Don't Laïk": Complicit Visual Languages and Malleable Signifiers

Médine's meta-commentary at the end of "11 septembre" attempts to account for the inherent vulnerability in its use of media referents. He ultimately accepts uncertainty and the chance that dominant narratives will overpower his search for greater contextualization and complexity. The rapper's 2015 single and music video, "Don't Laïk," play with media referents as malleable vessels that can be cohabitated and instrumentalized by contradictory, even diametrically opposed views. The song denounces what Médine considers to be political and media actors' harmful, self-serving manipulations of France's particular vision of secularism, *laïcité*. Over the past few decades, public debate over *laïcité* has increasingly shifted the obligation of religious neutrality from the state and its institutions to individual citizens in public space.[46] Médine confronts this debate and ultimately stages an exorcism to banish its principal participants from the doctrine's metaphorical body.

In "11 septembre," Médine preempts and acknowledges complicity with dominant media narratives. This complicity is both a powerful tool in his performance's urgent search for truth and a potential negative side effect, the result of a fundamental misinterpretation of the geopolitical narrative he pieces together. "Don't Laïk," however, treats polarized interpretations as inevitable. Médine counts upon the audience's familiarity with rigid, discursive binaries and structures the performance around them. This cynicism perhaps

[46] Numerous pieces of legislation and media polemics have targeted Muslim women's signs of religiosity, including the 2004 law banning the hijab in public schools, the 2010 ban on full face coverings, municipal ordinances seeking from 2016 onward to ban the "burkini" on beaches and in public swimming pools, and, most recently, directives from the Minister of Education to ban the abaya. For more on *laïcité* debates, see Jean Baubérot, *Les 7 laïcités françaises: le modèle français de laïcité n'existe pas* (Éditions de la Maison des sciences de l'homme, 2015).

reflects the rapper's increased visibility within the debates he critiques. As discussed in Chapter 1, from the mid-2010s onward, Médine has routinely found himself in the midst of media polemics regarding his affiliations with controversial figures, such as the comedian Dieudonné and Pan-Africanist Kémi Séba. At the time of "Don't Laïk's" creation, his immersion in potentially distorted media coverage was less a distant eventuality to be preempted than an ever-present reality and a possible fuel source for his own aesthetic techniques of provocation.

Médine's stylistic ambitions with "Don't Laïk" reflect this increased complicity with the objects of his critique. In his "La Plume et le bitume" appearance, he cited journalistic jargon as a major influence in his creative process:

> *Je trouve que [les journalistes] ont un esprit de néologisme, des mots valises, des mots synthétiques, des contractions entre des termes que je trouve incroyables, alors que ça fait partie de mes cibles de prédilection, le monde du journalisme. Et ses dérives en tout cas quand il n'y a pas de sourcing, quand il y a des approximations, etc.*[47]
>
> I find that journalists have a sense of neologisms, portmanteau words, synthesized words, contradictions between terms that I find incredible, even though the world of journalism is one of my preferred targets. And its misconduct in any case when there's no sources, when there are approximations, etc.

The rapper acknowledged that while his music often targets journalists, he also marvels at their craftiness with language.

The concise nature of journalistic discourse reverberates in Médine's description of how new subgenres, such as trap music, have influenced his writing style.[48] Trap, marked by crisp, accelerated hi-hats, a slow beat, and 808 drum machines, has encouraged rappers to be succinct with their lyrics, leave more gaps between their rhymes, and opt for less rhythmically complex flows.[49] Médine explained in the seminar how trap beats have altered the content of his lyrics and the way he transmits ideas through them:

[47] "Rencontre avec le rappeur Médine," 51:31.

[48] Originating in the US Deep South, particularly in Atlanta, trap began to take coherent, sonic form in the late 1990s. Over these beats, rappers narrated experiences of dealing drugs out of abandoned (trap) houses. By the early 2010s, the subgenre was a mainstream staple of rap and began to infuse and inspire other regional styles. Shawn Setaro, "How Trap Music Came to Rule the World," *Complex*, February 14, 2018, https://www.complex.com/music/2018/02/how-trap-music-came-to-rule-the-world.

[49] Brice Miclet, "Comment la trap a bouleversé l'univers du rap français," *Slate*, July 4, 2015, http://www.slate.fr/story/102455/trap-bouleverse-univers-rap-francais.

> *Là où j'aurais, sur du boom bap,*[50] *exprimé une idée sur 8 à 12 mesures, équivalent 45 secondes, je l'exprime peut-être en deux phrases sur de la trap. Certains vont parler d'appauvrissement, de novlangue-Georges-Orwell-1984, "la trap ça va mettre fin aux idées," moi je le vois vraiment comme un esprit de synthèse. Ça a précisé mes idées, ça a mieux calibré ma plume dans le sens où ça endigue les éventuelles descriptions qui viennent parasiter le message central. Parfois à force de dialoguer, de broder, de discuter d'un sujet, tu sais même plus de quoi tu parles au final. Viens, on balance une phrase, claire, qui va peut-être résumer le morceau: "Dieu est mort selon Nietzsche/ Nietzsche est mort signé Dieu." On peut arrêter le morceau-là si on veut.*[51]
>
> Where, with boom bap, I would have expressed an idea in 8 to 12 measures, the equivalent of 45 seconds, I can express it in two lines with trap. Some are going to talk about impoverishment, a George Orwell *1984* Newspeak, "trap will be the end of ideas," but I really see it as a spirit of synthesis. It clarified my ideas and better calibrated my pen, in the sense that it restrains descriptions that might parasite the central message. Sometimes by dialoguing, weaving, discussing a subject, you don't even know what you're talking about anymore. Come, spit out a clear line, that might summarize the whole song: "God is dead, according to Nietzsche/ Nietzsche is dead, signed God." We can stop the song there if we want.

Citing a punchline from "Don't Laïk," which features a trap beat by Proof, Médine illustrated how the flow typical of this subgenre has allowed him to synthesize the form of his writing, all while infusing it with a higher concentration of content. The title of "Don't Laïk" marries Médine's critical and aesthetic ambitions, as it blends the adjective form of *laïcité* with a nod to Chicago rapper (and influential figure in drill, a subgenre sonically close to trap) Chief Keef's 2012 hit "I Don't Like." Situating himself within the style and constraints of journalistic language allows Médine to not only articulate his stance toward media debates surrounding *laïcité* and Islamophobia but also assert his adaptability to new musical trends while remaining true to his thematic repertoire and critical intent. These intertwined aesthetic influences, however, play into media logics of succinct language and fetishized events that can be distilled into evocative moments and archetypes ripe for decontextualization and recirculation.

The punchline Médine uses to illustrate the evolution of his writing, "*Dieu est mort selon Nietzsche/Nietzsche est mort signé Dieu*," is indeed emblematic of the song's lyrics, in that numerous lines work within shared

[50] Boom Bap, the style most associated with "conscious" rap and the rap of the 1990s, features a faster tempo and the alternate use of kick and snare drums, usually on beats one and three and two and four, respectively.
[51] "Rencontre avec le rappeur Médine," 41:51.

logics or symbolism between different cultural repertoires. In the first verse, Médine offers streamlined idiomatic play: "*Je porte la barbe, j'suis de mauvais poil/Porte le voile t'es dans de beaux draps*."[52] Here, the recourse to idioms collapses Islamophobic assumptions into the expressions' textural logics. Médine interjects familiar, everyday phrases with images and references to signs that society deems non-normative. The punchline "*Si j'applique la Charia les voleurs pourront plus faire de main courante*" pivots on corporeal imagery of justice present in both the highly mediated specter of Sharia law and the routine jargon of the French legal system.[53] Médine relies on a system French citizens take for granted as a guarantor of security and disrupts it with a reference to a media talking point that seeks to induce anxiety. He takes signs of Otherness or failures to assimilate and highlights their common visual language with elements of quotidian social functioning. The potency of Médine's lyrical imagery lies in hinging together supposed antagonisms and counting on the ready-made emotional weight these concepts carry in media discourse.

In addition to lyrical slippages between supposedly contradictory registers of language, the music video, directed by Florin Defrance, mobilizes the visual referents, essentialized characters, and newsworthy moments that structure televisual and social media debates over secularism and Muslim identities in France.[54] The music video relies on viewers' cultural knowledge to project value onto the people and objects offered up for observation. The lyrics repeat qualities or actions considered "Don't Laïk," while the music video flashes this judgment as a hashtag across the screen, reinforcing the essentializing gesture through social media codes. Filming techniques further seduce viewers into these kinds of categorical perceptions. During the first verse, we see a body holding a red, leather-bound book and dressed in a judge's robe, the head cropped out of the frame. In France, the penal code typically has this color binding. The shot thus invites viewers to invest in their ability to read this person as a judicial representative of the Republic. However, upon closer inspection, the finely stamped cover reads, *Le Noble Coran*—the Noble Qur'an. Seconds later, the video cuts back to the figure, panning up to reveal that the judge also wears a hijab (see Fig. 5.5). The props and the woman's bodily stylizations express meaning in both Republican and Muslim visual languages, undermining the security

[52] "I wear a beard/I'm in a bad mood (literally: I'm of a bad hair)/Wear the veil you're in a right mess (literally: you're in beautiful sheets)."

[53] "If I apply Sharia law, robbers will no longer be able to log complaints with the police."

[54] "Médine—Don't Laïk (Official Clip)," YouTube Video, 3:46, January 1, 2015, https://www.youtube.com/watch?v=E7B45h_lAEk.

Fig. 5.5 Stills from the music video, "Don't Laïk"

of perceptual categories often presented as dichotomous in public debate. The image's suggestion of a Muslim judge administering faith-informed justice—an inherent violation of *laïcité's* principle of State neutrality—fuels the provocative visual parallel.

In a subsequent scene, a person, whose face is obscured by a black veil, dominates the center of the frame. The series of preceding shots may tempt viewers expecting continuity to read this veiled person through the prism of Muslim religiosity. However, a fleeting glitch disrupts this perception, revealing, if only for a fraction of a second, a Black woman in a nun's habit. She eventually turns around, confirming the perceptual trap by displaying a sign that states "no burqa." "Don't Laïk" counts on viewers' immersion in the media landscape and sets them up to interpret these scenes accordingly. If successful in priming this familiarity, the framing renders viewers complicit with the value judgments and categories the music video disrupts.[55]

[55] In this sense, "Don't Laïk" recalls the performances discussed in Chapter 3, including one from Médine, that draw in and destabilize the racializing gaze.

"Don't Laïk" alludes to various events framed around *laïcité* and racial discrimination, yet inscribes these moments in a surrealist aesthetic that challenges television news or social media's logic of engaging with and commenting upon a continuous, self-referential feed of events. The music video's slow panning and rotational shots contrast with the fast-paced momentum of 24-hour television news. Through props and staging, the video distills these events into metonymic objects or phrases that push the media's desire for salient, succinct, shareable stories to the extreme. This technique resonates with short-format video segments, or *zappings*, on French talk shows that mash up notable media events into an easily digestible visual form.[56] It further points to cross-contamination of television and social media imperatives for viral content.[57] The video notably displays a plate of *pains au chocolat*, referencing a media polemic in which right-wing politician Jean-François Copé asserted that a schoolboy had a pastry ripped from his hands by his Muslim peers during Ramadan. The image prompts viewers to harness their media knowledge and pinpoint the reference. The video lays bare the media's circulation of sensational stories by condensing the anecdote even further into one ordinary food item. The conspicuous display further underscores how convergent television and social media frames over-invest significance in the story as indicative of far-reaching social dysfunction.

As a solution to pervasive manipulations of *laïcité* and the discriminatory conceptual categories they create, the performance stages an exorcism of *Dame laïcité*. As a raspy, demonic voice calls out "*ça brûle*" (it burns), Médine calls out the right-wing French politicians and activists that have taken control of *laïcité*: "*Nadine Morano, Jean-François Copé, Pierre Cassen et tous les autres/je vous chasse de ce corps, et vous condamne à l'exil pour l'éternité/Vade retro satana.*"[58] However, amid cries of physical pain, the exorcism does not produce resolution, but preserves lingering unease, as it ultimately recalls *laïcité's* nature as a vulnerable linguistic "body." Médine's lyrics and the music video's aesthetics methodically draw upon the shared visual languages of seemingly diametrically opposed discourses and media tropes. Granting

[56] Pierre Leroux and Philippe Riutort, "Les émissions de divertissement: de nouveaux lieux de valorisation des petites phrases?" *Communication & langages* 168, no. 2 (2011): 75.

[57] Media scholar Henry Jenkins refers to the flow of content and audiences across media platforms as "convergence," *Convergence Culture: Where Old and New Media Collide* (New York University Press, 2006). He has subsequently theorized the built-in logics facilitating sharing of digestible bytes of content across media as "spreadability." Henry Jenkins, Sam Ford, and Joshua Green, *Spreadable Media: Creating Value and Meaning in a Networked Culture* (New York University Press, 2013).

[58] "Nadine Morano, Jean-François Copé, Pierre Cassen, and all the others/I chase you from this body/ and condemn you to exile for eternity/Vade retro satana." Morano featured in Chapter 2 for her role in the Sniper affair.

these antagonisms a central place in "Don't Laïk," Médine and his video director intertwine the aesthetic experience of the performance with the polarization of the media landscape it denounces. The performance collapses the distance that Médine's earlier work preserves between his own narrative and the ideological power of the media frames he combats. In working within the succinct codes of journalistic jargon and trap music, and perhaps in implicitly acknowledging the rapper's own embeddedness in polemical news coverage, "Don't Laïk" turns the normative weight of media narratives into the crux of the performance. In so doing, Médine leaves "Don't Laïk," at the level of interpretation, as exposed as the metaphorical body it exorcises.

In a tragic twist of fate, Médine released the music video for "Don't Laïk" a mere six days before the deadly terrorist attack on the offices of satirical magazine *Charlie Hebdo.* In the fraught aftermath, media commentary accused the rapper of artistic irresponsibility in his diffusion of words, images, and emotions saturated with rage and glorifications of "the worst."[59] Throughout Médine's cyclical experiences with controversy, including the polemic that would eventually lead him to cancel his concerts at the Bataclan, journalists, political figures, and far-right militants routinely pull one punchline from "Don't Laïk" to the surface: "*Crucifions les laïcards comme à Golgotha.*"[60] Albeit for ideological reasons that exceed the scope of its aesthetic form or journalistic source material, "Don't Laïk" anchors Médine's place in polarized media debate in ways that have left a significant mark on his creative process and posture.[61]

In a 2020 radio interview with *France Culture's* Marie Richeux, the rapper cited "Don't Laïk" as an error in his artistic ambition to "plant a debate, use that debate for provocation, but then quickly defuse it afterwards."[62] He locates the error in the music video that, in his view, piled an extra layer on top of the song's aggressive tone. Richeux pushes back on this disarming objective: "yes, but all while placing mines. You do see the ambivalence?"[63] Médine recognizes

[59] Vincent Cespedes, "'Islamo-racaille': le droit de haïr?" *Huffington Post,* January 8, 2015, https://www.huffingtonpost.fr/vincent-cespedes/-islamo-racaille-le-droit-de-hair-charlie-hebdo_b_6434686.html.

[60] "Let's crucify the *laïcards* (die-hard, anti-religion proponents of secularism) like in Golgotha." Chapter 1 discussed the cancelation of Médine's concerts at the Bataclan, a site of the November 2015 terrorist attacks, as well as his musical responses to that cancelation.

[61] It is not only virulent media debates that have left consequential marks on Médine. The rapper has been subject to death threats from the Islamic State, as well as a far-right, domestic terrorist plot targeting him and other public figures for assassination.

[62] "*Poser un débat . . . et de provoquer par ce débat-là, mais aussi de désamorcer, de déminer très vite derrière.*" Marie Richeux, *Par les temps qui courent,* "Médine: 'Pour moi, une idée qui n'est pas dangereuse, n'est pas une idée,'" *France Culture,* October 16, 2020, https://www.radiofrance.fr/franceculture/podcasts/par-les-temps-qui-courent/medine-pour-moi-une-idee-qui-n-est-pas-dangereuse-n-est-pas-une-idee-7049689.

[63] "*Oui, mais tout en minant, vous voyez bien l'ambivalence?*"

in turn that he manipulates explosive substances, but as an artist. This precision echoes an earlier distinction in the interview, in which he opposes expectations that he organize his rap around arguments and sources as would an intellectual, instead affirming his artistic prerogative to remain evasive, muddled, and to solicit ambivalent emotions, even disgust. Throughout the interview, Médine acknowledges and defends an inherently risky strategy of complicity with volatile debates as a means to transform his representational space. In this sense, "Don't Laïk's" complicity with the form and antagonisms of the media discourse it challenges engenders its inherent susceptibility to interpretations that are overdetermined by those same debates, and, in the rapper's own view, brings about its eventual failure.

Eurotrap: Authentic Inauthenticity and the Ambivalences of Decontextualization

Up until this point, this chapter has analyzed performances that foreground their situatedness in the media landscape in order to carve out oppositional stances. They engage in a form of complicity in which they rely upon dominant media logics, all while portraying themselves as alternatives to existing media narratives. Over the course of the chapter, these performances have shown increasing reflexivity toward their complicity with the targets of their critique, as well as increasing awareness of their susceptibility to the weight of dominant media frames. In the final case study, the rapper Vald inverses this logic of oppositionality by exposing his performance to a seemingly infinite number of interpretations as a means of questioning rap's critical vocation. Born Valentin Le Du, Vald grew up in the Parisian suburb of Aulnay-sous-Bois, first in the housing projects of *La Cité des Mille-Mille*, and then in a single-family home. He has released six studio albums to great commercial success, including multiple diamond certifications. His single "Eurotrap," off his first album *Agartha*, takes up media logics of decontextualization and circulation to reinforce a posture rooted in detached humor. His irreverence seeks an "alternative" stance within the rap scene by flouting the legitimizing power of socially conscious positions.

The nonconformist intent of "Eurotrap" hinges upon the song's bridge, which reappropriates the same Ärsenik lyric that, as discussed in Chapter 2, Youssoupha's "Menace de Mort" transforms into a rallying cry for rappers who have faced legal battles: "*Qui peut prétendre faire du rap sans prendre position?*"[64]

[64] "Who can claim to rap without taking a stance?"

Ärsenik's original line decisively brushes off anyone who would claim to rap without taking clear stances. Vald, however, adapts the adage to ponder making apathetic refusal to take anything seriously the core of his posture: "*Comment faire du rap sans être dissident?*"[65] Vald's nasal interpretation gives the question a taunting tone, as if he were mocking those who think rap must be radical, and offering up his song as proof that the alternative is possible. In a 2017 appearance on Thierry Ardisson's primetime talk show, *Salut les Terriens*, Vald explained the bridge as "a kind of funny phrase in a song that's really not radical. But I for sure find it interesting to question rap's antisocial commentary."[66] The rapper simultaneously commits to the lyric's humor and to its more serious intent to pose an existential question to those who would see firm social stances as a prescriptive rule for rap. The bridge frames "Eurotrap" as a potential model of dissidence toward this very rule.

Vald provides meta-commentary to reinforce the paradoxically serious unseriousness of his song's supposed innovation within French rap. His introduction sets up the aesthetic project in tongue-in-cheek tone: "*C'est le moment où on va enregistrer 'Eurotrap,' voilà. Pour l'moment, ça n'vous dit rien, vous n'connaissez pas la trap de viking, encore. On va faire d'la trap de viking, mec.*"[67] The claim to be inventing a new subgenre alludes to the existing style of Afro Trap, popularized by French rapper MHD in the 2010s. While Afro Trap blends West African musical styles with trap music, the beat for "Eurotrap," produced by Seezy, pulls from the highly synthesized sounds of Eurodance and rave techno. Vald exaggerates a Nordic lineage and alludes to his blond-hair and blue-eyed physique to nickname his invented subgenre, "Viking trap," placing whiteness at the center of this fictional musical trend. The introduction plays off Afro Trap's global success and musical heritage to reinforce and racialize the performance's irreverent take on a notion of rap authenticity rooted in dissidence. Vald's approach diverges from previous models of white French rappers, many of whom navigated their social privilege and place within hip-hop culture to articulate anti-racist critiques and solidarity with their multiracial, working-class neighborhoods.[68] It does, however, align with

[65] "How to rap without being radical?"

[66] "*Une phrase un peu marrante dans un morceau qui n'est vraiment pas dissident. Mais c'est sûr que je trouve intéressant de remettre le rap en question sur son propos antisocial,*" Les Terriens, "L'invité OVNI: VALD, le Eminem français," YouTube Video, 6:38, September 23, 2017, https://www.youtube.com/watch?v=_uCYeC_o-OY.

[67] "It's the moment when we're going to record 'Eurotrap', voilà. For the moment, that doesn't mean anything to you, you don't know Viking trap yet. We're going to make some Viking trap, man."

[68] Chong J. Bretllion, "'Ma Face Vanille': White Rappers, 'Black Music', and Race in France," *International Journal of Francophone Studies* 17, nos. 3 & 4 (2014): 421–443.

an international repertoire of white rappers using humor to preempt and deflect critiques of inauthenticity.[69]

The festive, kitschy beat anchors the song's non-response to the existential musings of its own bridge, as the chorus simply repeats the injunction to, "*Turn up dans le club!*" The lyrics reference sex, drugs, and money in an ode to meaninglessness, with abrupt shifts in topic serving as the only constant in the song's structure. Vald makes this dedication to randomness plain with self-conscious commentary in the third verse: "*Je pper-ra des phases qui n'ont rien à voir entre elles.*"[70] The declaration coincides with the beat dropping back into synthesized Eurodance after a brief piano interlude, playing with the expectation of profound, emotionally resonant lyrics to accompany such a melody. As a closer look at the music video and a televised performance of "Eurotrap" will show, this commitment to absurdity, decontextualization, and unseriousness when earnestness is most expected takes root in niche Internet codes and televisual infotainment aesthetics. Instead of acknowledging openness to interpretation as a potential point of vulnerability, these performances make that susceptibility their driving force.

On January 6, 2017, Vald performed "Eurotrap" on the nightly news and talk show, *Le Grand Journal*.[71] *Le Grand Journal* launched in 2004 on the premium cable channel Canal+. Emerging after the end of public-only broadcasting in France, Canal+ sought to appeal to a socially liberal upper- to middle-class audience with cosmopolitan tastes. *Le Grand Journal* played a key role in the channel's ambitions with its mix of more argumentative reporting, interviews, entertainment segments, and parodic sketches, such as *Les Guignols de l'Info*, a mock news segment with puppet versions of French broadcast journalists and politicians. Taking cues from *Le Grand Journal's* specific blend of the serious and the playful, and acknowledging the performance's timing—two weeks before Donald J. Trump's investiture as the 45th President of the United States—Vald appeared dressed as the then-president-elect. The rapper performed from behind a lectern featuring a promotional poster for his new album in the style of Trump's campaign posters, replacing "Make America Great Again," with the chorus of "Eurotrap,"—*Turn up dans le club.* The album's release date, January 20, coincided with that of Trump's investiture. The *Grand Journal* performance therefore inserts itself into the media agenda and the

[69] See Justin A. Williams, *Brithop*, 119–142; Antti-Ville Kärjä, "Humour and Parody as Strategies of Securing the Ethnic Other in Popular Music," in *Migrating Music*, ed. Jason Toynbee and Byron Dueck (Routledge, 2011), 83–88.

[70] "I'm rapping bars that have nothing to do with one another."

[71] Le Grand Journal, "Eurotrap—Vald—Le live du 06/01—Canal+," YouTube Video, 4:01, January 8, 2017, https://www.youtube.com/watch?v=PVSTd2GzpjY&t=9s.

perceived gravity of the political moment to create tension with its lyrical ode to nonchalance.

Vald stands behind the lectern in a suit jacket, Trump's signature bright red tie, and a heavily bronzed face. Side-angle shots reveal the rapper to be in his boxer shorts, reinforcing the performance's clownish nature. The staging makes a transatlantic allusion to Eminem's 1999 music video for "My Name Is," in which he impersonates then-President Bill Clinton giving a speech while receiving oral sex from a Monica Lewinsky lookalike. As Loren Kajikawa has argued, "My Name Is" introduced Eminem to the mainstream and implicitly responded to charges of racial inauthenticity by parodying whiteness through nasal vocal interpretation, "square" turns of phrase, a rhythmically rudimentary backbeat, and a music video imitating canonical TV sitcoms such as *The Brady Bunch*.[72] The reference nods to routine comparisons between Vald and Eminem in the French media, and reinforces an in-joke with fans familiar with Vald's boredom with the parallel. Underneath this layer of irony, however, the allusion reinforces the link between white masculinity, authenticity, and vulgar humor at the heart of "Eurotrap" and Vald's self-positioning in the French rap scene.[73]

The televised performance echoes the music video for the single, which places Vald before a green screen and invites fans to download the video and submit their own compilations to his record label. The televised performance's editing makes this reference apparent by alternating between frontal shots that project various images onto the green screen behind Vald, and wide-angle side views that show the performance's artifice. The staging also nods to the aesthetics of *Le Grand Journal* itself, whose studio features a giant screen onto which the program projects archival images, press snippets, or polling results as "gotcha" proof to confront invited politicians with their ambiguous or contradictory positions.[74] Vald's performance mirrors this aesthetic by filling the green screen with b-roll footage of the New York Stock Exchange, protests, refugee camps, and melting glaciers (see Fig. 5.6). Each image carries geopolitical significance, yet within the performance remains purely gratuitous and detached from the song.

[72] Loren Kajikawa, *Sounding Race in Rap Songs*, 127–133.

[73] Comparisons to Eminem are not purely imposed on Vald. In 2011, he released the freestyle "Holehe" over the beat of Eminem's "Without Me," which featured a punchline that prefigures "Eurotrap's" mock aesthetic innovation: "*Et quand certains font dans la Négritude, j'fais la maigritude/Naturel et blanc comme apéricube*" ("And when some do it in the Negritude tradition, I do skinny-tude/Natural and white like cheese cubes.")

[74] Patrick Amey, "Du traitement journalistique des acteurs politiques dans *Le Grand Journal*," *Questions de communication* 24, no. 2 (2013): 68.

Fig. 5.6 Stills from the television program *Le Grand Journal*

The form recalls the music video for Orelsan's "L'odeur de l'essence" that opened this chapter. However, whereas Orelsan seeks to embolden his social critique by coopting the media's modus operandi of soliciting reactions to its own content, Vald makes no effort to draw focus to the images behind him. On television news, these clips would accompany urgent stories, but the reuse of the music video's green screen format portrays them as one of an infinite number of possibilities alongside fan compilations, diluting their politicized weight, evidentiary value, and journalistic incisiveness. The hollowed-out images work within and extend the existing remove between traditional news programs and *Le Grand Journal's* blend of irony, parody, and critique. As such, it holds up a distorted mirror to the ambiguous, and often apolitical effects of such programs, which use media footage, quoted text, or snippets of speeches to ridicule politicians less for their policies than for their personality traits or breaks with decorum.[75] Vald's performance inserts itself in *Le Grand Journal's* tautological logic of parodying media representations of politics to reinforce his own humor's ideological ambivalence.

Vald's assertion of a deeply disengaged rap through green screens and b-roll footage also resonates with the authentic inauthenticity of Internet memes, in which witty truths and perspicacious social observations come through repurposed content and stock photographs.[76] Vald's diluted, randomized use of geopolitically significant and emotionally heavy images particularly echoes the practice of online trolling. Trolling's dissociative brand of humor lies in exploiting the most absurd and sensational details of an event, disconnecting them from their emotional context, and circulating them to increasingly incongruous settings.[77] This fetishization of the grisliest elements of a disastrous event or tragic testimony marks a parallel between Internet trolls and an economic model of television news built on sensationalized stories.[78] Vald's performance makes these complicit logics apparent by using footage of various crises to legitimize his quest to rap without having to care about anything, thus underscoring the dissociation that stems from television news' heavy-handed use of these same images.

The trolling logic creates a tenuous barrier between absurd and sardonic humor, which becomes the most salient when background dancers emerge—seemingly from within the screen itself—dressed as reptiles, invoking the historically antisemitic and anti-immigrant conspiracy theory of lizard people controlling humans. The dancing reptiles use moves inspired from the video game *Fortnite*. Within the confines of the game, dance moves enable players to celebrate their kills and humiliate their opponents, but through their use in reaction videos or "stiches" on YouTube and TikTok, enable young, white men to mock social media content of women or other marginalized young people discussing mental health or emotionally charged issues.[79] The privileged

[75] Patrick Amey, "Du traitement journalistique," 74; for discussions of the apolitical ridicule of Anglophone satirical news programs, see Nicholas Holm, *Humour as Politics. The Political Aesthetics of Contemporary Comedy* (Palgrave Macmillan, 2017), 65.

[76] Jay Owens, "Post-Authenticity and the Ironic Truths of Meme Culture," in *Post-Memes: Seizing the Memes of Production*, ed. Alfie Brown and Dan Bristow (Punctum Books, 2019), 105.

[77] Whitney Phillips, *This Is Why We Can't Have Nice Things: Mapping the Relationship Between Online Trolling and Mainstream Culture* (The MIT Press, 2015), 30.

[78] Ibid., 86.

[79] Wayne Marshall, "Social Dance in the Age of (Anti-) Social Media: Fortnite, Online Video, and the Jook at a Virtual Crossroads," *Journal of Popular Music Studies* 31, no. 4 (2019): 7.

social positions entangled with these social media aesthetics and codes of humor align with Vald's fictionalized aesthetic innovation of "Viking trap" as an alternative to Afro Trap. Just as "Eurotrap" lays claim to apathetic rap as a niche alternative to the existing, politically engaged musical offering, it replicates social media logics of trolling, as well as the normative positions of whiteness and heterosexual masculinity enveloped therein.

As coincidence (or market ruthlessness) would have it, Vald performed during *Le Grand Journal's* last weeks on the airwaves. The show's cancelation came after years of free-falling ratings and clashes over political ideology, journalistic values, and business models following right-wing media mogul Vincent Bolloré's takeover of Canal+ in 2015. In addition to a revolving door of hosts and constant shifts between unencrypted and encrypted broadcasts, Bolloré's arrival exacerbated the already apolitical effects of the program's ironic critique by axing segments, such as *Zapping*, deemed too politically dissident.[80] The billionaire's vision for the media group would privilege the populist model of depoliticized, spectacular clashes of opinion of *Touche pas à mon poste!* on sister-channel C8.[81] Helmed by polemical host Cyril Hanouna, *Touche pas à mon poste!* faces frequent criticism for veering into heterosexist vulgarity.

While not endowed with clairvoyance regarding *Le Grand Journal*'s imminent fate, Vald nevertheless slips ad-libbed commentary into his performance that impetuously acknowledges the state of French televisual offerings. In the recorded song, the rapper owns up to his phoned-in lyrics by imitating an automated answering system: "*Vous avez demandé le refrain, ne quittez pas/ Un conseiller va vous prendre dans quelques minutes.*"[82] In the televised performance, Vald answers the phone as if Hanouna were calling: "*Ouais, Baba, le patron du PAF? Ouais, on se voit lundi, j'suis dans une émission sérieuse, là.*"[83] Using Hanouna's self-imposed nickname as the boss of the French audiovisual landscape, Vald plays up the opposition between the two programs and underscores *Le Grand Journal*'s comparative seriousness. The rapper's commentary reinforces his dissociative approach in response to the show's political tone, all while underlining an affinity with its more ideologically ambiguous and profitable counterpart.

"Eurotrap" self-consciously espouses the media logics of decontextualization and dissociative humor to position Vald's irreverent posture as subversive

[80] Jérôme Lefilliâtre, "Et Bolloré acheva le 'Grand Journal,'" *Libération*, February 13, 2017, https://www.liberation.fr/futurs/2017/02/13/et-bollore-acheva-le-grand-journal-de-canal_1548200/.

[81] See Claire Sécail, *Touche pas à mon peuple* (Éditions du Seuil, 2024).

[82] "You've requested the chorus, remain on the line/An agent will take your call in a few minutes."

[83] "Yeah Baba, the boss of the French audiovisual landscape? Yeah, we'll see each other on Monday. I'm on a serious show here."

within the rap scene. Vald posits his authentic inauthenticity not only through a larger web of media practices, images, and narratives, but in opposition to the ways other rappers position themselves vis-à-vis this material. "Eurotrap" thus points to a further evolution of the complicit relationship between rap and media, in which immersion in the latter's norms becomes the starting point to dissent from the very expectation that rap be critical at all. Beneath its nonchalance, "Eurotrap" puts forth a vision of rap that presents disinterest in denouncing social injustices as a radical gesture. It is in this sense that Keny Arkana's "V pour Vérités" and "Eurotrap" serve as mirror-like oppositions that bookend this chapter. Whereas Keny Arkana's entanglement with television news' self-referential authority fuels her activist posture and efforts to ensure the audience's adhesion to her political message, Vald presents his performance as an unmoored, floating signifier in the media landscape, making susceptibility to multiple interpretations and recontextualization the driving force of his dissent from the injunction to take stances in his rap.

* * *

The complicit position from which this chapter's case studies critique their surrounding media landscape opens space for the logics of those media to shape rappers' postures. The friction between alternativeness and immersion requires a move beyond a purely subversive, oppositional relationship between rap and media, toward a relationship of complicity. Recognizing complicity does not deny the divergent, critical viewpoints rappers may share through their craft, nor the various aesthetic techniques they employ to do so. Rather, complicity acknowledges that this divergence stems from *within* the media systems they may oppose. It is from that implicated position that these performances derive meaning and strength, but that situatedness is also what makes the reception of their critique vulnerable to the narratives, frames, and affects that circulate in the broader media landscape. The lens of complicity leaves room for rappers to reflexively experiment with that strength and susceptibility. They create from a place of recognition of the role media forms play in framing and diffusing their music, which can lead them to explore alternatives to that fraught relationship, play off its antagonisms, or challenge the very presumption of its oppositionality.

Conclusion

Validé, Nouvelle École, and the Futures of French Rap's Reflexivity

In 2020, Canal+ launched the fictional series *Validé.* The series, created by director Franck Gastambide, follows the rapid ascent to stardom of a young talented rapper, thanks to his "validation" by a veteran artist. While fictional in nature, the series cast rapper Hatik in the lead role of Apash. The driving force of the series is the consistently blurred line between fiction and the reality of the French music industry. As such, throughout his spectacular trajectory, Apash encounters rappers, music video directors, journalists, and tastemakers from the real-life French rap scene, including Kool Shen from NTM, Fred Musa, and Laurent Bouneau of the radio station Skyrock, and Cyril Hanouna of *Touche pas à mon poste!* (Chapter 5). As its name suggests, *Validé* offers constant reflection on the relationship between a given rapper's creative abilities and the numerous trials of artistic legitimation, authentication, and commercial validation they face from the music industry, the media, their peers, and even their neighborhood.

This reflection, however, results in the writers jamming into one season nearly all of the possible hurdles a rapper might face—lingering consequences of past involvement in the drug trade and violence in their native *banlieue*, spectacularly mediated clashes with other artists, and politicized polemics due to songs deemed "anti-France." Season 2, which features the rapper Laeti in the role of Lalpha, multiplies obstacles through a gendered lens: single motherhood, domestic violence, sexism in the music industry, and the non-consensual leak of intimate photographs. In its exaggerated effort to pack in as many clichés as possible into a single artist's trajectory, *Validé* incorporates meta-reflections on the possibility for novelty in a cultural landscape in which rap is an increasingly mainstream fixture. This commentary often occurs through both explicit and thinly veiled references to what real-life rappers have already done in their songs, music videos, or publicity stunts. Apash shies away from blocking the highway for a music video since Sofiane has already done so, while the character Mastar hesitates before filming in the Naples housing project where the Italian organized crime drama *Gomorrah* was set, since PNL

Reflexivity in French Rap. Emily Q. Shuman, Oxford University Press. © Oxford University Press 2026.
DOI: 10.1093/9780197781609.003.0007

and SCH have already played out that décor. Despite the gauntlet of challenges thrown at each rapper, they rise to the occasion through strokes of individual genius in which they channel those obstacles into seemingly even more impressive creative and promotional choices—whether it is a freestyle over a beat destined for another rapper, an impromptu concert outside a rival artist's prison cell, or a music video that reclaims leaked private photos. In making the tension between tired tropes and artistic innovation the motor of the series, *Validé* reflects on the established contours of rap's representational space.

In their review of the series, *Libération* notes the heavy use of clichés and risk of "déjà vu" for the audience. The review highlights these hackneyed plot points as a means of elaborating a more general critique of the contemporary rap scene: "Isn't French rap itself, at least in its most exposed subgroup, a ball of clichés?"[1] The reviewer's leap from the television show's scenario to the French rap scene itself reinforces the porous boundaries between the two in the series. In an interview with the same critic, the rapper and actor Sam's, who plays Mastar, the veteran mentor-turned-rival of Apash, recognizes the intentionally self-critical relationship between *Validé* and the rap scene it models itself after. For Sam's, "French rap, a family withdrawn in on itself, needed to see itself through a fiction one millimeter away from reality."[2] In his view, *Validé* holds up a much-needed mirror to French rap's insular creative community. In its desire to bring the "French rap family" face to face with the inner workings of their professional world, the series contributes to the complicit relationship between rap performances, cultural criticism, and representational expectations explored in the preceding chapters. The series' narrative structure and its web of characters microcosmically reproduce the kinds of self-aware creativity I have explored throughout this book. *Validé* is less a festival of clichés than a meta-reflection on those clichés. It fictionally stages the ways French rappers reflexively experiment with the legitimizing mechanisms and conventions of reception their music faces.

The advent of series such as *Validé* extends even further the final chapter's reflection on rap's immersion within the larger media landscape and complicity with the latter's logics. *Validé* exemplifies this situatedness by intertwining its fictional narrative of a rapper's ascent to stardom with a *mise en abyme* of the radio programs and primetime talk shows that frame French rappers' public visibility. The final chapter demonstrated how rappers pull the

[1] *"Est-ce que le rap français lui-même, du moins sa frange la plus exposée, n'est pas une pelote de clichés?"* Ramès Kefi, "'Validé'. Des flows et des bas," *Libération*, March 20, 2020, https://www.liberation.fr/images/2020/03/20/serie-valide-des-flows-et-des-bas_1782500/.

[2] *"Le rap français, famille repliée sur elle-même, avait besoin de se regarder au travers d'une fiction à un millimètre du réel,"* Ibid.

creative strength and salience of their postures and aesthetic experimentations from the mainstream media they are often expected to oppose—whether it's television's self-referential authority in the case of Keny Arkana, journalists' pithy language in the case of Médine, deliberately exoticized frames for NTM, or ideologically unmoored irreverence for Vald. *Validé* broadens this complicity by enveloping rap's capacity for self-reflection and innovation within the codes of a television series. The series accentuates Apash and Lalpha's abilities to one-up their critics and peers through encounters with television drama's preferred tropes and narrative arcs, including suspense, larger-than-life villains, violence, and romantic tension.

The release of Netflix's French rap competition show, *Nouvelle École*, modeled after the American predecessor *Rhythm + Flow*, adapts this reflection on the pursuit of rap stardom, the possibility for creative innovation, and established frames of reception to reality television. In *Nouvelle École,* the jury the jury—featuring Shay, Niska, and SCH in Seasons 1 and 2; SCH, Aya Nakamura, and SDM in Season 3; and SCH and SDM in Season 4—evaluates "up-and-coming" rappers through a series of challenges that range from freestyles, rap battles, music videos, and guest verses on some of French rap's biggest hits.[3] The trials, such as battles and cyphers,[4] challenges the jury likely never had to engage in on their own paths to discovery, reflect an almost mythologized view of hip-hop culture and the creative abilities needed to prove a rapper's worth. Battles for territory and prestige between breakdance crews, rappers, or DJs were key aesthetic and social practices in early hip-hop culture. While battles and cyphers certainly occur within the contemporary French rap scene, they represent relatively underground practices, and thus do not entirely reflect current paths to success in the music industry, nor do they always match the contestants' range of styles.[5] These challenges, however, align seamlessly with the competitive format of the show, as well as reality television's thirst for (supposedly unscripted) drama.

Nouvelle École's modus operandi lies in the tension between the contestants' artistic ambitions and the show's mission of finding the next rare "gem," or *pépite*, that will prove a profitable investment for its 100,000-euro reward.

[3] Despite the premise being the search for the "new school" of French rap, the contestants vary in age, and some have already released EPs or albums prior to appearing on the show.

[4] A cypher is a collective freestyle, with rappers, beatboxers, and/or break-dancers gathered in a circle performing together and feeding off each other's creative energy.

[5] A notable exception is the battle rap series, "Rap Contenders," which debuted in 2010. The format launched Alpha Wann (Chapter 4). For more on rap battles and open mics in France, see Cyril Vettorato, " 'Ça va être un viol': Formes et fonctions de l'obscénité langagière dans les joutes verbales de rap," *Cahiers de littérature orale* 71 (2012), DOI: 10.4000/clo.1492; Séverin Guillard, " 'To be in the place': les *open mics* comme espaces de légitimation artistique pour les scènes rap à Paris et Atlanta," *Belgeo* 3, no. 3 (2014), DOI: 10.4000/belgeo.13025.

Reviews of the first season found the jury's critical eye lacking in this pursuit and contextualized that flaw both within French rap's difficult relationship with rigorous, aesthetic critique from music journalists,[6] and within the complex balance between criticism and entertainment specific to reality talent competitions.[7] The jury's evaluations illustrate the friction between the search for a rapper who will propose something refreshing and a rapper who checks the tried-and-true boxes to go far not only in the competition, but in the market for French rap. In Season 1, Elyon, a contestant whose eccentric gimmick is to perform in a bathrobe, debuts a somber music video in which he raps over a piano melody about mental health struggles and suicide attempts.[8] During the jury's deliberations, Niska finds Elyon's song a bit too "crazy" and counsels him to "stay a bit normal." Marseille rapper SCH, who was visibly moved to the brink of tears by the performance, retorts that Elyon is an "artist" and compares him to Stromae, whose acclaimed music blurs the lines between rap, electronic music, and pop. The discussions oppose Niska's normative—albeit vague—preference for rap that stays in its lane to SCH's legitimizing notion of the elevated, experimental artist.

The struggle between fidelity to expected codes and aesthetic risk-taking continues as the jury moves on to the contestant Fresh, whose music video primarily features him in the concrete décor of parking garages or basements, bathed in the red and blue of police car lights.[9] SCH describes the music video as standard, but "they're standards that we really like." Fresh goes on to win the competition. The Season 2 finale, however, replays this debate to different ends. After Yuz Boy's live performance, which opened with a female griot singing in the Malinke language, SCH wonders if the song could have staying power in the top streams on Spotify. When Shay firmly expresses doubt in that regard, SCH muses, "but doesn't France need an artist like that to raise the bar for rap?"[10] Niska, for his part, wonders if there is market demand for this kind of song, admitting that they will never know for sure, but following what is generally released, likely not. Before deciding to crown Yuz Boy the winner, SCH adjudicates that, while Yuz Boy doesn't have the format, he does have DNA, recognizing the candidate's artistic idiosyncrasy.

[6] Shkyd, "Les médias musicaux n'osent plus critiquer les albums de rap français," *Yard*, March 2, 2018, https://yard.media/medias-musicaux-france-critique-albums-rap-francais/.

[7] Brice Miclet, "Pourquoi j'ai détesté 'Nouvelle École', le nouveau télé-crochet rap de Netflix," *Slate*, June 14, 2022, http://www.slate.fr/story/229179/pourquoi-deteste-nouvelle-ecole-tele-crochet-rap-francais-netflix-niska-sch-shay.

[8] Netflix France, "ELYON—À la recherche CLIP OFFICIEL (Nouvelle École—Netflix)," YouTube video, 1:43, https://www.youtube.com/watch?v=WLVpC_RCueQ.

[9] Netflix France, "FRESH LAPEUFRA—Drama Queen CLIP OFFICIEL (Nouvelle École—Netflix)," YouTube Video, 1:31, https://www.youtube.com/watch?v=KvMHSuUVeQI.

[10] "*Mais est-ce que la France n'a pas besoin d'artiste comme ça pour élever le propos du rap?*"

These discussions transpose the debates over standardization and commodification I examined in Chapter 4 to a reality competition program whose avowed priority is return on investment for a global giant of content production like Netflix. In Chapter 4, I posited the relationship between aesthetic complexity and commodification as one of imbrication, rather than mutually exclusive opposition. *Nouvelle École* represents an accelerated and staged version of the reflexive commentary on market appetites I found in the works of PNL, Alpha Wann, and Shay. The show constantly holds the financial reward over the contestants' heads and incites them to showcase their talents with this monetary value in mind. In Chapter 4, the metaphor of the drug trade articulated the relationship between perceived alterity and rap's commercial appeal. In *Nouvelle École,* the aesthetics of the different contestants' performances are interlaced with the conditions under which they are produced. They therefore speak to the imperatives of performative labor specific to reality competitions, including time and material constraints, the desire to be idiosyncratic to retain attention, expectations of emotional divulgence to create a salient personal backstory, and the delicate balance between risk-taking and anticipating the jury's tastes. The meta-commentary on the creation, commodification, and reception of French rap in *Nouvelle École* and *Validé* extends this book's focus on the relationship between reflexivity and stylistic exercises. As television programs, these two cultural productions are in the unique position of representing both exterior forms of critical commentary that may influence rap's creative processes and stagings of aesthetic self-consciousness in their own right.

Some contestants have responded through music to the criticism they received on *Nouvelle École.* These releases garner significant attention when the candidate's dismissal has sparked heated debate among viewers. After the first season's debut, the rapper Ben PLG, whom Shay quickly axed during the audition segment (for not seeming sufficiently motivated), released a music video addressing his rejection from the show—"Mauvaise nouvelle" ("Bad News"). The video, directed by Anastasia Salomé, begins with Netflix's signature *dun-dun* intro, and stages Ben PLG in the parking garage setting where he auditioned, rapping before a motionless Shay lookalike and camera crew.[11] When the beat drops, Ben PLG hoarsely cries out, "*J'suis l'meilleur rappeur de la Terre (Ouh)/Si j'le pense pas, qui va m'sortir de la merde? (Qui?).*"[12] As the video progresses, he moves in circles through the building's labyrinth of hallways,

[11] Ben_plg, "BEN plg—Mauvaise nouvelle (prod. Murer)," YouTube Video, 3:49, January 15, 2022, https://www.youtube.com/watch?v=85d4uAx9nvs&t=6s.

[12] "I'm the best rapper on Earth/If I don't believe that, who will get me out of this shit?"

returning each time to the scene of the rejection as the chorus repeats, "*Encore une mauvaise nouvelle.*" The lyrics attest to Ben PLG's determination to forge ahead despite these waves of bad news, but they also sketch out the somber themes and disenchanted mood that make up the Tourcoing native's artistic signature. At the end of the video, Ben PLG finally locates his vehicle in the maze-like garage. The camera pauses on the side mirror, showing a doubled version of the rapper beginning his *Nouvelle École* audition. The *huis clos* frames exposure to rejection and defiant critique of Shay's judgment as the performance's creative core.

Nouvelle École's second season saw another much-debated rejection, with audiences turning this time on Niska's aesthetic discernment. In the Parisian auditions, Niska, accompanied by Zed (former member of the group 13 Block), evaluates freestyles from two male rappers from the 18th arrondissement, Slkrack and Bayass, as well as from Nayra, a rapper from the Saint-Denis suburb. By the time Nayra enters the room, the two men have already performed, and the judges treat her to an awkward welcome. After Nayra politely greets her competitors, Zed—stumbling over his words—wonders if, as a woman, she isn't uncomfortable in this situation. When she immediately asks why that would be the case, Zed is taken aback at her retort—"*Ah ouais, t'as du répondant.*" (Ah yeah, you're quick off the mark.) Niska, in schoolboy fashion, laughs, slaps his friend's arm, and observes, "*elle s'est fâchée*" (she's mad). Not willing to let them off the hook, Nayra inquires, "*Ça change quelque chose?*" (Does that change anything?), to which the answer is a sheepish no. In deliberations, Zed ends up counseling Niska to take Nayra, convinced that there is an audience for her style of music, even if it does not appeal to their personal tastes. However, despite repeatedly observing that Slkrack and Bayass propose exactly the same type of rap, Niska "follows his instinct" and takes both to the next round instead. The choice exposed him to numerous critiques on social media when the show aired.

In the weeks following the season's premiere on Netflix, Nayra released the single "Le nord." The chorus affirms her attachment to both her North African roots and Saint-Denis neighborhood, located north of Paris and affectionately dubbed the "*le Grand Nord*" by local legends NTM.[13] Nayra sings: "*J'perds pas le nord/Invasion sonore j'suis dans le thème.*"[14] The track, produced by Khalil Cherradi, loops in traditional Moroccan chants to create a galloping rhythm. In addition to the beat, the song crystallizes the rapper's multi-faceted artistic identity as she flows from French to Arabic. The music video, directed

[13] The nickname appears frequently on the group's 1993 album, *J'appuie sur la gâchette* . . . .
[14] "I don't lose the north/Sonic invasion I'm on theme."

by Samuel Colin, stages Nayra getting a touch-up of her traditional Amazigh tattoo—a straight line connecting her mouth to her heart symbolizing integrity.[15] "Le nord" interlaces these elements with the artist's ode to her fighting spirit when faced with closed doors. This ode takes the form of a defiant, scholastically themed punchline at *Nouvelle École's* expense: "*Fuck les règles j'compte pas mourir avec mes rêves/Ils ont fini par prendre des notes je leur ai fait croire que j'étais l'élève.*"[16] The punchline is not the only subliminal strike toward the reality competition show. In the final moments, the group of women who encircle Nayra throughout the video step away to reveal the rapper's retort to Zed—*Ça change quelque chose?*—on the wall behind them. The message takes the A4 white paper and thick black lettering style of the feminist collages that, in recent years, have covered French cities with slogans targeting the nation's alarming rate of femicides. Nayra looks back at the collage and casts a cheeky glance toward the camera before walking out of frame.

More than straightforward reactions to rejection, these two performances represent deliberate strategies to capitalize on the visibility *Nouvelle École* affords to announce—or reannounce—their artistic universes to a wider audience. The performances draw upon and stylistically integrate not only the show's competitive format but also its difficult relationship to rigorous, aesthetic judgments and struggles to accommodate an eclectic range of styles. *Nouvelle École*'s affordances and shortcomings therefore become potential motors to propel rap's dynamic relationship between stylistic experimentation and critical expectations.

My attention to reflexivity, complicity, and representational space throughout this book has highlighted the creative ambitions of those involved in the production of French rap music and its visual culture. The aim has been to challenge portrayals of rap as a fundamentally misunderstood, maligned musical genre caught up in an imbalanced struggle against political ideologies or purely subject to the music industry's whims. My approach has demonstrated the entanglement of rap's aesthetic qualities with judgments of the genre's value. I have argued that idealized notions of rap's autonomy are untenable in light of the genre's situatedness in the forces of commodification at work in the cultural industries, as well as within the logics of the larger media landscape, of which *Validé* and *Nouvelle École* represent the next frontier.

[15] NAYRA, "Nayra—le nord," YouTube Video, 3:00, June 15, 2023, https://www.youtube.com/watch?v=hbPHulk0OZ0; K. Gloire Savula Mbongo, host, "Nayra, mythologie arabo-amazigh," Backstory (podcast), September 2023, https://open.spotify.com/episode/06AT5pJ6mHRxvweZdk4GAW?si=8bd6f7911a184eb2.

[16] "Fuck the rules I don't plan on dying with my dreams/They ended up taking notes, I made them believe I was the student."

The complicity between French rap and the social forces that condition its reception is not inherently disqualifying, nor morally compromising, as certain connotations of the word may suggest. This folded togetherness instead sparks much of the aesthetic innovation and complex postures that drive the genre forward.

Investments in rap's political import risk glossing over this stylistic complexity when privileging arguments about the music's end results, such as societal interventions achieved through visibility and representation. In Chapter 3, I argued that scholarship highlighting French rappers' public visibility as an inherent challenge to Republican colorblind ideology asks rap to do a tremendous amount of work to solve far-reaching political problems. I further argued that this lens portrays race as a pre-established reality that French rap reflects, rather than a construct resulting from a social and perceptual process that rap's aesthetic qualities can shape. In close readings of performances by Médine, Abd al Malik, and Casey, I explored how these rappers draw in and entangle the racializing gaze with rap's stylistic conventions in ways that highlight the interpretive work behind racialization. Each performance's emphasis on circulating, decoding, and unsettling markers of alterity troubles racialization's dependence on visible, intelligible performers of difference. Médine, Abd al Malik, and Casey thus make exposure to and potential complicity with the racializing gaze the crux of their aesthetic techniques, anti-racist stances, and connections to their audience.

In the political and legal spheres, racialization propels belief in the capacity of French rappers' lyrics to enact harm and incite violence against the Republic. In Chapter 2, Tandem, La Rumeur, Sniper, and Youssoupha staged rap's penalization, as well as their own typecasting as ideal culprits therein. These rappers balanced a fine line between aestheticizing the legal parameters of their cases and limiting their representational space to counteraccusations and defensive subject positions. I have argued in Chapter 1 that frames of reception intended to aesthetically validate rap, notably the comparison to the literary, are conditioned by normative scripts of creative genius, as well as the fixed doses of alterity and artistic detachment that determine solubility within France's pantheon. I examined how MC Solaar, Médine, and Booba acknowledge the weight of France's literary patrimony in evaluations of rap music, as well as the limits to the creative privileges associated with the venerated figure of the author. I pointed to the various postures these rappers adopt toward the literary, ranging from reverence for MC Solaar, to provocative appropriation for Médine, to performed disinterest and outsourced consecration for Booba. In highlighting the range of self-positioning strategies toward the boundaries of inclusion in France's literary patrimony, Chapter 1 threw into relief the role of image and tone that underlie the critical focus on French rap as text.

Recognizing French rap's aesthetic ambiguities is critical for pushing back against rigid definitions of its representational space. It is also critical for understanding representational space not as something rap is subjected to, but something rappers and all the actors involved in the creation of rap performances co-construct with critics, industry professionals, audiences, and even political figures. My analyses have demonstrated this complicit co-construction by attending to the reflexivity with which rappers treat various conventions of reception and cultural expectations of them, from the selectively validating frame of the literary, to mechanisms of penalization that invest in rap lyrics' performative power, to the representational task of performing race, to the standardizing effects of commodification and finally to the expectation of media critique. In the preceding chapters, these frames of reception became fuel for stylistic experimentation and the crux of how rappers articulate their postures. These frames of reception have also maintained porous boundaries between rap and other aesthetic forms, social power dynamics, and industry logics. Such porous boundaries ultimately leave the interpretation of French rap performances susceptible to the weight of those external forces.

Through reflexivity at the level of aesthetics and artistic posture, many French rappers recognize and rework their ambivalent, complicit relationship to the dominant frames of reception their music faces. Rap's dependence on and immersion within the logics of the cultural industries and larger media landscape create points of vulnerability, but also opportunities for artists to harness and instrumentalize these mechanisms for their own aims. Through such reflexivity, rappers intervene in their representational space, seeking to expand, renew, shift, or indeed shore up its borders. While this book has examined the effects of such reflexivity within performances themselves, they do not stop at the limits of the recorded track, concert, album cover, or music video. Rap performances may play off conventions of reception, but their interpretations remain open to collective acts of meaning-making from fans, peers, industry professionals, critics, and politicians. Though, as I have argued, reflexivity enables French rappers to negotiate that susceptibility, it cannot ultimately prescribe or control reception once the music is put out into the world.

As *Validé*'s dramatized universe suggests, the narrative of the self-aware virtuoso who succeeds through a seemingly inexhaustible, innate ability to innovate and one-up their peers still holds a great deal of weight in popular representations of rap, even as they gravitate toward other media. The reflexive relationship between conventions of reception and aesthetics continues to be a driving force in the creation of French rap music, as well as in the genre's self-image. However, filtered through the codes of reality competition television, *Nouvelle École* points to the ambivalence of reflexivity and the risk that it serves to preempt, neutralize, and integrate criticism. While there is a risk that wishy-washy decisions will alienate the audience, controversial choices also generate buzz for the show. This buzz can serve the strategies of rappers rejected from the competition, but it also enables the show's formula.[17] In Season 2, the producers and judges absorbed critiques into the show's metanarrative, cyclically promising viewers that this time, they would be more demanding of the contestants. The jury also slips in self-aware comments as to the lack of women in the cast, with Shay adamantly refusing that they save the last woman standing from elimination purely to fulfill a quota. With attention to their distinct genres, *Validé* and *Nouvelle École* nevertheless beg the question—what happens when rap's taste for reflexivity comes to serve an idealized self-image and the status quo?

In this regard, I can only join calls for sustained, constructive criticism and audience expectations for ambitious, impactful, and entertaining music. Indeed, studies of French rap fans show levels of reflexivity toward their listening practices, tastes, and values that rival those of the artists themselves. Women and members of the LGBTQ+ community in particular navigate moral dilemmas in their consumption of the music, rooting intersectional feminist critiques in aesthetic and political arguments that situate their judgments from within the world of French rap.[18] As such, these fans refuse moralizing, delegitimizing judgments seen as external to rap for their associations with whiteness and bourgeois socioeconomic status.[19] As seen in Chapter 2, such moralizing and discriminatory judgments have notably fueled French rap's penalization. This kind of situated critique aligns with the hip-hop feminism Joan Morgan and other feminist and queer voices in hip-hop studies have long called for, one "brave enough to fuck with the grays," and navigate gaps between feminist praxis and the pleasures found in rap.[20] As a scholar who became a fan through my work, I have sought to adopt a

[17] Both Ben PLG and Nayra featured in Netflix's 2025 documentary, *Nouvelle École: Et après? Réussir ou mourir* (*Nouvelle Ecole: After the Beat*), which follows former contestants' trajectories after their appearances on the show.

[18] Emmanuelle Carinos Vasquez, "Le son qui tue," 377.

[19] Ibid.

[20] Joan Morgan, *When Chickenheads Come Home to Roost: A Hip-Hop Feminist Breaks It Down* (Simon & Schuster, 1999), 59; Gwendolyn D. Pough, *Check It While I Wreck It: Black Womanhood, Hip-hop Culture, and the Public Sphere* (Northeastern University Press, 2004); Aisha S. Durham, *Home with Hip Hop Feminism. Performances in Communication and Culture* (Peter Lang, 2014).

similar degree of self-consciousness as to the expectations that often underlie academic treatments of French rap and of popular culture more broadly. Questioning these often-politicized assumptions throws into relief the intertwined relationship between aesthetics and social power dynamics, not only in the creation of popular culture objects but also in the consumption and criticism of them.

In calling this book *Reflexivity in French Rap: More Than a Mirror to the Republic*, my objective was twofold. First, I aimed to nuance the notion of rap as a reflection of its environment by attuning to its complicit and reflexive strategies of working within various expectations projected onto it. Second, my objective was to expand critical discussions of French rap beyond the genre's relationship to Republican ideologies and institutions by integrating its complex back-and-forth with media logics, literary patrimony, and industry imperatives. Rap's taste for reflexivity allows it to both push against and re-entrench its representational space. Reflexivity is something that draws the audience in, creating space to form community and to rest on shared knowledge. Reflexivity can further engender critique, producing situated knowledge about social power dynamics and colonial histories. It is also a source of aesthetic pleasure and appreciation. The close readings that make up this book left me more deeply aware of the nature of my work as a critic and of the enjoyment I derive from the music and its visual culture. Each reading and rereading brought new subtleties to appreciate and thus left me with firmer belief in French rap's proven capacity for stylistic experimentation and artistic reflexivity that will continue to shape its evolution.

Audiovisual Corpus

Abd al Malik. "Allogène (j'suis un stremon)." *Scarifications.* 2015. Gibraltar/ Le Label.

Abd al Malik. "Allogène (j'suis un stremon)." YouTube Video, 3:04. September 22, 2015. https://www.youtube.com/watch?v=MSHcJgup4Z4.

Alpha Wann. "Stupéfiant et noir." *Une main lave l'autre.* 2018. Don Dada Records.

DonDada Television. "Alpha Wann—Stupéfiant et noir." YouTube Video, 3:30, July 19, 2018. https://www.youtube.com/watch?v=2UMML7hPDec.

Alpha Wann. "Pour celles." *Une main lave l'autre.* 2018. Don Dada Records.

Ärsenik. "Boxe avec les mots." *Quelques gouttes suffisent.* 1998. Warner Music.

Ben_plg. "BEN plg—Mauvaise nouvelle (prod. Murer)." YouTube Video, 3:49. January 15, 2022. https://www.youtube.com/watch?v=85d4uAx9nvs&t=6s.

Le bitume avec une plume. "Le Bitume avec une plume/Teaser." YouTube video, 1:04. November 24, 2018. https://www.youtube.com/watch?v=_K4JJVM40fM&t=60s.

Booba. "Le Duc de Boulogne." *Ouest Side.* 2006. Tallac Records.

Booba. "Temps mort 2.0." *D.U.C.* 2015. Tallac Records.

Casey. "Créature ratée." *Libérez la bête.* 2010. A-parté.

CASEY Anfalsh. "Créature ratée (Clip Officiel)." YouTube Video, 4:38. January 17, 2020. https://www.youtube.com/watch?v=Fa7nN1YXQv0.

IAM. "Red, Black and Green." *De la planète Mars.* 1991. Delabel.

"IAM—Independenza (Clip officiel)." YouTube Video, 3:54. June 12, 2015. https://www.youtube.com/watch?v=UPrpwzpdzWI.

Keny Arkana. "V pour Vérités." *L'Esquisse 2.* 2011. Because Music.

Keny Arkana. "V pour Vérités (Clip Officiel)." YouTube Video, 4:09. https://www.youtube.com/watch?v=eQwxh68kKYc.

Lunatic. "Le crime paie." *Hostile Hip-Hop.* 1996. Hostile Records.

Lunatic ft. Mala. "Hommes de l'ombre." *Boulbi 9.2 Spécial Boulogne Vol. 1.* 2000. 45 Scientific.

MC Solaar. "À temps partiel." *Qui sème le vent récolte le tempo.* 1991. Polydor Records.

MC Solaar. "Bouge de là." *Qui sème le vent récolte le tempo.* 1991. Polydor Records.

MC Solaar. “À dix de mes disciples.” *Prose combat.* 1994. Polydor Records.
MC Solaar. “Temps mort.” *Prose combat.* 1994. Polydor Records.
Médine. “11 septembre.” *11 septembre, récit du 11e jour.* 2004. Din Records.
Médine. “Code Barbe.” *Arabian Panther.* 2008. Din Records/Because Music.
Médine. “Code Barbe (Official Clip).” YouTube Video, 4:00. https://www.youtube.com/watch?v=XWWj6Kr9yVQ.
Médine. “Don’t Laïk.” *Démineur.* 2015. Din Records.
Médine. “Don’t Laïk (Official Clip).” YouTube Video, 3:45. January 1, 2015. https://www.youtube.com/watch?v=E7B45h_lAEk.
Médine. “MC Soraal.” *Démineur.* 2015. Din Records.
Médine. “Médine—11 Septembre (Official Clip).” YouTube Video, 6:04. March 25, 2012. https://www.youtube.com/watch?v=YYsXaQeesqI&rco=1.
Médine. “Prose Élite.” *Prose Élite.* 2017. Din Records.
Médine. “Speaker Corner.” *Démineur.* 2015. Din Records.
Médine. “Speaker Corner (Official Video).” YouTube Video, 4:33. May 14, 2015. https://www.youtube.com/watch?v=i_FCAOM8GG8.
Médine. “Voltaire.” *Grand Médine.* 2020. Din Records.
Monsieur R. “FranSSe.” *Politikement Incorrekt.* 2005. Diamond Entertainment.
NAYRA. “Nayra—le nord.” YouTube Video, 3:00. June 15, 2023. https://www.youtube.com/watch?v=hbPHulk0OZ0.
Nouvelle École. Seasons 1–2. Aired 2022–2023 on Netflix.
Orelsan. “RaelSan.” YouTube Video, 3:29. August 24, 2011. https://www.youtube.com/watch?v=Qu3WOFqoQbQ.
Orelsan. “L’odeur de l’essence.” *Civilisation.* 2021. 7th Magnitude/3ème Bureau/Wagram Music.
Orelsan. “L’odeur de l’essence [CLIP OFFICIEL].” YouTube Video, 4:44. November 17, 2021. https://www.youtube.com/watch?v=Arve4ZB8jog.
PNL. “Je vis je visser.” *Que la famille.* 2015. PNL/Musicast.
PNL. “DA.” *Dans la légende.* 2016. QLF Records.
PNL. “91’s.” *Deux frères.* 2019. QLF Records.
PNL. “A l’Ammoniaque [Official Video].” YouTube Video, 5:47. June 22, 2018. https://www.youtube.com/watch?v=Vl-GJaitlNs.
PNL. “À l’ammoniaque.” *Deux frères.* 2019. QLF Records.
La Rumeur. “Inscrivez Greffier.” *Regain de tension.* 2004. La Rumeur Records.
La Rumeur. “Maître Mot, Mots de Maître.” *Regain de tension.* 2004. La Rumeur Records.
Shay. “Cocorico.” *Antidote.* 2019. Capitol Music.
Shayofficiel. “Cocorico.” YouTube Video, 2:51. January 11, 2019. https://www.youtube.com/watch?v=7z_38QNOgHM.

SNIPER. "La France." *Du rire aux larmes.* 2001. Desh Musique.

SNIPER. "La France, itinéraire d'une polémique." *Trait pour trait.* 2006. Desh Musique/Warner Music France.

"Sniper—La France, itinéraire d'une polémique (Clip officiel)." YouTube video, 6:48. January 3, 2013. https://www.youtube.com/watch?v=C1mSAMhYLHY.

Suprême NTM. "Authentik." *Authentik.* 1991. Sony Music Entertainment.

Suprême NTM. "Authentik." YouTube Video, 3:58. https://youtu.be/z_ffMoV-qpE.

Tandem, Mac Tyer, Mac Krégor, Diam's, Kery James,El Runisiano, Faf La Rage, Kazkami, Lino, "Le Jugement." *C'est toujours pour ceux qui savent.* 2005. Kilomaitre/Because Music.

Mac Tyer. "Tandem—Le jugement (feat. Diam's, Kery James, Faf La Rage, Lino, Kazkami, Tunisiano) [Officiel]." YouTube Video, 7:16. February 23, 2011. https://www.youtube.com/watch?v=_o9PUU1Yx9w.

Vald. "Eurotrap." *Agartha.* 2017. Mezoued Records/Capitol Music.

Le Grand Journal. "Eurotrap—Vald—Le live du 06/01—Canal+." YouTube Video, 4:01. January 8, 2017. https://www.youtube.com/watch?v=PVSTd2GzpjY&t=9s.

Vald. "Holehe." *NQNT.* 2014. Mezoued Records.

Validé. Seasons 1–2. Directed by Franck Gastambide. Aired 2020-21 on Canal+.

Youssoupha. "Menace de mort." YouTube Video, 5:02. September 15, 2011. https://www.youtube.com/watch?v=Arve4ZB8jog.

Youssoupha. "Menace de mort." *Noir D****.* 2012. *Bomaye muzik.*

Bibliography

Abd al Malik. *Camus, l'art de la révolte.* Fayard, 2016.

Abd al Malik. *Le jeune Noir à l'épée.* Flammarion, 2019.

Adorno, Theodor W. "On the Fetish Character of Music and the Regression of Listening." In *The Culture Industry: Selected Essays on Mass Culture*, edited by J.M. Bernstein. Routledge, 1991.

Ahmed, Sara. *The Cultural Politics of Emotion.* Routledge, 2004.

Aidi, Hisham. *Rebel Music: Race, Empire, and the New Muslim Youth Culture.* Pantheon Books, 2014.

Alim, H. Samy, Awad Ibrahim, and Alastair Pennycook, eds. *Global Linguistic Flows: Hip Hop Cultures, Youth Identities, and the Politics of Language.* Routledge, 2008.

Alix, Florian. "'Stendhal me connaît pas': reconnaissances littéraires et pratiques transmédiales dans le rap français." *XXI/XX- Reconnaissances littéraires* 1, no. 1 (2020): 187–207.

Almeida, Cristina Moreno. *Rap Beyond Resistance: Staging Power in Contemporary Morocco.* Palgrave Macmillan, 2017.

Amad, Paula. "Visual Riposte: Looking Back at the Return of the Gaze as Postcolonial Theory's Gift to Film Studies." *Cinema Journal* 52, no. 3 (2013): 49–74.

Amey, Patrick. "Du traitement journalistique des acteurs politiques dans *Le Grand Journal.*" *Questions de communication* 24, no. 2 (2013): 61–76.

Amnesty International. "France: Fatal Shooting by Police Officer of 17-Years-Old Habib Ould Mohamed." April 21, 1999. https://www.amnesty.org/en/documents/eur21/004/1999/en/.

Arzoumanov, Anna. "Le style peut-il être un bouclier juridique? Réflexions sur l'argument du style dans les procès contemporains." *Romantic Review* 109 (2019): 31–52.

Aterianus-Owanga, Alice. *"Le rap, ça vient d'ici!" Musiques, pouvoirs et identités dans le Gabon contemporain.* Éditions de la maison des sciences de l'homme, 2017.

Auslander, Philip. "Performance Analysis and Popular Music: A Manifesto." *Contemporary Theatre Review* 14, no. 1 (2004): 1–13.

Austin, J.L. *How to Do Things with Words.* Harvard University Press, 1962.

Baker, Geoffrey. "Preachers, Gangsters, Pranksters: MC Solaar and Hip-Hop as Overt and Covert Revolt." *The Journal of Popular Culture* 44, no. 2 (2011): 233–255.

Baldassarra, Julien. "Rappe pour Nike!" *Le Monde Diplomatique*, October 2018. https://www.monde-diplomatique.fr/2018/10/BALDASSARRA/59127.

Balibar, Étienne. "Uprisings in the *Banlieues.*" *Constellations* 14, no. 1 (2007): 47–71.

Baouche, Amine. "*Négrographèse: être noir•e, s'écrire noir•e. L'écriture de la 'race' chez Casey.*" *Itinéraires. Littérature, textes, cultures* 2021-2 (2022). https://doi.org/10.4000/itineraires.11324.

Bar-David, Gérard. "MC Solaar à Versailles." *Ramdam.* France 3, January 13, 1992.

Barret, Julien. *Le Rap ou l'artisanat de la rime.* L'Harmattan, 2008.

Baubérot, Jean. *Les 7 laïcités françaises: le modèle français de laïcité n'existe pas.* Éditions de la Maison des sciences de l'homme, 2015.

Benjamin, Walter. "The Work of Art in the Age of Mechanical Reproduction." Translated by Harry Zohn. In *Illuminations*, edited by Hannah Arendt. Schocken Books, 1969.

Bénech, Clément. "Booba, Faim de reparties." *Libération*, April 20, 2015.

Berrada, Taïeb. "La Rumeur et son rap: emploi de la rumeur comme fonction discursive contestataire." *Contemporary French Civilization* 37, no. 1 (2012): 59–77.

Béru, Laurent. "Le rap français, un produit musical postcolonial?" *Volume!* 6, nos. 1–2 (2008): 61–79.

Béthune, Christian. *Le rap, une esthétique hors la loi.* Éditions Autrement, 2003.

Béthune, Christian. *Pour une esthétique du rap.* Klincksieck, 2004.

Bhabha, Homi K. *The Location of Culture.* Routledge, 1994.

Binet, Stéphanie. "Orelsan: 'Le monde n'a plus besoin de cynisme.'" *Le Monde*, November 19, 2021, https://www.lemonde.fr/culture/article/2021/11/19/orelsan-le-monde-n-a-pas-besoin-de-plus-de-cynisme_6102677_3246.html.

Binet, Stéphanie. "Que raconte le rap aujourd'hui?" *Le Monde*, November 15, 2019. https://www.lemonde.fr/culture/article/2019/11/15/que-raconte-le-rap-aujourd-hui_6019347_3246.html.

Bishop, Cécile. "Photography, Race and Invisibility." *photographies* 11, nos. 2–3 (2018): 193–213.

Bishop, Cécile and Zoë Roth. "Introduction: Race and the Aesthetic in French and Francophone Cultures." *L'Esprit Créateur* 59, no. 2 (2019): 1–11.

Blondeau, Thomas. "La Rumeur, 'au-delà de l'acharnement.'" *Le Monde Diplomatique.* September 30, 2008. https://www.monde-diplomatique.fr/carnet/2008-09-30-La-Rumeur.

Boëtsch, Gilles and Pascal Blanchard. "The Hottentot Venus: Birth of a 'Freak' (1815)." In *Human Zoos: Science and Spectacle in the Age of Colonial Empires*, edited by Pascal Blanchard, Nicolas Bancel, Gilles Boëtsch, Éric Deroo, Sandrine Lemaire, and Charles Forsdick. Liverpool University Press, 2008.

"Booba, De la Prison à Harvard." *Sept à huit.* TF1, May 22, 2016.

Booba. *Le bitume avec une plume. Un puzzle de mots et de pensées.* Hoëbeke, 2022.

Bordier, Julien. "Futur, un Booba sombre et musclé." *L'Express*, December 10, 2012.

Boucher, Manuel. *Rap, Expression des Lascars. Significations et enjeux du rap dans la société française.* L'Harmattan, 1998.

Bourderionnet, Olivier. "A 'Picture-Perfect' Banlieue Artist: Abd al Malik or the Perils of a Conciliatory Rap Discourse." *French Cultural Studies* 22, no. 2 (2011): 151–161.

Bourdieu, Pierre. *On Television.* Translated by Priscilla Parkhurst Ferguson. The New Press, 1996.

Bourdieu, Pierre. *The Rules of Art: Genesis and Structure of the Literary Field.* Translated by Susan Emanuel. Stanford University Press, 1996.

Bretillon, Chong J. "'Double Discours': Critiques of Racism and Islamophobia in French Rap." In *Post-Migratory Cultures in Postcolonial France*, edited by Kathryn Kleppinger and Laura Reeck. Liverpool University Press, 2018.

Bretillon, Chong J. "'Ma Face Vanille': White Rappers, 'Black Music' and Race in France." *International Journal of Francophone Studies* 17, no. 3&4 (2014): 421–433.

Briggs, Jonathyne. *Sounds French: Globalization, Cultural Communities & Pop Music, 1958–1990.* Oxford University Press, 2015.

Brinker, Virginie. "Actualité de la pensée de Frantz Fanon dans le rap de Casey." *Mouvements* 96, no. 4 (2018): 36–42.

Butler, Judith. *Gender Trouble: Feminism and the Subversion of Identity.* Routledge, 1990.

Butler, Judith. *Excitable Speech: A Politics of the Performative.* Routledge Classics Edition. Routledge, 2021.

Caffin, Patrick. "La Rumeur: le groupe de rap qui derange." *Le Parisien,* November 12, 2004. https://www.leparisien.fr/oise-60/la-rumeur-le-groupe-rap-qui-derange-12-11-2004-2005448201.php.

Carinos Vasquez, Emmanuelle. "Fuck le 17! Rap français et forces de l'ordre." In *Droit(s) et Hip-hop*, edited by Arnaud Montas. Mare & Martin, 2020.

Carinos Vasquez, Emmanuelle and Karim Hammou, eds. *Perspectives esthétiques sur les musiques hip-hop.* Presses universitaires de Provence, 2020.

Carinos Vasquez, Emmanuelle. "Le rap au prétoire: luttes politico-judiciaires autour de deux clips de rap (Jo le Phéno et Nick Conrad)." *Biens symboliques* 10 (2022). https://journals.openedition.org/bssg/1025.

Carinos Vasquez, Emmanuelle. "'Anti-White Racism' and 'Anti-France Hatred': Prosecution of Rap Music and the Paradox of Racist Use of Anti-Racist Legislation in France (2003–2019)." *POMEPS Studies* 52 (2024). https://pomeps.org/anti-white-racism-and-anti-france-hatred-prosecution-of-rap-music-and-the-paradox-of-racist-use-of-anti-racist-legislation-in-france-2003-2019.

Carinos Vasquez, Emmanuelle. "Le son qui tue. Dénoncer, justifier, performer la violence dans le rap français (2000–2024)." PhD diss., Université Paris 8, 2024.

Cespedes, Vincent. "'Islamo-racaille': le droit de haïr?" *Huffington Post*, January 8, 2015. https://www.huffingtonpost.fr/vincent-cespedes/-islamo-racaille-le-droit-de-hair-charlie-hebdo_b_6434686.html.

Chang, Jeff. *Total Chaos: The Art and Aesthetics of Hip-Hop*. Basic Books, 2006.

Chapman, Herrick and Laura L. Frader, eds. *Race in France: Interdisciplinary Perspectives on the Politics of Difference*. Berghahn Books, 2004.

Cheng, Anne Anlin. *Second Skin: Josephine Baker and the Modern Surface*. Oxford University Press, 2011.

Chirat, Alexandre. *Booba. Poésie, musique et philosophie*. L'Harmattan, 2015.

Citton, Yves. *Mediarchy*. Translated by Andrew Brown. Polity Press, 2019.

Clark, Priscilla Parkhurst. *Literary France: The Making of a Culture*. University of California Press, 1987.

Clement, Pierre-Alain. "La signification du politique dans le rap. L'exemple du 'rap de fils d'immigrés' (1997–2012)." *Cultures et conflits* 97 (2015): 123–141.

Collins, Patricia Hill. *Black Sexual Politics. African Americans, Gender, and the New Racism*. Routledge, 2005.

Collins, Patricia Hill. "Selling Blackness in a Global Marketplace." *Ethnicities* 6, no. 3 (2006): 297–317.

Condry, Ian. *Hip-Hop Japan: Rap and the Paths of Cultural Globalization*. Duke University Press, 2006.

Couldry, Nick. "Mediatization or Mediation? Alternative Understandings of the Emergent Space of Digital Storytelling." *New Media & Society* 10, no. 3 (2008): 373–391.

Craske, Helen. *Complicity in Fin-de-siècle Literature*. Oxford University Press, 2024.

Curtius, Anny Dominique and Simonne Henry-Valmore. "Quimbois." In *The Encyclopedia of Caribbean Religions*, vol. 2, edited by P. Taylor et al. The University of Illinois Press, 2013.

Dalibert, Marion. "Les masculinités ethnoracialisées des rappeur-se-s dans la presse." *Mouvements* 96, no. 4 (2018): 22–28.

Dalibert, Marion. "Du 'bon' et du 'mauvais' rap? Les processus médiatiques de hiérarchisation artistique." *Volume! La revue des musiques populaires* 17, no. 2 (2020): 82–97.

Davet, Stéphane. "MC Solaar, héritier rappeur du dandysme à la française." *Le Monde*, June 11, 1997.

Davet, Stéphane. "Les Transmusicales accueillent un hip-hop nouveau, progressiste et poétique." *Le Monde*, December 2, 1999.

Deltombe, Thomas. *L'islam imaginaire: la construction médiatique de l'islamophobie en France, 1975–2005*. La Découverte: 2005.

DeNora, Tia. "Music into Action: Performing Gender on the Viennese Concert Stage, 1790–1810." *Poetics* 30 (2002): 19–33.

Deslogis, Thomas. "Comment le rap français a réécrit (et dépassé) l'Histoire de la poésie." *Les Inrocks*, June 12, 2016. https://www.lesinrocks.com/musique/rap-francais-a-reecrit-depasse-lhistoire-de-poesie-65047-12-06-2016/.

Diamond, Elin. *Performance and Cultural Politics*. Routledge, 1996.

Djavadzadeh, Keivan. "Colonialité du pouvoir, postcolonialité du rap: l'émergence et la répression d'un rap français structuré autour de la critique postcoloniale dans les années 2000." *The Postcolonialist* 3, no. 1 (2015): 1–9.

Djavadzadeh, Keivan. *Hot, Cool & Vicious. Genre, race et sexualité dans le rap états-unien.* Éditions Amsterdam, 2021.

Dotson-Renta, Lara. "'On n'est pas condamné à l'échec': Hip-hop and the *Banlieue* Narrative." *French Cultural Studies* 26, no. 3 (2015): 354–367.

Drott, Eric. *Streaming Music, Streaming Capital.* Duke University Press, 2023.

Drucker, Johanna. *Sweet Dreams: Contemporary Art and Complicity.* Chicago University Press, 2005.

Dufau, Benoît. "Humour et violence dans le rap français." In *Le sens de l'humour. Style, genres, contextes*, edited by Florence Leca-Mercier and Anne-Marie Paillet. Academia-l'Harmattan, 2018.

Dugowson, Pierre. *Les grands entretiens du cercle.* France 2, May 5, 1998.

Duneier, Mitchell. *Slim's Table. Race, Respectability, and Masculinity.* University of Chicago Press, 1992.

Durand, Alain-Philippe, ed. *Black, Blanc, Beur: Rap Music and Hip-Hop Culture in the Francophone World.* Scarecrow Press, 2002.

Durand, Alain-Philippe, ed. *Hip-Hop en français. An Exploration of Hip-Hop Culture in the Francophone World.* Rowman & Littlefield, 2020.

Durham, Aisha S. *Home with Hip Hop Feminism. Performances in Communication and Culture.* Peter Lang, 2014.

Dyer, Richard. *Stars.* Bloomsbury, 1979.

Dyer, Richard. *The Culture of Queers.* Routledge, 2002.

École normale supérieure. "Rencontre avec la rappeuse Casey." YouTube Video, 1:48:14. May 2, 2016. https://www.youtube.com/watch?v=jJsqvpG6Gfk.

Elam Harry J. "Change Clothes and Go: A Postscript to Postblackness." In *Black Cultural Traffic: Crossroads in Global Performance and Popular Culture*, edited by Harry J. Elam and Kennell A. Jackson. University of Michigan Press, 2005.

English, Darby. *How to See a Work of Art in Total Darkness.* The MIT Press, 2007.

"Éric Zemmour perd son procès en appel contre le rappeur Youssoupha." *Le Monde*, June 28, 2012. https://www.lemonde.fr/societe/article/2012/06/28/eric-zemmour-perd-son-proces-en-appel-contre-le-rappeur-youssoupha_1726665_3224.html.

Etoke, Nathalie. "Black Blanc Beur: Ma France à moi." *Nouvelles Études Francophones* 24, no. 1 (2009): 151–171.

Fallon, Kris. *Where Truth Lies: Digital Culture and Documentary Media After 9/11.* University of California Press, 2019.

Fanon, Frantz. *Black Skin, White Masks.* Translated by Charles Lam Markmann. Pluto Press, 1967.

Fassin, Didier and Éric Fassin, eds. *De la question sociale à la question raciale? Représenter la société française.* La Découverte, 2006.

Fisher, Anna Watkins. *The Play in the System: The Art of Parasitical Resistance.* Duke University Press, 2020.

Fitts, Mako. "'Drop It Like It's Hot': Cultural Industry Laborers and Their Perspectives on Rap Music Video Production." *Meridians* 8, no. 1 (2008): 211–235.

Fleetwood, Nicole R. *Troubling Vision: Performance, Visuality, and Blackness.* University of Chicago Press, 2011.

Forman, Murray. *The 'Hood Comes First: Race, Space, and Place in Rap and Hip-Hop.* Wesleyan University Press, 2002.

Foster Wallace, David. "E Unibus Pluram: Television and U.S. Fiction." *Review of Contemporary Fiction* 13, no. 2 (1993): 151–194.

Freitas, Franck. "'Blackness à la demande.' Production narrative de 'l'authenticité raciale' dans l'industrie du rap américain." *Volume! La revue des musiques populaires* 8, no. 2 (2011): 93–121.

Galonnier, Juliette. "Barbes et foulards: les marqueurs genrés de l'islamophobie." In *Genre et islamophobie. Discriminations, préjugés et représentations en Europe*, edited by Éléonore Lépinard, Oriane Sarrasin, and Lavinia Gianettoni. ENS Éditions, 2021.

Garcia, Paco. "L'indépendance est morte, vive l'indépendance. Entre contraintes matérielles et enjeux symboliques: une analyse de l'évolution de 'l'indépendance' dans le rap en France." *Les Enjeux de l'information et de la communication* 22, no. 1 (2021): 19–34.

Gates, Henry Louis, Jr. *The Signifying Monkey: A Theory of African-American Literary Criticism.* Oxford University Press, 1989.

Genono. "Time Bomb Explose!" *Vice.* July 7, 2014. https://www.vice.com/fr/article/6va8mr/time-bomb-explose-revolution-rap-francais.

Ghio, Bettina. *Sans Fautes de frappe: rap et littérature.* Le Mot et le reste, 2016.

Gillett, Rachel Anne. *At Home in our Sounds. Music, Race, and Cultural Politics in Interwar Paris.* Oxford University Press, 2021.

Gilroy, Paul. *The Black Atlantic: Modernity and Double-Consciousness.* Harvard University Press, 1993.

Gilroy, Paul. "'After the Love Has Gone': bio-politics and etho-poetics in the black public sphere." *Public Culture* 7 (1994): 49–76.

Glissant, Édouard. *Poetics of Relation,* Translated by Betsy Wing. The University of Michigan Press, 1997.

Guénif-Souilamas, Nacira and Éric Macé. *Les féministes et le garçon arabe.* Éditions de l'aube, 2004.

Guibert, Gérôme and Catherine Rudent, eds. *Made in France: Studies in Popular Music.* Routledge, 2018.

Guillard, Séverin. "'To Be in the Place': les *open mics* comme espaces de légitimation artistique pour les scènes rap à Paris et Atlanta." *Belgeo* 3, no. 3 (2014). DOI: 10.4000/belgeo.13025.

Hajjat, Abdellali and Marwan Mohammed. *Islamophobie: Comment les élites françaises fabriquent le problème musulman.* La Découverte, 2013.

Hall, Stuart. "What Is This 'Black' in Black Popular Culture?" *Social Justice* 20, no. 1/2 (1993): 104–114.

Hall, Stuart. "Notes on Deconstructing the Popular." In *Essential Essays, Volume 1*, edited by Stuart Hall and David Morley. Duke University Press, 2018.

Hamé. "Insécurité sous la plume d'un barbare." *La Rumeur magazine*, no. 1 (2002).

Hammou, Karim. "Quand la Rumeur Pointe Les Violences Policières." *Sur un son rap*, July 26, 2010. https://surunsonrap.hypotheses.org/1452.

Hammou, Karim. *Une histoire du rap en France.* La Découverte, 2014 [2012].

Hammou, Karim. "Rap et banlieue: Crépuscule d'un mythe?" *Informations sociales* 190, no. 4 (2015): 74–82.

Hammou, Karim. "Mainstreaming French Rap Music. Commodification and Artistic Legitimation of Othered Cultural Goods. *Poetics* 59 (December 2016): 67–81.

Hammou, Karim. "Das Gedächtnis der Vielheit. Minderheitsuniversalismus im französischen Rap." Translated by Gesa zur Nieden. *Die Tonkunst*, no. 4 (2020): 380–392.

Hammou, Karim. "Du web au prétoire. Comment l'affaire Orelsan est devenue une question de droit," In *Droit(s) et Hip-hop*, edited by Arnaud Montas. Mare & Martin, 2020.

Hammou, Karim, "Forty Years of French Rap: Identities in Crescendo." Translated by Katie B. Angus. In *Hip-Hop en français. An Exploration of Hip-Hop Culture in the Francophone World*, edited by Alain-Philippe Durand. Rowman & Littlefield, 2020.

Hammou, Karim. " 'J'suis une femme d'affaires/viens m'faire le café.' L'articulation des rapports sociaux de pouvoir dans la mobilité sociale des rappeuses françaises des années 1990." *Biens symboliques/Symbolic Goods* 10 (2022). DOI: 10.4000/bssg.935.

Hammou, Karim. "Une exclusion qui ne dit pas son nom?" Les rappeuses face aux appariements genrés des carrières artistiques." *Travail, genre et sociétés* 53, (2025): 55–56.

Hammou, Karim and Marie Sonnette-Manouguian. "Mesurer les processus d'(il)légitimation des musiques hip-hop en France. Méthodologie et premiers résultats d'une recherche en cours sur la période 1990–2019." *Volume! La revue des musiques populaires* 17, no. 2 (2020): 99–127.

Hammou, Karim and Marie Sonnette-Manouguian, eds. *40 ans de musiques hip-hop en France.* Presses de Sciences po, 2022.

Harchi, Kaoutar. *Je n'ai qu'une langue, ce n'est pas la mienne. Des écrivains à l'épreuve.* Pauvert, 2016.

Hargreaves, Alec G. *Multi-Ethnic France. Immigration, Politics, Culture and Society.* 2nd edition. Routledge, 2007.

Harsin, Jayson. "Cultural Racist Frames in TF1's French *Banlieue* Riots Coverage." *French Politics, Culture & Society* 33, no. 3 (2005): 47–73.

Hawkins, Peter. "The Re-Invention of the French Singer-Songwriter in the Liberation Years: Léo Ferré and the French Poetic Heritage." In *The Singer-Songwriter in Europe: Paradigms, Politics, and Place,* edited by Isabelle Marc and Stuart Green. Routledge, 2016.

Hawkins, Peter. *Chanson: The French Singer-Songwriter from Aristide Bruant to the Present Day.* Ashgate, 2000.

Helenon, Veronique. "Africa on Their Mind: Rap, Blackness, and Citizenship in France." In *The Vinyl Ain't Final: Hip Hop and the Globalization of Black Popular Culture*, edited by Dipannita Basu and Sidney J. Lemelle. Pluto Press, 2006.

Heysch de la Borde, Clara. "Les codes d'une masculinité 'cool': discours et performance de genre dans les clips du rappeur MC Solaar." *Genre en séries: cinéma, télévision, médias* 15 (2023). https://doi.org/10.4000/ges.3904.

Hill, Edwin C., Jr. *Black Soundscapes White Stages: The Meaning of Francophone Sound in the Black Atlantic.* The Johns Hopkins University Press, 2013.

Hjarvard, Stig. *The Mediatization of Culture and Society.* Taylor & Francis, 2013.

Holm, Nicholas. *Humour as Politics. The Political Aesthetics of Contemporary Comedy.* Palgrave Macmillan, 2017.

Hoofd, Ingrid Maria. "Complicit Subversions: Cultural New Media Activism and 'High' Theory." *First Monday* 13, no. 10 (2008). https://doi.org/10.5210/fm.v13i10.2147.

Huggan, Graham. *The Postcolonial Exotic: Marketing the Margins.* Taylor & Francis Group, 2001.

Husson, Anne-Charlotte. "Genre et violence verbale: l'exemple de 'l'affaire Orelsan.'" *Pratiques* 163–164 (2014). https://journals.openedition.org/pratiques/2315.

Jackson, Kennell A. "The Shadows of Texts: Will Black Music and Singers Sell Everything on Television?" In *Black Cultural Traffic: Crossroads in Global Performance and Popular Culture,* edited by Harry J. Elam and Kennell A. Jackson. University of Michigan Press, 2005.

Jacono, Jean-Marie. "Pour une analyse des chansons de rap." *Musurgia* 5, no. 2 (1998): 65–76.

Jacono, Jean-Marie. "Musique et politique: le cas du RAP." In *Arts, transversalités et questions politiques,* edited by Sylvie Coëllier et Louis Dieuzayde. Publications de l'Université de Provence, 2011.

Jefferies, Michael P. *Thug Life: Race, Gender, and the Meaning of Hip-Hop.* University of Chicago Press, 2011.

Jefferson, Ann. *Genius in France: An Idea and its Uses.* Princeton University Press, 2014.

Jenkins, Henry. *Convergence Culture: Where Old and New Media Collide.* New York University Press, 2006.

Jenkins, Henry, Sam Ford, and Joshua Green, *Spreadable Media: Creating Value and Meaning in a Networked Culture.* New York University Press, 2013.

Jhally, Sut (director). *bell hooks: Cultural Criticism and Transformation.* Media Education Foundation, 1997. 1hr.

Johnson, E. Patrick. *Appropriating Blackness: Performance and the Politics of Authenticity.* Duke University Press, 2003.

Jouili, Jeanette S. "Rapping the Republic: Utopia, Critique, and Muslim Role Models in Secular France." *French Politics, Culture & Society* 31, no. 2 (2013): 58–80.

Kajikawa, Loren. *Sounding Race in Rap Songs.* University of California Press, 2015.

Kärjä, Antti-Ville. "Humour and Parody as Strategies of Securing the Ethnic Other in Popular Music." In *Migrating Music,* edited by Jason Toynbee and Byron Dueck. Routledge, 2011.

Keaton, Tricia Danielle, Tracey Denean Sharpley-Whiting, and Tyler Stovall, eds. *Black France/France Noire. The History and Politics of Blackness.* Duke University Press, 2012.

Kefi, Ramès. "'Validé'. Des flows et des bas." *Libération,* March 20, 2020. https://www.liberation.fr/images/2020/03/20/serie-valide-des-flows-et-des-bas_1782500/.

Kelley, Robin D.G. "Playing for Keeps: Pleasure and Profit on the Postindustrial Playground." In *The House that Race Built: Black Americans, U.S. Terrain,* edited by Wahneema Lubiano. Pantheon, 1997.

Keyes, Cheryl L. "Empowering Self, Making Choices, Creating Spaces: Black Female Identity via Rap Music Performance." *The Journal of American Folklore* 113, no. 449 (Summer 2000): 255–269.

Kleppinger, Kathryn. "When Parallels Collide: Social Commentary and Satire in French Rap Before and After *Charlie Hebdo.*" *Contemporary French Civilization* 41, no. 2 (2016): 197–216.

Knox, Katelyn E. "Rapping Postmemory, Sampling the Archive: Reimagining 17 October 1961." *Modern & Contemporary France* 22, no. 3 (2014): 381–397.

Knox, Katelyn E. *Race on Display in 20th- and 21st Century France.* Liverpool University Press, 2016.

Knox, Katelyn E. "Abd al Malik's 'Meta-French' Perspective: An Audiovisual Approach to French Universalism and Difference Consciousness." *L'Esprit Créateur* 59, no. 2 (2019): 120–133.

Krims, Adam, ed. *Music/Ideology. Resisting the Aesthetic.* Gordon and Breach, 1998.

Krims, Adam. *Rap Music and the Poetics of Identity.* Cambridge University Press, 2000.

Lafargue de Grangeneuve, Loïc. *Politique du hip-hop: Action publique et cultures urbaines.* Presses universitaires du Mirail, 2008.

Lafrance, Marc, Lori Burns, and Alyssa Woods. "Doing Hip-Hop Masculinity Differently: Exploring Kanye West's 808s & Heartbreak through Word, Sound, and Image." In *The Routledge Companion to Popular Music and Gender,* edited by Stan Hawkins. Routledge, 2017.

Lapassade, Georges and Philippe Rousselot. *Le Rap ou la fureur de dire.* Éditions Talmart, 1990.

LaRocca, David, ed. *Metacinema: The Form and Content of Filmic Reference and Reflexivity.* Oxford University Press, 2021.

Lebrun, Barbara. *Protest Music in France. Production, Identity, and Audiences.* Ashgate, 2009.

Lefilliâtre, Jérôme. "Et Bolloré acheva le 'Grand Journal.'" *Libération,* February 13, 2017. https://www.liberation.fr/futurs/2017/02/13/et-bollore-acheva-le-grand-journal-de-canal_1548200/.

"Le procureur demande la relaxe des rappeurs de Sniper." *Agence France Presse.* May 25, 2005.

Leroux, Pierre and Philippe Riutort, "Les émissions de divertissement: de nouveaux lieux de valorisation des petites phrases?" *Communication & langages* 168, no. 2 (2011): 69–80.

Les Terriens. "L'invité OVNI: VALD, le Eminem français." YouTube Video, 6:38. September 23, 2017. https://www.youtube.com/watch?v=_uCYeC_o-OY.

Lesacher, Claire. " 'Le rap est sexiste': ou quand les représentations sur le rap en France engagent une réflexion à partir de l'intrication et de la coproduction des rapports de pouvoir." In *Genre et migrations postcoloniales: lectures croisées de la norme,* edited by Yolaine Parisot and Nadia Ouabdelmoumen. Presses Universitaires de Rennes, 2013.

Levine, Caroline. *Forms: Whole, Rhythm, Hierarchy, Network.* Princeton University Press, 2015.

Lipsitz, George. *Dangerous Crossroads: Popular Music, Postmodernism, and the Poetics of Place.* Verso, 1994.

Little, William G. "24: Time, Terror, Television." *Journal of Popular Film and Television* 42, no. 1 (2014): 3–15.

Looseley, David. *Popular Music in Contemporary France: Authenticity, Politics, Debate.* Berg, 2003.

Looseley, David. "Authenticity and Appropriation: A Discursive History of French Popular Music." In *Imagining the Popular in Contemporary French Culture*, edited by Diana Holmes and David Loosely. Manchester University Press, 2013.

Mahiou, Idir. "Du flow binaire au flow polyrythmique, 'de la rime scolaire à la rime rappeuse': une histoire des performances formelles dans le rap en France de Chagrin d'amour à Ärsenik." *Itinéraires. Littérature, textes, cultures* 2020-3 (2021). DOI: 10.4000/itineraires.9222.

Malela, Buata B. "Le sujet afro-féministe dans le discours de l'œuvre musicale de Shay." *Transposition. Musique et sciences sociales* 12 (2024). https://doi.org/10.4000/12fpv.

Mandel, Naomi. "Toward a New Complicity for New Media." *Comparative Literature Studies* 56, no. 4 (2019): 693–710.

Marc Martínez, Isabelle. *Le rap français. Esthétique et poétique des textes* (1990–1995). Peter Lang, 2008.

Marquet, Mathieu. "Politisation de la parole: du rap ludique au rap engagé." *Variations* 18 (2013). DOI: 10.4000/variations.645.

Marshall, Wayne. "Social Dance in the Age of (Anti-) Social Media: Fortnite, Online Video, and the Jook at a Virtual Crossroads." *Journal of Popular Music Studies* 31, no. 4 (2019): 3–15.

Marx, Karl. *Capital.* Translated by Samuel Moore and Edward Aveling. Encyclopedia Britannica, 1955.

Mbongo, K. Gloire Savula, host. "Nayra, mythologie arabo-amazigh." Backstory (podcast). September 2023. https://open.spotify.com/episode/06AT5pJ6mHRxvweZdk4GAW?si=8bd6f7911a184eb2.

McCarren, Felicia. *French Moves. The Cultural Politics of Le Hip-Hop.* Oxford University Press, 2013.

Meizoz, Jérôme. *Postures littéraires. Mises en scène modernes de l'auteur* Éditions Slatkine, 2007.

Miclet, Brice. "Comment la trap a bouleversé l'univers du rap français." *Slate*, July 4, 2015. http://www.slate.fr/story/102455/trap-bouleverse-univers-rap-francais.

Miclet, Brice. "Pourquoi j'ai détesté 'Nouvelle École', le nouveau télé-crochet rap de Netflix." *Slate,* June 14, 2022. http://www.slate.fr/story/229179/pourquoi-deteste-nouvelle-ecole-tele-crochet-rap-francais-netflix-niska-sch-shay.

Mitchell, Robin. *Vénus Noire: Black Women and Colonial Fantasies in Nineteenth-Century France.* University of Georgia Press, 2020.

Mitchell, Tony, ed. *Global Noise: Rap and Hip Hop Outside the USA.* Wesleyan University Press, 2001.

Moore, Celeste Day. *Soundscapes of Liberation.* Duke University Press, 2021.

Morano, Nadine. "Question au gouvernement no. 897." *Journal officiel.* November 6, 2003. https://questions.assemblee-nationale.fr/.

Morgan, Joan. *When Chickenheads Come Home to Roost: A Hip-Hop Feminist Breaks It Down.* Simon & Schuster, 1999.

Moten, Fred. *In the Break: The Aesthetics of the Black Radical Tradition.* University of Minnesota Press, 2003.

Myard, Jacques. "Question écrite no. 2618." *Journal officiel.* September 16, 2002. https://questions.assemblee-nationale.fr/.

Ndiaye, Pap. *La Condition noire: essai sur une minorité française.* Calmann-Lévy, 2008.

Neal, Mark Anthony. "Sold Out on Soul: The Corporate Annexation of Black Popular Music." *Popular Music and Society* 21, no. 3 (Fall 1997): 117–135.

Ngai, Sianne. *Theory of the Gimmick: Aesthetic Judgment and Capitalist Form.* Harvard University Press, 2020.

Nielson, Erik and Andrea L. Dennis. *Rap on Trial: Race, Lyrics, and Guilt in America.* The New Press, 2019.

Owens, Jay. "Post-Authenticity and the Ironic Truths of Meme Culture." In *Post-Memes: Seizing the Memes of Production,* edited by Alfie Brown and Dan Bristow. Punctum Books, 2019.

Parthonnaud, Aymeric and Steven Bellery. "Avec l'Odeur de l'essence', OrelSan dit leurs 4 vérités aux Français avant 2022." *RTL,* November 18, 2021. https://www.rtl.fr/culture/medias-people/avec-l-odeur-de-l-essence-orelsan-dit-leurs-4-verites-aux-francais-avant-2022-7900097594.

Pecqueux, Anthony. *Voix du rap: essai de sociologie de l'action musicale.* L'Harmattan, 2007.

Perry, Imani. *Prophets of the Hood: Politics and Poetics in Hip Hop.* Duke University Press, 2004.

Phillips, Whitney. *This Is Why We Can't Have Nice Things: Mapping the Relationship Between Online Trolling and Mainstream Culture.* The MIT Press, 2015.

Potter, Russel A. *Spectacular Vernaculars: Hip-Hop and the Politics of Postmodernism.* State University of New York Press, 1995.

Pough, Gwendolyn D. *Check It While I Wreck It: Black Womanhood, Hip-hop Culture, and the Public Sphere.* Northeastern University Press, 2004.

Prévos, André J.M. "The Evolution of French Rap Music and Hip Hop Culture in the 1980s and the 1990s." *The French Review* 69, no. 5 (1996): 713–725.

Prévos, André J.M. "Hip-hop, Rap, and Repression in France and in the United States." *Popular Music and Society* 22, no. 2 (1998): 67–84.

Proposition de loi tendant à renforcer le contrôle des provocations à la discrimination, à la haine ou à la violence, no. 2957, 12th legislature. (2006).

Provenzano, Catherine. "Making Voices: The Gendering of Pitch Correction and the Auto-Tune Effect in Contemporary Pop Music." *Journal of Popular Music Studies* 31, no. 2 (2019): 63–83.

Puig, Stève. "Redefining Frenchness Through Urban Music and Literature: The Case of Rapper-Writers Abd al Malik and Disiz." In *Post-Migratory Cultures in Postcolonial France,* edited by Kathryn Kleppinger and Laura Reecks. Liverpool University Press, 2018.

Quemener, Nelly. "'Vous voulez réagir?' L'étude des controverses médiatiques au prisme des intensités affectives." *Questions de communication* 33 (2018): 23–41.

Raengo, Alessandra. *On the Sleeve of the Visual: Race as Face Value.* Dartmouth College Press, 2013.

Ramdani, Karima. "Bitch et beurette, quand féminité rime avec liberté. Représentation du corps féminin noir et maghrébin dans la musique rap et le R'n'B." *Volume!* 8, no. 2 (2011): 13–39.

Rami, Anissa. "Figurantes de clips: les précaires du rap français." *Médiapart* and *The Bondy Blog,* July 23, 2022. https://www.mediapart.fr/journal/france/230722/figurantes-de-clips-les-precaires-du-rap-francais.

Rancière, Jacques. *Le partage du sensible: esthétique et politique.* La Fabrique Éditions, 2000.

Rapido TV. "Interviews de membres de 93 NTM." TF1. 1990.

Ravier, Thomas A. "Booba ou le démon des images." *La Nouvelle Revue Française,* no. 567 (October 2003): 37–56.

Reivax. "Chronique: La Rumeur, Regain de tension." *Abcdrduson,* November 14, 2004. https://www.abcdrduson.com/chroniques/regain-de-tension/.

Riboni, Ulrike Lune. *Vidéoactivismes. Contestation audiovisuelle et politisation des images.* Éditions Amsterdam, 2023.

Richeux, Marie. *Par les temps qui courent.* "Médine: 'Pour moi, une idée qui n'est pas dangereuse, n'est pas une idée." *France Culture,* October 16, 2020. https://www.radiofrance.fr/franceculture/podcasts/par-les-temps-qui-courent/medine-pour-moi-une-idee-qui-n-est-pas-dangereuse-n-est-pas-une-idee-7049689.

Rigouste, Mathieu. *L'ennemi intérieur. La généalogie coloniale et militaire de l'ordre sécuritaire dans la France contemporaine.* La Découverte, 2011.

Rolland, Nina. "'Dans la rue et le bitume ne poussent que les fleurs du mal': jouer et déjouer Charles Baudelaire et sa poésie dans le rap français." *Itinéraires. Littérature, textes, cultures* 2020-3 (2021). https://doi.org/10.4000/itineraires.9377.

Rollefson, J. Griffith. *Flip the Script: European Hip Hop and the Politics of Postcoloniality* University of Chicago Press, 2017.
Rose, Tricia. *Black Noise: Rap Music and Black Culture in Contemporary America.* Wesleyan University Press, 1994.
Rose, Tricia. *The Hip Hop Wars: What We Talk About When We Talk About Hip-Hop—And Why It Matters.* Basic Books, 2008.
Rubin, Christophe. "Le texte de rap: une écriture de la voix." In *Actes du 22ème colloque d'Albi.* CALS-CPST, 2002.
Rubin, Christophe. "Le rap est-il soluble dans la chanson française?" *Volume!* 3, no. 2 (2004): 29–42.
Rubin, Christophe. "Configurations rythmiques et progression textuelle dans un extrait d'un rap de Casey." *Revue critique de Fixxion française contemporaine* 5 (2012). https://journals.openedition.org/fixxion/5498.
Sagnard, Arnaud. "L'autre affaire Booba, le tabou littéraire." *L'Obs,* September 4, 2018. https://bibliobs.nouvelobs.com/actualites/20180904.OBS1773/l-autre-affaire-booba-le-tabou-litteraire.html.
Saha, Anamik. *Race and the Cultural Industries.* Polity Press, 2018.
Sapiro, Gisèle. *La responsabilité de l'écrivain. Littérature, droit et morale en France (XIXe – XXIe siècle).* Éditions du Seuil, 2011.
Sapiro, Gisèle. "La responsabilité pénale de l'écrivain au prisme des procès littéraires (France, XIXe – XXe siècles)." *Histoire de la justice* 23, no. 1 (2013): 13–23.
Savoirs ENS. "La Plume et le Bitume: rencontre avec le rappeur Médine." 1:40:40. March 28, 2017. https://savoirs.ens.fr/expose.php?id=3114.
Sécail, Claire. *Touche pas à mon peuple.* Éditions du Seuil, 2024.
Selod, Saher. "Citizenship Denied: The Racialization of Muslim American Men and Women Post-9/11." *Critical Sociology* 41, no. 1 (2015): 77–95.
Setaro, Shawn. "How Trap Music Came to Rule the World." *Complex*, February 14, 2018. https://www.complex.com/music/2018/02/how-trap-music-came-to-rule-the-world.
Schloss, Joseph G. *Foundation. B-Boys, B-Girls, and Hip-Hop Culture in New York.* Oxford University Press, 2009.
Scott, Joan Wallach. *The Politics of the Veil.* Princeton University Press, 2007.
Sharpley-Whiting, T. Denean. *Black Venus: Sexualized Savages, Primal Fears, and Primitive Narratives in French.* Duke University Press, 1999.
"Shay, l'interview par Mehdi Maïzi—Le Code." YouTube Video, 39:06. January 19, 2024. https://www.youtube.com/watch?v=H6Ljp2JWUE8.
"SHAY: son album, le féminisme, Niska, Bruxelles, son frère . . . " *Mouv'*. Dailymotion Video, 28:21. May 14, 2019. https://www.dailymotion.com/video/x78b1q6.
Shepard, Todd. *Sex, France, and Arab Men, 1962–1979.* University of Chicago Press, 2018.
Shkyd. "Les médias musicaux n'osent plus critiquer les albums de rap français." *Yard*, March 2, 2018. https://yard.media/medias-musicaux-france-critique-albums-rap-francais/.
Shuman, Emily Q. "'Tout de noir vêtu': Skin and Surface in the Rap of Abd al Malik." *French Cultural Studies* 29, no. 3 (2018): 209–217.
Shuman, Emily Q. "Esthétique et performativité de la race dans 'Créature ratée' de Casey." *Itinéraires. Littérature, textes, cultures* 2020-3 (2021). DOI: https://doi.org/10.4000/itineraires.8805.
Shuman, Emily Q. "Fantasies of Power: Sex, Humour and Complicities in French Rap." *Modern & Contemporary* France 33, no.4 (2025): 523–540. DOI: https://doi.org/10.1080/09639489.2025.2519085.
Shusterman, Richard. *Pragmatist Aesthetics: Living Beauty, Rethinking Art* 2nd edition. Rowman & Littlefield Publishers, 2000.
Stélandre, Thomas. "Booba, le cru et l'écrit." *Libération,* November 24, 2013. https://next.liberation.fr/musique/2013/11/24/booba-le-cru-et-l-ecrit_961653.

Stone Peters, Julie. "Legal Performance Good and Bad." *Law, Culture and the Humanities*, no. 4 (2008):179–200.

Sonnette-Manouguian, Marie. "Qu'est-ce qu'on attend pour foutre le feu: le rap sur le banc des accusés." In *Une esthétique de l'outrage?*, edited by Jean-Marc Lachaud and Olivier Neveux. L'Harmattan, 2012.

Sonnette-Manouguian, Marie. "Des Manières critiques de faire du rap: Pratiques artistiques, pratiques politiques. Contribution à une sociologie de l'engagement des artistes." PhD diss., Université Sorbonne Nouvelle, 2013.

Sonnette-Manouguian, Marie. "Des mises en scène du 'nous' contre le 'eux' dans le rap français." *Sociologie de l'art* 23/24, no. 1 (2015): 153–177.

Sterne, Jonathan. "The Burden of Culture." In *The Aesthetics of Cultural Studies*, edited by Michael Berubé. Blackwell Publishing, 2005.

Tchokokam, Rhoda. *Sensibles. Une histoire du R&B français.* Audimat Éditions, 2023.

Thompson, Krista A. *Shine: The Visual Economy of Light in African Diasporic Aesthetic Practice.* Duke University Press, 2015.

Tshimanga, Charles. "Let the Music Play: The African Diaspora, Popular Culture, and National Identity in Contemporary France." In *Frenchness and the African Diaspora: Identity and Uprising in Contemporary France*, edited by Charles Tshimanga, Ch. Didier Gondola, and Peter J. Bloom. Indiana University Press, 2009.

Vernallis, Carol. *Experiencing Music Video: Aesthetics and Cultural Context.* Columbia University Press, 2004.

Vernallis, Carol. *The Media Swirl, Politics, Audiovisuality, and Aesthetics.* Duke University Press, 2023.

Vettorato, Cyril. "'Ça va être un viol': Formes et fonctions de l'obscénité langagière dans les joutes verbales de rap." *Cahiers de littérature orale* 71 (2012). DOI: 10.4000/clo.1492.

Vidalie, Christian. dir. *Ciel, mon mardi!* TF1. February 5, 1991.

Vieille, Jean-Baptiste. "Prose Combat, histoire d'un classique," *Abcdrduson*, April 24, 2021, https://www.abcdrduson.com/special/mc-solaar-prose-combat/.

Vîrus x Jehan-Rictus. *Les Soliloques du Pauvre* (Livre-CD). Au Diable Vauvert, 2017.

Wallon, Rémi. "Booba." *Vice.* November 20, 2008. https://www.vice.com/fr/article/vdwmy9/booba-187-v2n11.

Wallon, Rémi. "'Va te faire niquer toi et tes livres': Time Bomb, le triomphe d'un rap français bête et méchant." *Revue critique de fixxion française contemporaine* 5 (2012): 117–129.

Waugh, Patricia. *Metafiction: The Theory and Practice of Self-Conscious Fiction (New Accents).* Routledge, 2002.

Watkins, S. Craig. *Hip Hop Matters. Politics, Pop Culture, and the Struggle for the Soul of a Movement.* Beacon Press, 2005.

Watts, Eric K. "An Exploration of Spectacular Consumption: Gangsta Rap as Cultural Commodity." In *That's the Joint! The Hip-Hop Studies Reader*, edited by Murray Forman and Mark Anthony Neal. Routledge, 2004.

Weber, Samuel. *Mass Mediauras: Form, Technics, Media.* Stanford University Press, 1996.

Williams, Justin A. *Rhymin' and Stealin': Musical Borrowing in Hip-Hop.* University of Michigan Press, 2013.

Williams, Justin A. *Brithop. The Politics of UK Rap in the New Century.* Oxford University Press, 2021.

Wolf, Werner, ed. *The Metareferential Turn in Contemporary Arts and Media. Forms, Functions, Attempts at Explanation.* Rodopi, 2011.

Index

For the benefit of digital users, indexed terms that span two pages (e.g., 52–53) may, on occasion, appear on only one of those pages.